INVESTIGATION OF THE BALTIMORE CITY POLICE DEPARTMENT

U.S. DEPARTMENT OF JUSTICE
CIVIL RIGHTS DIVISION

August 10, 2016

TABLE OF CONTENTS

EXECUTIVE SUMMARY

Today, we announce the outcome of the Department of Justice's investigation of the Baltimore City Police Department (BPD).[1] After engaging in a thorough investigation, initiated at the request of the City of Baltimore and BPD, the Department of Justice concludes that there is reasonable cause to believe that BPD engages in a pattern or practice of conduct that violates the Constitution or federal law. BPD engages in a pattern or practice of:

(1) making unconstitutional stops, searches, and arrests;

(2) using enforcement strategies that produce severe and unjustified disparities in the rates of stops, searches and arrests of African Americans;

(3) using excessive force; and

(4) retaliating against people engaging in constitutionally-protected expression.

This pattern or practice is driven by systemic deficiencies in BPD's policies, training, supervision, and accountability structures that fail to equip officers with the tools they need to police effectively and within the bounds of the federal law.

We recognize the challenges faced by police officers in Baltimore and other communities around the country. Every day, police officers risk their lives to uphold the law and keep our communities safe. Investigatory stops, arrests, and force—including, at times, deadly force—are all necessary tools used by BPD officers to do their jobs and protect the safety of themselves and others. Providing policing services in many parts of Baltimore is particularly challenging, where officers regularly confront complex social problems rooted in poverty, racial segregation and deficient educational, employment and housing opportunities. Still, most BPD officers work hard to provide vital services to the community.

The pattern or practice occurs as a result of systemic deficiencies at BPD. The agency fails to provide officers with sufficient policy guidance and training; fails to collect and analyze data regarding officers' activities; and fails to hold officers accountable for misconduct. BPD also fails to equip officers with the necessary equipment and resources they need to police safely, constitutionally, and effectively. Each of these systemic deficiencies contributes to the constitutional and statutory violations we observed.

---

[1] The Special Litigation Section of the Civil Rights Division conducted the investigation pursuant to the Violent Crime Control and Law Enforcement Act of 1994, 42 U.S.C. § 14141 ("Section 14141"), Title VI of the Civil Rights Act of 1964, 42 U.S.C. § 2000d, the Omnibus Crime Control and Safe Streets Act of 1968, 42 U.S.C. § 3789d ("Safe Streets Act"); and the Americans with Disabilities Act of 1990, 42 U.S.C. §§ 12131–12134. The investigation did not examine the actions of officers involved in Freddie Gray's arrest on April 12, 2015, or the merits of any criminal or civil proceedings connected to that incident.

Throughout our investigation, we received the full cooperation and assistance of BPD and the City of Baltimore. We interviewed current and former City leaders, including current BPD Commissioner Kevin Davis and former commissioners. We also interviewed current and former officers throughout the BPD command structure. We participated in ride-alongs in each district, interviewed numerous current and former officers individually, and met with the leadership of the Baltimore City Lodge No. 3 of the Fraternal Order of Police, which represents all sworn BPD officers. We also heard from hundreds of people in the broader Baltimore community who shared information with our investigation. We met with religious organizations, advocacy groups, community support organizations, neighborhood associations, and countless individuals who provided valuable information about their experiences with BPD. We thank everyone for sharing their experiences and insights with us.

In addition to these interviews, we reviewed hundreds of thousands of pages of documents, including all relevant policies and training materials used by the Department since 2010; BPD's database of internal affairs files from January 2010 through March 2016; BPD's data on pedestrian stops, vehicle stops, and arrests from January 2010 to May 2015; incident reports describing stops, searches, arrests, and officers' use of non-deadly force from 2010 to 2015; all files on deadly force incidents since 2010 that BPD was able to produce to us through May 1, 2016; and investigative files on sexual assault cases from 2013 to 2015. We were assisted by a dozen current and former law enforcement leaders and experts with experience on the issues we investigated, and we retained statistical experts to analyze BPD's data on its enforcement activities.[2]

In the course of our investigation, we learned there is widespread agreement that BPD needs reform. Almost everyone who spoke to us—from current and former City leaders, BPD officers and command staff during ride-alongs and interviews, community members throughout the many neighborhoods of Baltimore, union representatives of all levels of officers in BPD, advocacy groups, and civic and religious leaders—agrees that BPD has significant problems that have undermined its efforts to police constitutionally and effectively. As we note in this report, many of these people and groups have documented those problems in the past, and although they may disagree about the nature, scope, and solutions to the challenges, many have also made efforts to address them. Nevertheless, work remains, in part because of the profound lack of trust among these groups, and in particular, between BPD and certain communities in Baltimore. The road to meaningful and lasting reform is a long one, but it can be taken. This investigation is intended to help Baltimore take a large step down this path.

Recent events highlight the critical importance of mutual trust and cooperation between law enforcement officers and the people they serve. A commitment to constitutional policing builds trust that enhances crime fighting efforts and officer safety. Conversely, frayed community relationships inhibit effective policing by denying officers important sources of information and placing them more frequently in dangerous, adversarial encounters. We found these principles in stark relief in Baltimore, where law enforcement officers confront a long history of social and economic challenges that impact much of the City, including the perception that there are "two

---

[2] In addition, the Department of Justice's Office of Community Oriented Policing Services (COPS) has been engaged in a collaborative reform process with the City and BPD. The COPS office has continued to provide technical assistance to BPD during our investigation, along with other components of the Department of Justice.

Baltimores:" one wealthy and largely white, the second impoverished and predominantly black. Community members living in the City's wealthier and largely white neighborhoods told us that officers tend to be respectful and responsive to their needs, while many individuals living in the City's largely African-American communities informed us that officers tend to be disrespectful and do not respond promptly to their calls for service. Members of these largely African-American communities often felt they were subjected to unjustified stops, searches, and arrests, as well as excessive force. These challenges amplify the importance of using policing methods that build community partnerships and ensure fair and effective enforcement without regard for affluence or race through robust training, close supervision, data collection and analysis, and accountability for misconduct.

Starting in at least the late 1990s, however, City and BPD leadership responded to the City's challenges by encouraging "zero tolerance" street enforcement that prioritized officers making large numbers of stops, searches, and arrests—and often resorting to force—with minimal training and insufficient oversight from supervisors or through other accountability structures. These practices led to repeated violations of the constitutional and statutory rights, further eroding the community's trust in the police.

Proactive policing does not have to lead to these consequences. On the contrary, constitutional, community-oriented policing is proactive policing, but it is fundamentally different from the tactics employed in Baltimore for many years. Community policing depends on building relationships with all of the communities that a police department serves, and then jointly solving problems to ensure public safety. We encourage BPD to be proactive, to get to know Baltimore's communities more deeply, build trust, and reduce crime together with the communities it serves.

Fortunately, the current leadership of the City and the BPD already have taken laudable steps to reverse this course, including by revising BPD's use of force policies, taking steps toward enhancing accountability and transparency throughout the Department by, for example, beginning to equip officers with body worn cameras, and taking steps toward improving and expanding its community outreach to better engage its officers with the community they serve. Still, significant challenges remain.

Unconstitutional Stops, Searches, and Arrests

BPD's legacy of zero tolerance enforcement continues to drive its policing in certain Baltimore neighborhoods and leads to unconstitutional stops, searches, and arrests. Many BPD supervisors instruct officers to make frequent stops and arrests—even for minor offenses and with minimal or no suspicion—without sufficient consideration of whether this enforcement strategy promotes public safety and community trust or conforms to constitutional standards. These instructions, coupled with minimal supervision and accountability for misconduct, lead to constitutional violations.

- Stops. BPD officers recorded over 300,000 pedestrian stops from January 2010–May 2015, and the true number of BPD's stops during this period is likely far higher due to under-reporting. These stops are concentrated in predominantly African-American neighborhoods and often lack reasonable suspicion.

o BPD's pedestrian stops are concentrated on a small portion of Baltimore residents. BPD made roughly 44 percent of its stops in two small, predominantly African-American districts that contain only 11 percent of the City's population. Consequently, hundreds of individuals—nearly all of them African American—were stopped on at least 10 separate occasions from 2010–2015. Indeed, seven African-American men were stopped more than 30 times during this period.

o BPD's stops often lack reasonable suspicion. Our review of incident reports and interviews with officers and community members found that officers regularly approach individuals standing or walking on City sidewalks to detain and question them and check for outstanding warrants, despite lacking reasonable suspicion to do so. Only 3.7 percent of pedestrian stops resulted in officers issuing a citation or making an arrest. And, as noted below, many of those arrested based upon pedestrian stops had their charges dismissed upon initial review by either supervisors at BPD's Central Booking or local prosecutors.

- Searches. During stops, BPD officers frequently pat-down or frisk individuals as a matter of course, without identifying necessary grounds to believe that the person is armed and dangerous. And even where an initial frisk is justified, we found that officers often violate the Constitution by exceeding the frisk's permissible scope. We likewise found many instances in which officers strip search individuals without legal justification. In some cases, officers performed degrading strip searches in public, prior to making an arrest, and without grounds to believe that the searched individuals were concealing contraband on their bodies.

- Arrests. We identified two categories of common unconstitutional arrests by BPD officers: (1) officers make warrantless arrests without probable cause; and (2) officers make arrests for misdemeanor offenses, such as loitering and trespassing, without providing the constitutionally-required notice that the arrested person was engaged in unlawful activity.

o Arrests without probable cause: from 2010–2015, supervisors at Baltimore's Central Booking and local prosecutors rejected over 11,000 charges made by BPD officers because they lacked probable cause or otherwise did not merit prosecution. Our review of incident reports describing warrantless arrests likewise found many examples of officers making unjustified arrests. In addition, officers extend stops without justification to search for evidence that would justify an arrest. These detentions—many of which last more than an hour— constitute unconstitutional arrests.

o Misdemeanor arrests without notice: BPD officers arrest individuals standing lawfully on public sidewalks for "loitering," "trespassing," or other misdemeanor offenses without providing adequate notice that the individuals were engaged in unlawful activity. Indeed, officers frequently invert the constitutional notice requirement. While the Constitution requires individuals to receive pre-arrest notice of the specific conduct prohibited as loitering or trespassing, BPD officers approach individuals standing lawfully on sidewalks in front of public housing complexes or private businesses and arrest them unless the individuals are able to "justify" their presence to the officers' satisfaction.

Discrimination against African Americans

BPD's targeted policing of certain Baltimore neighborhoods with minimal oversight or accountability disproportionately harms African-American residents. Racially disparate impact is present at every stage of BPD's enforcement actions, from the initial decision to stop individuals on Baltimore streets to searches, arrests, and uses of force. These racial disparities, along with evidence suggesting intentional discrimination, erode the community trust that is critical to effective policing.

- BPD disproportionately stops African-American pedestrians. Citywide, BPD stopped African-American residents three times as often as white residents after controlling for the population of the area in which the stops occurred. In each of BPD's nine police districts, African Americans accounted for a greater share of BPD's stops than the population living in the district. And BPD is far more likely to subject individual African Americans to multiple stops in short periods of time. In the five and a half years of data we examined, African Americans accounted for 95 percent of the 410 individuals BPD stopped at least 10 times. One African American man in his mid-fifties was stopped 30 times in less than 4 years. Despite these repeated intrusions, none of the 30 stops resulted in a citation or criminal charge.

- BPD also stops African American drivers at disproportionate rates. African Americans accounted for 82 percent of all BPD vehicle stops, compared to only 60 percent of the driving age population in the City and 27 percent of the driving age population in the greater metropolitan area.

- BPD disproportionately searches African Americans during stops. BPD searched African Americans more frequently during pedestrian and vehicle stops, even though searches of African Americans were less likely to discover contraband. Indeed, BPD officers found contraband twice as often when searching white individuals compared to African Americans during vehicle stops and 50 percent more often during pedestrian stops.

- African Americans similarly accounted for 86 percent of all criminal offenses charged by BPD officers despite making up only 63 percent of Baltimore residents.

  o Racial disparities in BPD's arrests are most pronounced for highly discretionary offenses: African Americans accounted for 91 percent of the 1,800 people charged solely with "failure to obey" or "trespassing"; 89 percent of the 1,350 charges for making a false statement to an officer; and 84 percent of the 6,500 people arrested for "disorderly conduct." Moreover, booking officials and prosecutors decline charges brought against African Americans at significantly higher rates than charges against people of other races, indicating that officers' standards for making arrests differ by the race of the person arrested.

o We also found large racial disparities in BPD's arrests for drug possession. While survey data shows that African Americans use drugs at rates similar to or slightly exceeding other population groups, BPD arrested African Americans for drug possession at five times the rate of others.

BPD deployed a policing strategy that, by its design, led to differential enforcement in African-American communities. But BPD failed to use adequate policy, training and accountability mechanisms to prevent discrimination, despite longstanding notice of concerns about how it polices African-American communities in the City. BPD has conducted virtually no analysis of its own data to ensure that its enforcement activities are non-discriminatory, and the Department misclassifies or otherwise fails to investigate specific complaints of racial bias. Nor has the Department held officers accountable for using racial slurs or making other statements exhibiting racial bias. In some cases, BPD supervisors have ordered officers to specifically target African Americans for stops and arrests. These failures contribute to the large racial disparities in BPD's enforcement that undermine the community's trust in the fairness of the police. BPD leadership has acknowledged that this lack of trust inhibits their ability to forge important community partnerships.

Use of Constitutionally Excessive Force

Our review of investigative files for all deadly force cases from 2010 until May 1, 2016, and a random sample of over eight hundred non-deadly force cases reveals that BPD engages in a pattern or practice of excessive force. Deficiencies in BPD's policies, training, and oversight of officers' force incidents have led to the pattern or practice of excessive force that we observed. We identified several recurring issues with BPD's use of force:

- First, BPD uses overly aggressive tactics that unnecessarily escalate encounters, increase tensions, and lead to unnecessary force, and fails to de-escalate encounters when it would be reasonable to do so. Officers frequently resort to physical force when a subject does not immediately respond to verbal commands, even where the subject poses no imminent threat to the officer or others. These tactics result from BPD's training and guidance.

- Second, BPD uses excessive force against individuals with mental health disabilities or in crisis. Due to a lack of training and improper tactics, BPD officers end up in unnecessarily violent confrontations with these vulnerable individuals. BPD provides less effective services to people with mental illness and intellectual disabilities by failing to account for these disabilities in officers' law enforcement actions, leading to unnecessary and excessive force being used against them. BPD has failed to make reasonable modifications in its policies, practices, and procedures to avoid discriminating against people with mental illness and intellectual disabilities.

- Third, BPD uses unreasonable force against juveniles. These incidents arise from BPD's failure to use widely-accepted tactics for communicating and interacting with youth. Instead, officers interacting with youth rely on the same aggressive tactics they use with adults, leading to unnecessary conflict.

- Fourth, BPD uses unreasonable force against people who present little or no threat to officers or others. Specifically, BPD uses excessive force against (1) individuals who are already restrained and under officers' control and (2) individuals who are fleeing from officers and are not suspected of serious criminal offenses.

  o Force used on restrained individuals: we found many examples of BPD officers using unreasonable force on individuals who were restrained and no longer posed a threat to officers or the public.

  o Force used on fleeing suspects: BPD officers frequently engage in foot pursuits of individuals, even where the fleeing individuals are not suspected of violent crimes. BPD's foot pursuit tactics endanger officers and the community, and frequently lead to officers using excessive force on fleeing suspects who pose minimal threat. BPD's aggressive approach to foot pursuits extends to flight in vehicles.

  We also examined BPD's transportation of detainees, but were unable to make a finding due to a lack of available data. We were unable to secure reliable records from either BPD or the jail regarding injuries sustained during transport or any recordings. Nonetheless, we found evidence that BPD: (1) routinely fails to properly secure arrestees in transport vehicles; (2) needs to continue to update its transport equipment to protect arrestees during transport; (3) fails to keep necessary records; and (4) must implement more robust auditing and monitoring systems to ensure that its transport policies and training are followed.

- Our concerns about BPD's use of excessive force are compounded by BPD's ineffective oversight of its use of force. Of the 2,818 force incidents that BPD recorded in the nearly six-year period we reviewed, BPD investigated only ten incidents based on concerns identified through its internal review. Of these ten cases, BPD found only one use of force to be excessive.

Retaliation for Activities Protected by the First Amendment

BPD violates the First Amendment by retaliating against individuals engaged in constitutionally protected activities. Officers frequently detain and arrest members of the public for engaging in speech the officers perceive to be critical or disrespectful. And BPD officers use force against members of the public who are engaging in protected speech. BPD has failed to provide officers with sufficient guidance and oversight regarding their interactions with individuals that implicate First Amendment protections, leading to the violations we observed.

Indications of Gender Bias in Sexual Assault Investigations

Although we do not, at this time, find reasonable cause to believe that BPD engages in gender-biased policing in violation of federal law, the allegations we received during the investigation, along with our review of BPD files, suggests that gender bias may be affecting BPD's handling of sexual assault cases. We found indications that officers fail to meaningfully investigate reports of sexual assault, particularly for assaults involving women with additional vulnerabilities, such as those who are involved in the sex trade. Detectives fail to develop and resolve preliminary investigations; fail to identify and collect evidence to corroborate victims' accounts; inadequately document their investigative steps; fail to collect and assess data, and report and classify reports of sexual assault; and lack supervisory review. We also have concerns that officers' interactions with women victims of sexual assault and with transgender individuals display unlawful gender bias.

Deficient Policies, Training, Supervision, and Accountability

BPD's systemic constitutional and statutory violations are rooted in structural failures. BPD fails to use adequate policies, training, supervision, data collection, analysis, and accountability systems, has not engaged adequately with the community it polices, and does not provide its officers with the tools needed to police effectively.

- BPD lacks meaningful accountability systems to deter misconduct. The Department does not consistently classify, investigate, adjudicate, and document complaints of misconduct according to its own policies and accepted law enforcement standards. Instead, we found that BPD personnel discourage complaints from being filed, misclassify complaints to minimize their apparent severity, and conduct little or no investigation. As a result, a resistance to accountability persists throughout much of BPD, and many officers are reluctant to report misconduct for fear that doing so is fruitless and may provoke retaliation. The Department also lacks adequate civilian oversight—its Civilian Review Board is hampered by inadequate resources, and the agency's internal affairs and disciplinary process lacks transparency.

- Nor does BPD employ effective community policing strategies. The Department's current relationship with certain Baltimore communities is broken. As noted above, some community members believe that the Department operates as if there are "two Baltimores" in which the affluent sections of the City receive better services than its impoverished and minority neighborhoods. This fractured relationship exists in part because of the Department's legacy of zero tolerance enforcement, the failure of many BPD officers to implement community policing principles, and the Department's lack of vision for engaging with the community.

- BPD fails to adequately supervise officers through policy guidance and training. Until recently, BPD lacked sufficient policy guidance in critical areas, such as bias-free policing and officers' use of batons and tasers. In other areas, such as its policy governing "stop and frisk," BPD policy conflicts with constitutional requirements. The Department likewise lacks effective training on important areas, such as scenario-based training for use of force, an adequate Field Training program; and supervisory or leadership training.

- BPD also fails to collect data on a range of law enforcement actions, and even when it collects data, fails to store it in systems that are capable of effective tracking and analysis.

Partly as a result, the BPD does not use an effective early intervention system to detect officers who may benefit from additional training or guidance to ensure that they do not commit constitutional and statutory violations.

- In addition, BPD fails to adequately support its officers with adequate staffing and material resources. The Department lacks effective strategies for staffing, recruitment and retention, forcing officers to work overtime after long shifts, lowering morale, and leading to officers working with deteriorated decision-making skills. Moreover, BPD lacks adequate technology infrastructure and tools that are common in many similar-sized law enforcement agencies, such as in-car computers. These technology deficits create inefficiencies for officers and inhibit effective data collection and supervision. The City must invest in its police department to ensure that officers have the tools they need to properly serve the people of Baltimore.

*   *   *

Notwithstanding our findings, we are heartened by the support for police reform throughout BPD the City, and the broader Baltimore community. Based on the cooperation and spirit of engagement we witnessed throughout our investigation, we are optimistic that we will be able to work with the City, BPD, and the diverse communities of Baltimore to address the issues described in our findings and forge a court-enforceable agreement to develop enduring remedies to the constitutional and statutory violations we found. Indeed, although much work remains, BPD has already begun laying the foundation for reform by self-initiating changes to its policies, training, data management, and accountability systems.

To that end, the Department of Justice and the City have entered into an Agreement in Principle that identifies categories of reforms the parties agree must be taken to remedy the violations of the Constitution and federal law described in this report. Both the Justice Department and the City seek input from all communities in Baltimore on the reforms that should be included in a comprehensive, court-enforceable consent decree to be negotiated by the Justice Department and the City in the coming months, and then entered as a federal court order.

As we have seen in jurisdictions across America, it is possible for law enforcement agencies to enhance their effectiveness by promoting constitutional policing and restoring community partnerships. Strengthening community trust in BPD will not only increase the effectiveness of BPD's law enforcement efforts, it will advance officer and public safety in a manner that serves the entire Baltimore community. Together with City officials and the people of Baltimore, we will work to make this a reality.

I. BACKGROUND

A. BALTIMORE, MARYLAND

Baltimore is the largest city in the state of Maryland with a population of approximately 621,000. The Baltimore metropolitan area's 2.7 million residents make it the nation's 21st largest urban center. The City's population is approximately 63 percent African American, 30 percent white, and 4 percent Hispanic or Latino.[3] While the City hosts a number of successful institutions and businesses,[4] most economic measures show that large portions of Baltimore's population struggle economically. Compared to national averages, Baltimore exhibits: lower incomes, with a median household income nearly 20 percent lower than the national average; higher poverty rates, with 24.2 percent of individuals living below the federal poverty level;[5] elevated unemployment, with a rate hovering around 7 percent, and average unemployment rates per month that were 50 percent higher than the national average from 2014 to 2015.[6] Baltimore also scores below national averages in education: 80.9 percent of the population has graduated from high school, while 27 percent has a bachelor's degree or higher.[7] In most grades and subjects, the percentage of students below basic proficiency in Baltimore was twice the rate seen in Maryland as a whole.[8]

These socioeconomic challenges are pronounced among Baltimore's African-American population, owing in part to the City's history of government-sponsored discrimination. Schools and many other public institutions in the City remained formally segregated until the 1950s, and stark residential segregation has marked the City's history. In 1910, Baltimore became the first city in America to pass an ordinance establishing block-by-block segregation, a policy that was followed by other discriminatory practices, including restrictive covenants, aggressive redlining, a contract system for housing loans, and racially targeted subprime loans.[9] This legacy continues to impact current home ownership patterns, as Baltimore remains among the most segregated cities in the country.[10] In 2008, the City of Baltimore sued Wells Fargo under the Fair Housing Act, alleging that the company steered minority homebuyers into subprime loans. To settle this litigation, Wells Fargo agreed to provide $4.5 million in lending assistance to Baltimore residents and $3 million to address

[3] U. S. Census Bureau, "American FactFinder - Results," accessed April 11, 2016, http://factfinder.census.gov/faces/tableservices/jsf/pages/productview.xhtml?src=CF.

[4] For example, Baltimore is the headquarters for Johns Hopkins University Hospital, Under Armour, Inc., and Legg Mason, Inc., among many others.

[5] U. S. Census Bureau, "American FactFinder - Results," accessed April 11, 2016, http://factfinder.census.gov/faces/tableservices/jsf/pages/productview.xhtml?src=CF.

[6] Department of Labor, Local Area Unemployment Statistics (LAUS) - Workforce Information & Performance, https://www.dllr.state.md.us/lmi/laus/.

[7] Bureau, "American FactFinder - Results." Nationally, over 88 percent of adult Americans have high school diplomas and 32 percent hold a bachelor's degree or higher.

[8] National Center for Education Statistics Institute of Education Sciences, 2009 National Assessment of Educational Proficiency data explorer, http://nces.ed.gov/nationsreportcard/naepdata/dataset.aspx.

[9] *See generally* Antero Pietila, NOT IN MY NEIGHBORHOOD (2010).

[10] Frey W.H., *New Racial Segregation Measures for States and Large Metropolitan Areas: Analysis of the 2005–2009 American Community Survey*, http://censusscope.org/ACS/Segregation.html

issues connected to foreclosures.[11] Certain neighborhoods, such as all of the census tracts in South Baltimore, have been at least 90 percent white since the 1970s. Other areas, including all of the tracts in Cherry Hill, Sandtown-Winchester, and Upton/Druid Hill, have been at least 90 percent black for the past five census periods and are currently more than 95 percent black.[12]

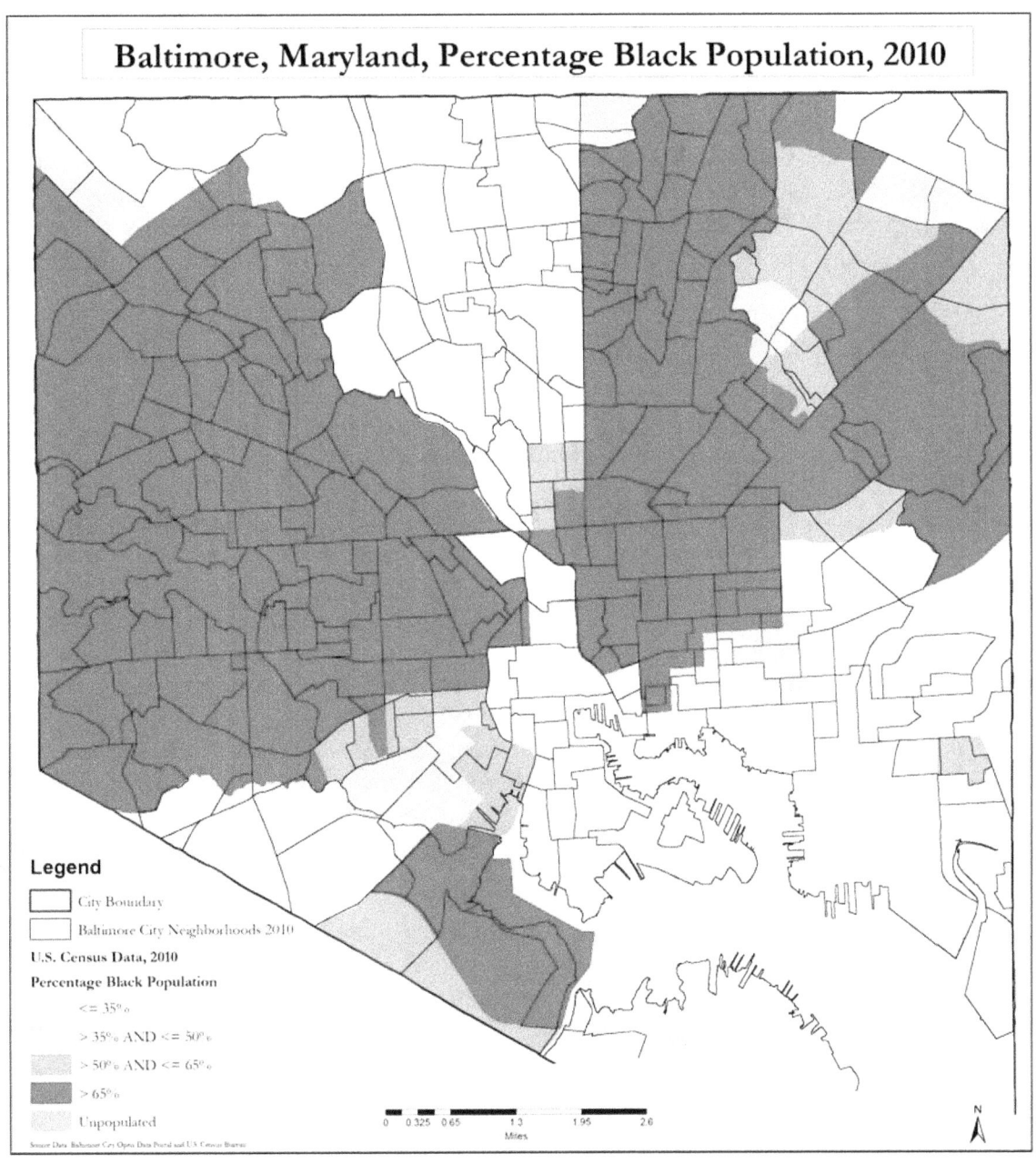

Baltimore, Maryland, Percentage Black Population, 2010

Legend

City Boundary

Baltimore City Neighborhoods 2010

U.S. Census Data, 2010

Percentage Black Population

<= 35%

> 35% AND <= 50%

> 50% AND <= 65%

> 65%

Unpopulated

0   0.325 0.65   1.3   1.95   2.6
Miles

---

[11] Similarly, Wells Fargo paid $234 million to settle a Fair Housing Act and Equal Credit Opportunity Act suit brought by the U.S. Department of Justice that alleged discriminatory lending practices against minorities, including payments to the City of Baltimore and many Baltimore residents that were alleged victims of the discriminatory practices. Wells Fargo agreed to provide $5.7 million in down payment assistance and pay an additional $1.6 million directly to victims with homes in the City.

[12] *Place Matters for Health in Baltimore: Ensuring Opportunities for Good Health for all*, Joint Center for Political and Economic Studies, November 2012, 19-20; 9. http://jointcenter.org/docs/40925_JCBaltimoreReport.pdf

This history of racial discrimination has created persistent racial disparities in economic opportunity and education. Roughly 100,000 African American Baltimore residents live in poverty, accounting for more than three-fourths of Baltimoreans who do so. Many communities, particularly low-income communities, confront grave challenges with respect to upward mobility. Indeed, a recent Harvard University study found that Baltimore has the least upward mobility in America. In the nation's 100 largest jurisdictions, Baltimore's children face the worst odds of escaping poverty.[13] Consequently, the unemployment rate among African Americans is roughly double that of white individuals. In addition, white adults are 3.5 times more likely than black adults to have earned a bachelor's degree. African Americans are also significantly less likely to hold a high school diploma.[14] Moreover, white children make up one percent or less of the student body in numerous schools that serve disproportionately low-income children, perpetuating segregation by race and class.[15]

The impacts of segregation and economic inequality are further evident in lead poisoning patterns across Baltimore. The City has nearly three times the national rate of lead poisoning among children. This burden weighs heaviest on poor, African-American communities. The areas with the highest percentage of children with elevated blood lead levels are the heavily African-American neighborhoods of Sandtown-Winchester/Harlem Park (7.4 percent), Midway/Coldstream (6.1 percent), and Edmondson Village (5.3 percent).[16] According to the Center for Disease Control, even low levels of lead are associated with learning and behavioral problems, including decreased cognitive performance.[17]

While crime rate in urban America has declined significantly since the 1990s, Baltimore has experienced violent crime rates relatively higher than many other large cities. According to data from the Federal Bureau of Investigation, in 2014 Baltimore had the sixth highest rate of violent crimes out of the country's 76 cities with at least 250,000 residents. Baltimore's violent crime rate is roughly equal to that of Cleveland, albeit lower than the rate of violent crime in Detroit, Memphis, and Milwaukee.[18] This past year reflected a notable surge in violence. On a per-capita basis, 2015 was the deadliest year in Baltimore's history with 344 homicides. The City's overall gun violence increased more than 75 percent compared to the previous year, with more than 900 people shot. As

[13] Raj Chetty and Nathaniel Hendren, *The Impacts of Neighborhoods on Intergenerational Mobility*, Harvard University, April 2015. http://www.equality-of-opportunity.org/images/nbhds_exec_summary.pdf

[14] *Place Matters for Health in Baltimore: Ensuring Opportunities for Good Health for all*, Joint Center for Political and Economic Studies, November 2012, 11. http://jointcenter.org/docs/40925_JCBaltimoreReport.pdf

[15] Ayscue, J. B., & Orfield, G. (2015). School district lines stratify educational opportunity by race and poverty. *Race and Social Problems*, 7(1), 5–20. doi:http://dx.doi.org.ezproxy.princeton.edu/10.1007/s12552-014-9135-0

[16] *Vital Signs*, Baltimore Neighborhoods Indicator Alliances, http://bniajfi.org/wp-content/uploads/2014/04/VS12_Children_and_Health.pdf.

[17] Center for Disease Control, "Childhood Lead Poisoning Data, Statistics, and Surveillance," accessed June 14, 2016, http://www.cdc.gov/nceh/lead/data/index.htm.; U.S. Department of Health and Human Services, *National Toxicology Program Monograph: Health Effects of Low-Level Lead*, June 2012, http://ntp.niehs.nih.gov/ntp/ohat/lead/final/monographhealtheffectslowlevellead_newissn_508.pdf; Aimin Chen et al., "Lead Exposure, IQ, and Behavior in Urban 5- to 7-Year-Olds: Does Lead Affect Behavior Only by Lowering IQ?," *Pediatrics* 119, No. 3 (March 1, 2007): e650–58, doi:10.1542/peds.2006-1973.

[18] In Section II.B, *infra*, we compare law enforcement activity in these cities with enforcement actions taken by BPD.

in other major cities, gang activity and a drug economy are also prominent features of Baltimore's crime landscape, although Baltimore residents use drugs at similar rates to the national average.[19]

Despite such challenges, Baltimore remains a vibrant cultural center in the region. It has a significant concentration of educational, medical, cultural, and sports institutions, and a rich collection of neighborhoods. As we heard throughout our investigation, residents take great pride in their neighborhoods and their City as a whole, and have invested deeply in them. These residents are supported by a vast array of community leaders, grassroots organizations, and service providers, and together they comprise a resilient and diverse collection of communities.

B. THE BALTIMORE POLICE DEPARTMENT

The Baltimore Police Department, or BPD, is the eighth largest municipal police department in the nation. BPD employs nearly 3,000 personnel, including approximately 2,600 sworn officers, although this number has declined over the last year. The Department is led by a police commissioner appointed by the mayor of Baltimore and approved by the Baltimore City Council. The current commissioner is Kevin Davis, who was appointed interim commissioner by Mayor Stephanie Rawlings-Blake on July 8, 2015, and sworn into the position permanently on October 19, 2015.

Most BPD officers work in either the Patrol Division or the Criminal Investigations Division, each of which is overseen by a chief.[20] Patrol officers are divided geographically among nine police districts that include local police stationhouses, referred to as district headquarters. Each district has a captain and is led by a major whose primary responsibility is directing enforcement activities and supervising officers. BPD currently employs approximately 1,300 patrol officers who have primary responsibility for responding to calls for service and patrolling Baltimore streets.

The Criminal Investigation Division and Operational Investigation Division house BPD's specialized units, such as the Homicide Section, and the Special Investigation Section, which focus on investigating violent offenders, gangs, and gun crimes across Baltimore. The Division includes units that perform tactical operations, use special weapons, and serve warrants. The names of these specialized enforcement units have changed several times over the past decade. Special enforcement units have previously been called the Violent Crime Impact Division (VCID), Violent Crime Impact Section (VCIS), and the Violent Repeat Offender Unit (VRO). BPD also assigns a small number of officers to its Community Collaboration Division, which focuses on building police-community relations throughout the City.

The Department has a complex process for accountability that is detailed in Section III(C), *infra*. BPD allows district supervisors to resolve complaints of officer misconduct that are deemed less serious offenses, carrying punishment of no more than a three-day suspension. Complaints deemed to allege more serious misconduct are assigned to the Internal Investigation Division. In

---

[19] According to data collected by the Substance Abuse and Mental Health Services Administration, 42.9 percent of Baltimore residents over age 12 have used marijuana, compared to 40.7 percent nationally. For drugs other than marijuana, SAMHSA reports that 3.28 percent of Baltimore adults have used these drugs within the past 30 days, compared to 3.35 percent nationally.

[20] BPD also has an Administrative Bureau that consists of booking, human resources, information services, inspections, and other management functions.

addition, Baltimore established a Civilian Review Board to provide a public voice in BPD's accountability process. Members of the public can lodge complaints with the Board directly, and BPD is required by statute to share with the Board all complaints it receives that fit within certain categories, including excessive force and discourtesy. The Board is authorized to conduct parallel investigations and make disciplinary recommendations. In practice, however, the Board's role has been diminished by severely limited investigative resources, inconsistent complaint referrals from BPD, and the City's failure to fill the Board's seats.

BPD officers are represented by the Fraternal Order of the Police Lodge No. 3 (FOP), which has a collective-bargaining contract with the City and serves as the sole collective-bargaining agent for officers below the rank of lieutenant, making membership inclusive of both line officers and their direct supervisors. In addition to the FOP, the Vanguard Justice Society, Inc., is a membership organization that advocates on behalf of minority officers. BPD did not hire its first African-American officer until 1937 and did not allow minority officers to drive patrol cars until 1966. Prior to 1966, the Department's small number of African-American officers were required to work foot patrol and were not permitted to work in predominantly white neighborhoods. In recent years, the Department has made efforts to attract and promote minority candidates. As of 2015, African Americans accounted for approximately 42 percent of BPD officers. About one-fifth of BPD officers are women. Most BPD officers are neither originally from Baltimore nor live in the City, and many commute long distances to work at the Department. Indeed, BPD leadership informed us that roughly three-fourths of BPD officers live outside the Baltimore City limits.

BPD coordinates with several auxiliary law enforcement agencies, and has done so increasingly in recent years to compensate when districts do not have sufficient officers to staff shifts. These agencies include the Baltimore School Police, the police force of the Baltimore City Public School System. Baltimore School Police officers have all the powers of law enforcement officers in the state, including arrest powers.[21] A memorandum of understanding between the Public School System and BPD authorizes the school police to "exercise full police power anywhere within the jurisdiction of the City of Baltimore," and to assist in investigations and follow-up in criminal cases.[22] The deployment plan for the school police indicates that these officers are assigned to foot patrol, bike units, and mobile response units outside of schools.[23] These officers also respond to calls for service in the City when BPD patrol shifts are understaffed.

C. BPD's ENFORCEMENT PRIORITIES AND RELATIONSHIP WITH THE BALTIMORE COMMUNITY

Baltimore's legacy of government-sanctioned discrimination, serious health hazards, and high rates of violent crime have persisted and compounded for years—making Baltimore a challenging city to police fairly and effectively. Indeed, officers convey that working in Baltimore affords a uniquely intense and demanding experience. One member of BPD recently asserted, "a

---

[21] Md. Code Ann., Educ. §§4–318 (c) and (d)(1) (2015).
[22] Memorandum of Understanding between the Baltimore City Public School System and Baltimore Police Department at 1–2 (June 27, 2007).
[23] Marshall T. Goddwin, Chief, Baltimore School Police Force, *Deployment For SY 2015/2016*, July 2, 2015.

five-year cop in the city has the equivalent experience of a ten-year cop anywhere else."[24] These challenges are amplified by long-simmering distrust of law enforcement from segments of the Baltimore community. Indeed, when asked when community distrust of Baltimore law enforcement began, a former top city official deadpanned to Justice Department officials, "1729"—the year of the City's founding. These tensions hardened during the 1990s and 2000s as the City responded to increasing violent crime rates by emphasizing an aggressive, "zero tolerance" policing strategy that prioritized making large numbers of stops, searches, and arrests—often for misdemeanor street offenses like loitering and disorderly conduct. Throughout the 1990s and 2000s, arresting large numbers of people for minor offenses was central to BPD's enforcement paradigm; in 2005, BPD made more than 108,000 arrests, most for nonviolent offenses.

Arrest numbers declined starting in the late 2000s in response to falling crime rates and efforts to move towards a more holistic policing model focused on building community partnerships. Indeed, current BPD Commissioner Davis and his predecessor, Anthony W. Batts, have both acknowledged publicly that the zero tolerance approach to policing eroded community trust and impeded efforts to build partnerships that are central to effective policing. Despite these efforts, however, the legacy of zero tolerance persists in many aspects of the Department's enforcement. Many supervisors who were inculcated in the era of zero tolerance continue to focus on the raw number of officers' stops and arrests, rather than more nuanced measures of performance. As one example of this approach, supervisors frequently encourage officers to "clear corners"—an instruction many officers understand to stop, disperse, or arrest groups of individuals standing on public sidewalks. The continued emphasis on these types of "stats" drives BPD's tendency to stop, search, and arrest significant numbers of individuals on Baltimore streets—often without requisite legal justification and in situations that put officers in adversarial encounters that have little connection to public safety. Although arrest numbers have declined from their peak in the mid-2000s, BPD officers made over 200,000 arrests and 300,000 pedestrian stops in the five years of data we examined.[25]

A diverse array of stakeholders has highlighted problems with BPD's policing strategy. For example, the Fraternal Order of Police's 2012 Blueprint for Improved Policing in Baltimore advocates discontinuing the practice of rewarding statistically driven arrests, noting:

> [N]umbers drive everything in the BPD, which has led to misplaced priorities. As a result, officers in the BPD feel pressure to achieve numbers for perception's sake… The focus on assigning blame for less-than-satisfactory numbers… rather than problem-solving, is completely unproductive and weakens the collective morale of the BPD.[26]

City officials also admit that the Department's approach has been problematic. Mayor Rawlings-Blake has long recognized the need for reform and repeatedly criticized the aggressive policing

---

[24] Fraternal Order of Police Lodge 3, *Blueprint for Improved Policing*, 5, http://www.fop3.org/wp-content/uploads/2015/05/blueprint.pdf.

[25] As explained further in Section II.A, the true number of pedestrian stops is likely several times higher than the recorded figure due to BPD's under-reporting.

[26] Fraternal Order of Police Lodge 3, *Blueprint for Improved Policing*, 8–9, http://www.fop3.org/wp-content/uploads/2015/05/blueprint.pdf

strategies championed in the years before her term. In September 2013, she told residents, "As this conversation is going on, there is an anxiety that is building in some of our communities that we're going back to a time when communities felt like their kids were under siege . . . I want to allay any concerns out there that that is the tactic we're going to return to. That's not going to happen."[27] And in the fall of 2014, her administration noted that the zero tolerance strategy "ignited a rift between the citizens and the police, which still exists today" and that there is a "broken relationship" between law enforcement officials and community members.[28]

The larger Baltimore community has voiced similar concerns. News outlets, community advocates, and grassroots organizations have frequently criticized Baltimore's approach to policing. In 2006, the ACLU of Maryland sued BPD over its alleged pattern of making high numbers of unlawful stops and arrests. In addition, the police department has long faced allegations of unreasonable force. In some of these allegations, the police interactions were fatal. In others, Baltimore residents were left severely and permanently injured. In September 2014, the Baltimore Sun published "Undue Force," an article documenting cases of alleged police brutality and the millions of dollars the city has paid to settle lawsuits alleging that officers used excessive force. The article notes that more than 100 people have won court judgments or settlements related to allegations of brutality and civil rights violations since 2010.[29] More recently, No Boundaries Coalition, a resident-led advocacy organization operating in West Baltimore, released a report in March 2016 detailing stories of police misconduct told by witnesses and victims in the Sandtown-Winchester neighborhood. The community recollections reveal a belief that there is racism in law enforcement, unnecessary force and verbal abuse, an "us-versus-them" attitude among police officers, a lack of positive interactions with the police, and strong feelings of recrimination, resentment, fear, and mistrust among residents.[30]

In 2012, Mayor Rawlings-Blake hired Commissioner Batts to initiate reforms throughout the police department. The following year, Commissioner Batts issued *Public Safety in the City of Baltimore*, a five-year plan intended to "reduce crime, improve service, increase efficiency, redouble community engagement, and provide for the highest standards of accountability and ethical integrity."[31] The report discussed numerous challenges facing BPD, including: equipment, accountability, training, and communication failures; strained police-community relations, and low community engagement; and decreased morale and motivation among officers.[32] The report included an internal survey that revealed that only 14 percent of BPD employees believed the Baltimore community supports the police department. The report also laid out a plan for improving BPD's work in these areas. During a similar time period, the City substantially increased the resources of the police department. While

[27] Luke Broadwater and Eric Cox, "Governor's Push for More Arrests Causing 'Anxiety' in Baltimore, Mayor Says," *Baltimore Sun*, September 25, 2013, http://www.baltimoresun.com/news/maryland/politics/blog/bs-md-ci-srb-arrests-20130925-story.html.

[28] John Fritze, "Rawlings-Blake Criticism Highlights Debate over Police Strategy under O'Malley," *Baltimore Sun*, October 13, 2014, http://www.baltimoresun.com/news/maryland/politics/bs-md-police-omalley-politics-20141007-story.html.

[29] Mark Puente, "Undue Force," *Baltimore Sun*, September 28, 2014, http://data.baltimoresun.com/news/police-settlements/.

[30] No Boundaries Coalition, *Over-Policed, Yet Underserved*, March 2016, http://www.noboundariescoalition.com/wp-content/uploads/2016/03/No-Boundaries-Layout-Web-1.pdf.

[31] Anthony Batts, *Public Safety in the City of Baltimore: A Strategic Plan for Improvement*, 2013, 5.

[32] *Id.* at 45–48.

the city faces serious budget constraints, the fiscal year 2016 police budget was approved at $476 million, representing a dramatic increase from the 2010 police budget of $340 million.

As the reform plans Commissioner Batts initiated were in their early stages, the unrest following the death of Freddie Gray in police custody in April 2015 demonstrated the deep and enduring divide between police officers and parts of the Baltimore community. Commissioner Davis acknowledged that BPD's legacy of zero tolerance enforcement contributed to these tensions: "Some of things that we did in the past, like zero tolerance policing, didn't work and arguably led in part to the unrest that we experienced in 2015."[33] He has also acknowledged that improved relations with City residents require BPD to change its culture.[34] The desire for such reform is apparent. Commissioner Davis began a "History of Baltimore" speakers-series in early 2016 to provide officers with an understanding of the City's historical background. The topics, which range from housing and segregation to the development of Baltimore's port, were selected to provide a deeper appreciation of the diverse communities that the police serve. The release of a new Core Operating Procedures Manual during the summer of 2016 also represents an attempt to improve standards and guidelines with respect to officers' use of force.

We commend these efforts, but find that significant obstacles remain to achieving the change necessary to ensure that BPD's policing is both effective and constitutional. As described below, we find that BPD has engaged in a pattern or practice of conduct that violates the constitutional and federal statutory rights of City residents, and that the Department lacks sufficient systems to minimize these violations.

D. FEDERAL INVOLVEMENT

Numerous federal components have assisted BPD's reform efforts in recent years. In October 2014, Mayor Rawlings-Blake and Commissioner Batts requested to enter a collaborative reform process with the Department of Justice's Office of Community Oriented Policing Services (COPS). This federal review involved an assessment of BPD's policies, training, and operations as they related to the use of force and interactions with the members of the community. Through this process, subject matter experts identified by the COPS office began to examine BPD's community policing and engagement efforts and provided additional resources and trainings, such as peer-to-peer exchanges to facilitate sharing best practices from other police departments. Over the past several years, the Office of Justice Programs also awarded Byrne Justice Assistance grants to BPD, to support certain initiatives, including: a comprehensive review of BPD's technology systems and capabilities; an analysis of BPD's grant development efforts and strategy; and a customized workshop for BPD command staff to effectively develop and manage crime analysis capabilities. In response to another request from City leadership, the Justice Department provided federal law enforcement resources to help the City combat its crime and public safety challenges in August 2015. Following this initial assistance, the Bureau of Alcohol, Tobacco, Firearms and Explosives, the Federal Bureau of Investigation, the Drug Enforcement Administration, and the U.S. Marshals

---

[33] Mary Rose Madden, "Baltimore Police Chief Wants To Reform Department," *NPR: All Things Considered*, April 24, 2016, http://www.npr.org/2016/04/24/475511963/baltimore-police-chief-wants-to-reform-department.
[34] Kevin Rector, Justin George, and Mark Puente, "Baltimore's New Police Commissioner Has a Full Plate — and an Opportunity," *Baltimore Sun*, July 12, 2015, http://www.baltimoresun.com/news/maryland/bs-md-davis-challenges-20150711-story.html.

Service all agreed to make a longer term commitment of resources to law enforcement efforts in Baltimore.[35]

The death of Freddie Gray and ensuing unrest occurred during the early stages of the collaborative reform efforts between BPD and COPS. These events underscored the critical lack of trust between BPD and a significant portion of the City's residents, especially African Americans. After reviewing information it had received about BPD's police practices and receiving requests from Mayor Rawlings-Blake, members of Congress, and numerous other members of the Baltimore community, the Justice Department determined BPD warranted a comprehensive civil rights investigation to determine whether the Department engaged in a pattern or practice of constitutional and statutory violations. The Civil Rights Division thus opened a formal investigation into BPD on May 8, 2015. Since the civil rights investigation opened, the COPS office has continued to provide technical assistance to BPD.

Our investigation recognizes that, as Commissioner Davis aptly noted, Baltimore officers "have the burden to address racism and poverty and education and homelessness." These problems, which confront officers every day on the street and are not their responsibility alone to fix, are nevertheless intertwined with crime conditions across the City. But this burden on officers does not excuse BPD's violations of the constitutional and statutory rights of the people living in these challenging conditions. We find that BPD's practices perpetuate and fuel a multitude of issues rooted in poverty and race, focusing law enforcement actions on low-income, minority communities in a manner that is often unnecessary and unproductive. In other words, BPD's law enforcement practices at times exacerbate the longstanding structural inequalities in the City by encouraging officers to have unnecessary, adversarial interactions with community members that increase exposure to the criminal justice system and fail to improve public safety.

---

[35] During this same time period, the Office of Justice Programs Office for Civil Rights initiated a language access compliance review of BPD, and that review is still ongoing.

II. BPD ENGAGES IN A PATTERN OR PRACTICE OF CONDUCT THAT VIOLATES THE UNITED STATES CONSTITUTION AND LAWS, AND CONDUCT THAT RAISES SERIOUS CONCERNS

The Civil Rights Division of the United States Department of Justice opened this investigation pursuant to the Violent Crime Control and Law Enforcement Act of 1994, 42 U.S.C. § 14141 ("Section 14141"), Title VI of the Civil Rights Act of 1964, 42 U.S.C. § 2000d ("Title VI"), and the Omnibus Crime Control and Safe Streets Act of 1968, 42 U.S.C. § 3789d ("Safe Streets Act" or "SSA"), and Title II of the Americans with Disabilities Act of 1990 (ADA), 42 U.S.C. §§ 12131–12134. Section 14141 prohibits law enforcement agencies from engaging in a pattern or practice of conduct that violates the Constitution or laws of the United States. Where such a pattern or practice exists, Section 14141 grants the Attorney General authority to bring suit for equitable and declaratory relief to remedy it. A pattern or practice exists where violations are repeated rather than isolated. *Int'l Bd. of Teamsters v. United States*, 431 U.S. 324, 336 n.16 (1977) (noting that the phrase "pattern or practice" "was not intended as a term of art," but should be interpreted according to its usual meaning "consistent with the understanding of the identical words" used in other federal civil rights statutes). An unlawful pattern or practice does not require any specific number of incidents. *United States v. W. Peachtree Tenth Corp.*, 437 F.2d 221, 227 (5th Cir. 1971) ("The number of [violations] . . . is not determinative. . . . In any event, no mathematical formula is workable, nor was any intended. Each case must turn on its own facts."); *see also Stastny v. S. Bell Tel. & Tel. Co.*, 628 F.2d 267, 278 (4th Cir. 1980) (holding in the context of employment discrimination that a plaintiff may show a pattern or practice through statistical evidence or a "sufficient number of instances of similar discriminatory treatment"). Title VI and its implementing regulations prohibit recipients of federal financial assistance, such as BPD, from discriminating on the basis of race, color, or national origin. Title VI provides that no person shall "be excluded from participating in, be denied the benefits of, or be subjected to discrimination under any program or activity receiving [f]ederal financial assistance" based on race. 42 U.S.C. § 2000d. The Title VI implementing regulations ban recipients of federal funds from using "criteria or methods of administration" that have an unnecessary disparate impact based on race. 28 C.F.R. § 42.104(b)(2). The Safe Streets Act likewise prohibits law enforcement practices that cause disparate impact based on race except where such impact is necessary to achieve nondiscriminatory objectives. *See* 28 C.F.R. § 42.203. The ADA, which applies to BPD's services, programs, and activities, including on-the-street encounters, arrests, and transportation to a hospital for mental health evaluation, *See* 42 U.S.C. § 12132; 28 C.F.R. § 35.130(a); requires BPD to "make reasonable modifications in policies, practices, or procedures when the modifications are necessary to avoid discrimination on the basis of disability." 28 C.F.R. § 35.130(b)(7); *Title II Technical Assistance Manual* § II-3.6100, at 14.

Our investigation finds that BPD engages in a pattern or practice of conduct that implicates our statutory authority. This pattern or practice is rooted in BPD's deficient supervision and oversight of officer activity, leading directly to a broad spectrum of constitutional and statutory violations. This lack of supervision and oversight includes BPD's failure to use effective and widely-accepted methods to supervise officers, collect and analyze data on officer activity, and classify, investigate, and resolve complaints of misconduct. This pattern or practice is also manifested in several ways that violate specific constitutional and statutory provisions: (1) BPD stops, searches, and arrests individuals on Baltimore streets without the reasonable suspicion or probable cause required by the Fourth Amendment; (2) BPD disproportionately stops, searches, and arrests African Americans in violation of Title VI and the Safe Streets Act, and this disparate impact, along with evidence suggesting intentional discrimination against African Americans, exacerbates community distrust of the police; (3) BPD uses unreasonable force in violation of the Fourth Amendment; (4) BPD violates the First Amendment rights of Baltimore residents by using force or otherwise retaliating against individuals exercising constitutionally protected activity, such as public speech and filming police activity; and (5) BPD's use of force against individuals with mental health disabilities or experiencing crisis violates the Americans with Disabilities Act. To illustrate these violations, throughout this letter we provide several examples of each type of violation that we found during our investigation. In some sections we provide more examples to illustrate the variety of circumstances in which the violation occurs, while in others we focus on one or two examples that demonstrate the nature of the violations we found. The number of examples included in a particular section is not indicative of the number of violations we found. These examples comprise a small subset of the total number of incidents upon which we base our conclusions.

We make these findings after a comprehensive 14-month investigation into BPD's practices. To gain the broadest possible perspective on the challenges facing BPD, our investigation involved reviewing an exhaustive set of documents and meeting with hundreds of officers, community members, city leaders, and other stakeholders. In total, we reviewed hundreds of thousands of pages of documents, including all relevant policies and training materials used by the Department since 2010; BPD's database of internal affairs files; a random sample of about 800 case files on non-deadly force incidents; files on all deadly force incidents since 2010 that BPD was able to produce to us through May 1, 2016; a sample of several hundred incident reports describing stops, searches, and arrests; investigative files on sexual assault cases; databases maintained by BPD and the State of Maryland containing information on hundreds of thousands of pedestrian stops, vehicle stops, and arrests; and many others. Throughout our review, we were assisted by a dozen law enforcement experts from across the country with expertise on the issues we investigated.

Our investigation also relied on numerous interviews with current and former BPD officers and city officials. At all times, BPD leadership took a cooperative and professional approach to our investigation and provided important insights into the challenges facing the Department. We met at length with current Commissioner Kevin Davis, former Commissioner Anthony Batts, and leaders throughout the BPD command structure. We visited each of BPD's nine police districts, where we met district leadership and spoke with line officers. We also accompanied line officers on dozens of ride-alongs that took place in every district. Line officers shared many key insights during these ride-alongs and other interviews. We are grateful for their candor in discussing the serious challenges they face and their genuine interest in preventing the types of issues discussed in our findings. We are likewise grateful to the leadership of the Baltimore Fraternal Order of Police, which met with us on multiple occasions and invited us to speak to union members at a lodge dinner. The Vanguard Justice Society similarly invited us to speak with their members and provided highly relevant information. To gain the broadest possible perspective on the challenges facing BPD, we also met with current and former officials in City government, including current and former elected officials and prosecutors from the State's Attorney's Office.

As in all of our investigations, we also met with large numbers of people in the broader Baltimore community. Our community outreach included meetings at churches and with religious leaders; meeting with advocacy and community support organizations; attending a variety of neighborhood gatherings, from formal meetings of neighborhood associations to summer barbecues; and canvassing neighborhoods on foot to collect stories about interactions with the police. We also met individually with numerous individuals who contacted us to share information. In sum, we met with more than 500 individuals during our investigation. We are extremely thankful for the many members of the Baltimore community who came forward to share information with us, even when doing so involved reliving difficult personal experiences. We are left with the firm impression that, despite the significant obstacles to restoring community trust in BPD, there is a deep desire across diverse elements of the City for a police force that is responsive, effective, and fair.

A. BPD MAKES UNCONSTITUTIONAL STOPS, SEARCHES, AND ARRESTS

We find that BPD engages in a pattern or practice of making stops, searches, and arrests in violation of the Fourth and Fourteenth Amendments and Section 14141. BPD frequently makes investigative stops without reasonable suspicion of people who are lawfully present on Baltimore streets. During stops, officers commonly conduct weapons frisks—or more invasive searches—despite lacking reasonable suspicion that the subject of the search is armed. These practices escalate street encounters and contribute to officers making arrests without probable cause,[36] often for discretionary misdemeanor offenses like disorderly conduct, resisting arrest, loitering, trespassing, and failure to obey. Indeed, BPD's own supervisors at Central Booking and prosecutors in the State's Attorney's Office declined to charge more than 11,000 arrests made by BPD officers since 2010.

1. BPD's Unconstitutional Stops, Searches, and Arrests Result in Part from Its "Zero Tolerance" Enforcement Strategy

The pattern of constitutional violations described below result in part from BPD's "zero tolerance" enforcement strategy, dating to the early 2000s. That strategy prioritized attempts to suppress crime by regularly stopping and searching pedestrians and arresting them on any available charges, including discretionary misdemeanor offenses. Recent BPD leadership, including the two most recent police commissioners, has acknowledged some of the problems created by this zero tolerance approach to enforcement and has attempted to shift BPD's focus to a more holistic policing model with greater emphasis on building community partnerships. For example, in April 2015 BPD enacted a new policy on misdemeanor "quality of life" offenses that instructed officers that "a verbal warning and counseling is preferable to a criminal/civil citation, and a criminal/civil citation is preferable to an arrest." Despite these laudable efforts, however, the legacy of the zero tolerance era continues to influence officer activity and contribute to constitutional violations.

Indeed, many BPD supervisors who were trained under the prior enforcement paradigm continue to encourage officers to prioritize short-term suppression, including aggressive use of stops, frisks, and misdemeanor arrests. A current BPD sergeant recently endorsed this approach to policing, posting on Facebook that the "solution to the murder rate is easy. Flex cuffs and a line at [Central Booking]. CJIS code 2-0055." CJIS 2-0055 is the offense code entered for loitering arrests. Similarly, a flyer celebrating loitering arrests was posted in several BPD districts. The flyer depicted three officers from one of BPD's specialized units known as Violent Crime Impact Division, or VCID, leading a handcuffed man wearing a hoodie along a city sidewalk towards a police transport van, with the text "VCID: Striking fear into loiters [sic] City-wide." And a deployment memo posted in one of BPD's districts in the summer of 2015 likewise encouraged officers to suppress crime through "proactive enforcement," including "stop and frisk," "street level drug enforcement," "warrant checks," "foot patrol," "car stops," and "quality of life" arrests.

---

[36] As detailed in Section II(C) below, these street encounters also contribute to officers' pattern or practice of using excessive force.

VCID

Striking fear into loiters City-Wide

These influences have contributed to BPD officers making large numbers of stops, searches, and arrests, often with dubious justification. From January 2010–May 2014, BPD officers recorded over 301,000 pedestrian stops. And the true number of stops is likely far higher because BPD officers do not document stops consistently. BPD's data suggests that stops are significantly under-reported. In 2014 alone, BPD officers recorded approximately 124,000 stops, but an internal audit found that officers completed reports for only 37 out of a sample of 123 investigative stops captured on the computer-aided dispatch (CAD) system. If this audit accurately captures BPD's overall rate of reporting stops in 2014, it indicates that officers made roughly 412,000 stops *that year alone*, which is more than seven times the average number of stops that BPD reported per year from 2010 to 2015. Other measures suggest that even this estimate may be conservative. BPD's 2014 audit of handgun charges that arose from stops found that officers did not complete a stop form in a single one of the 335 cases. These data are consistent with interviews and observations during the Justice Department's investigation, which revealed that many officers fill out stop reports rarely, if at all. In short, our investigation suggests that BPD officers likely make several hundred thousand pedestrian stops per year[37] in a city with only 620,000 residents.

---

[37] During this period, BPD policy required officers to record all stops on a form titled "Stop and Frisk." Some of the activity recorded by officers on this form may reflect encounters that do not require reasonable suspicion, such as

Moreover, BPD's data show that these stops are concentrated on a small segment of the City's population. From 2010–2014, BPD officers in the Western and Central Districts recorded more than 111,500 stops—roughly 44 percent of the total stops for which officers recorded a district location.[38] Yet these are the two least populated police districts in Baltimore, with a combined population of only 75,000, or 12 percent of City residents.[39] These districts include the City's central business district and several poor, urban neighborhoods with mostly African-American residents.[40] In these districts, police recorded nearly 1.5 stops per resident over a four-year period. This data reveals that certain Baltimore residents have repeated encounters with the police on public streets and sidewalks. Indeed, the data show that one African-American man was stopped 34 times during this period in the Central and Western Districts alone, and several hundred residents were stopped at least 10 times. Countless individuals—including Freddie Gray—were stopped multiple times in the same week without being charged with a crime.[41]

The data likewise indicate that these encounters produce large numbers of arrests. While a significant portion of these arrests reflect BPD's efforts to combat violent crime in Baltimore City, more than 25,000 arrests were for non-violent misdemeanor offenses for which officers have significant discretion about whether to make an arrest. BPD arrested approximately 6,500 people for disorderly conduct, 4,000 for failing to obey a police officer, 6,500 for trespassing, 1,000 for "hindering" or impeding, 3,200 for "interference," 760 for being "rogue and vagabond," and 650 for playing cards or dice. These highly discretionary offenses often are not an effective way to promote public safety and are subject to abuse. Indeed, supervisors at Central Booking and local prosecutors dismissed a significant percentage of these charges upon their initial review of arrest documents. This initial review resulted in dismissal of 1 in 6 of these highly discretionary charges. Over 20 percent of all disorderly conduct charges and 25 percent of failure to obey charges were dismissed.

Careful oversight is necessary to ensure that these frequent street encounters and arrests do not result in constitutional violations. Our investigation finds, however, that BPD has amplified the risk of constitutional violations in its street enforcement efforts by relying on inadequate policies, training, supervision, and accountability mechanisms. The Department does not collect reliable data on stops and searches, has no mechanism for identifying patterns or trends in its officers' stops,

---

voluntary social contacts and witness interviews. The large majority of stops recorded, however, appear to reflect situations in which the subject is not free to leave and reasonable suspicion is required. This conclusion stems from interviews with officers who explained that they completed a "Stop and Frisk" form only when making an investigative stop, and analysis of a sample of over 7,000 stops examined by Justice Department investigators, which revealed that 73 percent of stops involved officers detaining subjects at least long enough to complete a warrant check. The stop data discussed here thus overwhelmingly reflect stops that require reasonable suspicion. In 2015, BPD addressed this issue by changing its documentation protocols so that officers complete "citizen/police contact" forms for voluntary field interviews and a "Form 309" for investigative detentions, weapons frisks, and searches.

[38] Officers recorded district information in approximately 254,000 out of 301,000 total recorded stops.

[39] Population data on BPD's police districts was provided by the Department and was compiled from the U.S. Census Bureau's 2014 American Community Survey 5-year data.

[40] According to 2014 estimates from the U.S. Census Bureau, African Americans account for 83 percent of the population in the Central District and 96 percent in the Western District.

[41] The data show that BPD recorded stops of Freddie Gray on February 16th and 20th, 2014. The data nonetheless record only three total stops of Freddie Gray between 2010 and 2015. These records further indicate that BPD officers under-report pedestrian stops. Although BPD arrested Mr. Gray at least four times from 2010–2014 on charges stemming from street encounters, none of these arrests have a corresponding stop report in BPD's data.

searches, and arrests, and conducts little substantive review of officers' reasons for taking particular enforcement actions. Indeed, BPD has failed to take corrective action even where third parties—including local prosecutors—have identified officers who may be making stops, searches, or arrests in violation of the Constitution. As a result, the pattern or practice of constitutional violations described below has persisted for many years, undermining trust in law enforcement and impeding BPD's ability to form community partnerships that are essential to effective policing.

2. BPD Unconstitutionally Stops and Searches Pedestrians

The Fourth Amendment protects individuals from unreasonable seizures "when they step from their homes onto the public sidewalks." *Delaware v. Prouse*, 440 U.S. 648, 663 (1979). Contrary to this principle, we find reasonable cause to believe that BPD officers regularly stop and search individuals who are lawfully present on Baltimore's streets, despite lacking the constitutionally-required indicia that criminal activity is afoot.

Our findings are based on statistical analysis of stop outcomes, interviews with officers and community members, complaints filed against BPD, and our review of a random sample of several hundred incident reports that officers completed for arrests that stemmed from pedestrian stops. Officers' descriptions of the underlying stops in these incident reports revealed frequent constitutional deficiencies. We were unable to systematically analyze the sufficiency of reasonable suspicion in *all* stops made by BPD officers—as opposed to the subset of stops leading to arrest—because most BPD stop reports do not describe the facts establishing reasonable suspicion for a stop.[42] By limiting our review to stops that resulted in arrest, we focused on cases where officers presumably had stronger indicia of criminality to justify a stop compared to stops in which the investigation proved fruitless. It is troubling that this review nonetheless found repeated constitutional violations during stops and searches by BPD officers.

a. BPD Stops Pedestrians Without Reasonable Suspicion

Our investigation reveals a widespread pattern of BPD officers stopping and detaining people on Baltimore streets without reasonable suspicion that they are involved in criminal activity. This conduct violates the Fourth Amendment, which allows police officers to briefly detain an individual for investigation where the officers possess reasonable suspicion that the person is involved in criminal activity, *Terry v. Ohio*, 392 U.S. 1, 21 (1968). To satisfy this standard, officers "must be able to point to specific and articulable facts" supporting an inference of criminal activity; an "inchoate and unparticularized suspicion or hunch" is insufficient. *Id.* at 27.

Terry's particularity requirement is not satisfied where an officer deems a person to be acting suspiciously but fails to explain the specific basis of that suspicion. The police "must do more than simply label a behavior as suspicious to make it so"; rather, the police must also be able to . . . articulate why a particular behavior is suspicious" *United States v. Massenburg*, 654 F.3d 480, 491 (4th Cir. 2011) (citations and internal quotation marks omitted). Standing alone, an individual's unexplained presence in a high crime area is not sufficient to establish reasonable suspicion. *Illinois*

---

[42] As explained further below, the failure to capture the facts supporting reasonable suspicion on stop forms also precludes BPD supervisors from substantively reviewing the basis for stops and correcting officer behavior, where necessary.

v. Wardlow, 528 U.S. 119, 124 (2000) (citation omitted); *United States v. Slocumb*, 804 F.3d 677, 682–83 (4th Cir. 2015) (finding that officers lacked reasonable suspicion to stop a man who was present in a high crime area late at night, acting nervously, and conducting himself in a way that seemed "inconsistent" with his stated reasons for being at the location). Nor is an individual's decision to move away from police "in a normal, unhurried manner." *United States v. Sprinkle*, 106 F.3d 613, 617–18 (4th Cir. 1997) (officers lacked reasonable suspicion to stop individual who covered his face with his hand to conceal his identity and drove away from police at normal speed); *cf. United States v. Bumpers*, 705 F.3d 168, 175–76 (4th Cir. 2013) (finding reasonable suspicion where an apparent trespasser in high crime area "dodge[d] the police" by "walking away 'at a fast pace'"). Notwithstanding these requirements, officers may always approach individuals to make social contact and ask them to answer questions voluntarily. The cases discussed in this section involve situations in which BPD officers' descriptions of an encounter indicate that the person stopped was not free to leave and reasonable suspicion was therefore required.

BPD officers routinely violate these standards by detaining and questioning individuals who are sitting, standing, or walking in public areas, even where officers have no basis to suspect them of wrongdoing. The lack of sufficient justification for many of BPD's pedestrian stops is underscored by the extremely low rate at which stops uncover evidence of criminal activity. In a sample of over 7,200 pedestrian stops reviewed by the Justice Department, only 271—or 3.7 percent—resulted in officers issuing a criminal citation or arrest. Expressed a different way, BPD officers did not find and charge criminal activity in 26 out of every 27 pedestrian stops. Such low "hit rates" are a strong indication that officers make stops based on a threshold of suspicion that falls below constitutional requirements. *See Floyd v. City of New York*, 959 F. Supp. 2d 540, 575 (S.D.N.Y. 2013) (finding that a hit rate of 12 percent in pedestrian stops indicated that the stops were not supported by reasonable suspicion).

Despite the low rate of stops uncovering evidence of crimes, BPD supervisors often direct officers to make frequent stops as a crime suppression technique. Many of the unlawful stops we identified appear motivated at least in part by officers' desire to check whether the stopped individuals have outstanding warrants that would allow officers to make an arrest or search individuals in hopes of finding illegal firearms or narcotics. *Cf. Utah v. Strieff*, 579 U.S. __, slip op. at 8 (June 20, 2016) (holding that search incident to arrest was valid based on the discovery of an arrest warrant, even when the initial stop was unconstitutional, because "the stop was an isolated instance of negligence" and there was "no indication that this unlawful stop was part of any systemic or recurrent police misconduct"); *see also* 579 U.S. __, slip op. at 10–11 (Sotomayor, J., dissenting) (warning that police may make unlawful stops in hopes of uncovering outstanding warrants, subjecting individuals to "humiliations" and "indignity").[43] Indeed, where individuals lack identification allowing officers to check for warrants, officers sometimes detain and transport them to booking facilities to check their identification via fingerprinting—an unconstitutional detention even where officers have reasonable suspicion to make the initial investigative stop. *See, e.g., United States v. Zavala*, 541 F.3d 562, 579–80 (5th Cir. 2008) (90-minute detention in which subject was handcuffed, placed in a police car, and transported to different location "morphed from a *Terry* detention into a de facto arrest").

---

[43] Consistent with this concern, BPD officers indicated that they conducted a warrant check in 73 percent of all pedestrian stops the Justice Department analyzed—including many stops that lacked reasonable suspicion.

Officers' own reports describe this facially unconstitutional conduct. For example, an officer in the Northeast District noted in an incident report that he observed a 22-year-old African American male walking through an area "known to have a high rate of crime and [drug] activity." After watching the subject turn into an alley, the officer—despite possessing no specific information indicating that the man was involved in criminal activity—stopped and questioned him. The officer's report does not identify any evidence of wrongdoing uncovered during the *Terry* stop. Nonetheless, the report explains that the officer transported the man to BPD's Northeast District headquarters to "properly identif[y]" him because the subject "was reluctant to give any information about himself or his actions." After this custodial detention likewise uncovered no evidence of wrongdoing, the subject was finally released. This stop lacked reasonable suspicion at the outset, far exceeded the temporal limits even for valid *Terry* stops, *see infra* at 39, and violates BPD's policy requiring officers to contact supervisors when a *Terry* stop lasts for more than 20 minutes. But a BPD supervisor nonetheless signed off on the incident report describing this unlawful stop and detention.

In some cases, unconstitutional stops result from supervisory officers' explicit instructions. During a ride-along with Justice Department officials, a BPD sergeant instructed a patrol officer to stop a group of young African-American males on a street corner, question them, and order them to disperse. When the patrol officer protested that he had no valid reason to stop the group, the sergeant replied "Then make something up." This incident is far from anomalous. A different BPD sergeant posted on Facebook that when he supervises officers in the Northeast District, he encourages them to "clear corners," a term many officers understand to mean stopping pedestrians who are standing on city sidewalks to question and then disperse them by threatening arrest for minor offenses like loitering and trespassing. The sergeant wrote, "I used to say at roll call in NE when I ran the shift: Do not treat criminals like citizens. Citizens want that corner cleared." Indeed, countless interviews with community members and officers describe "corner clearing" scenarios, in which BPD officers stop, question, disperse, or arrest individuals in public areas based on minimal or no suspicion of highly discretionary offenses.

Such unlawful stops erode public confidence in law enforcement and escalate street encounters, sometimes resulting in officers deploying unnecessary force or committing additional constitutional violations. For example, on a cold January evening in 2013, an officer approached and questioned an African-American man crossing the street in a "high crime area" while wearing a hooded sweatshirt. The officer lacked any specific reason to believe the man was engaged in criminal activity, but, according to the incident report prepared by the supervisory officer on the scene, the officer "thought it could be possible that the individual could be out seeking a victim of opportunity."[44] This unsupported speculation furnishes no basis to conduct a stop. Nonetheless, multiple officers questioned the man and seized a kitchen knife that the man acknowledged carrying.

---

[44] To justify the stop, officers also noted that the man put his hands in the pockets of his sweatshirt as they approached. However, given that the encounter occurred on a cold January evening and officers observed the man "shivering," placing hands inside a sweatshirt adds minimally, if at all, to any objective suspicion the officers possessed. *See United States v. Burton*, 228 F.3d 524, 529 (4th Cir. 2000) (holding that where suspect refused to speak with police or remove his hand from his pocket, "something more is required to establish reasonable suspicion that criminal activity is afoot"); *United States v. Patterson*, 340 F.3d 368, 370–72 (6th Cir. 2003) (holding that officers lacked reasonable suspicion where suspect placed hands in his pockets and walked away from police); *United States v. Davis*, 94 F.3d 1465, 1468–649 (10th Cir. 1996) (holding that officers lacked reasonable suspicion to stop a known gang member who ignored officers' orders to take his hands out of his pockets).

When the man asked the officers to return his knife, the officers ordered the man to sit down and then forced him to the ground when the man "persisted to ask for his knife." The man yelled "you can't arrest me" and resisted his detention. Although there was no basis to detain the man, two officers attempted to handcuff and shackle him, while one officer struck him "in the face, ribs, and back" with fists. The man continued to resist being shackled as additional officers arrived, one of whom tased the man twice to prevent him from "escap[ing] the scene." After officers handcuffed the man, they transported him to Union Memorial Hospital for medical care. The man was not charged with any offense. The sergeant who responded to the scene confirmed that the involved officers tased the man twice and hit him in the face with their fists, yet the sergeant's report of the incident concluded that the "officers showed great restraint and professionalism."

In sum, we find that BPD officers frequently stop pedestrians on Baltimore streets without reasonable suspicion that they are engaged in criminal activity. This pattern is evidenced by the extremely low rate at which BPD's investigative stops yield evidence of criminality and officers' own descriptions of their conduct. The frequency of these unlawful stops subjects certain Baltimore communities to repeated constitutional harms.

b. BPD Searches Individuals During Stops Without Legal Justification

During pedestrian and vehicle stops, BPD officers regularly escalate encounters by conducting unlawful searches. This practice includes two types of conduct: (1) officers conducting weapons pat downs or "frisks" where they lack reasonable suspicion that a subject is armed and dangerous; and (2) pre-arrest strip searches in public areas. Both types of conduct result from systemic deficiencies in policy, training, and oversight.

i. Unconstitutional Frisks

BPD officers commonly frisk people during stops without reasonable suspicion that the subject of the frisk is armed and dangerous. This practice contravenes the principle that "before an officer places a hand on the person of a citizen in search of anything, he must have constitutionally adequate, reasonable grounds for doing so." *United States v. Powell*, 666 F.3d 180, 185 (4th Cir. 2011) (citation and internal quotation marks omitted). Before frisking a person stopped on the street or in a vehicle, officers must have reasonable suspicion—based on specific, particularized information— that a person is armed and dangerous. *See, e.g., Arizona v. Johnson*, 555 U.S. 323, 326–27 (2009). This requirement is distinct from the justification needed to make the underlying stop. *See Powell*, 666 F.3d at 186 n.5 (noting that the justification for making a stop "differs from . . . whether a lawfully detained person may be armed and dangerous and thus subject to a *Terry* frisk"). The assessment of reasonable suspicion to frisk is based on the totality of the circumstances; it is insufficient, standing alone, that a subject has a prior record of arrests for violent charges, *id. at* 184–86, was stopped in a high crime area, *Maryland v. Buie*, 494 U.S. 325, 335 (1990), or was stopped late at night, *Papachristou v. City of Jacksonville*, 405 U.S. 156, 163 (1972). Where reasonable suspicion to conduct a frisk exists, officers must limit the scope of the search to a pat down of "the outer layers of the suspect's clothing." *United States v. Holmes*, 376 F.3d 270, 275 (4th Cir. 2004). Once an officer establishes that a person is not armed, "that officer exceeds the permissible scope of a *Terry* frisk if he continues to search the suspect." *United States v. Swann*, 149 F.3d 271, 274–75 (4th Cir. 1998); *Minnesota v. Dickerson*, 508 U.S. 366, 378 (1993) (an officer exceeds the scope of a permissible frisk by

– 30 –

"squeezing, sliding and otherwise manipulating the contents of defendant's pocket" after determining that the pocket did not contain a weapon) (citation and internal quotation marks omitted).

Yet for many years, suspicionless frisks have been a common feature of BPD's street enforcement efforts. Officers and community members told Justice Department investigators that frisks—often made under the guise of "officer safety" but without identifying any specific basis for believing that a person is armed—are a common feature of BPD's stops. Officers' own descriptions of frisks in their incident reports support this conclusion. For example, on a spring evening in 2010 officers responded to a call complaining that drug sales were occurring at a particular location. Officers arrived at the scene and observed several African-American individuals "standing and sitting at the location." Absent information that these individuals were armed or otherwise dangerous, the officers nonetheless approached and immediately frisked them. Officers disclosed the frisk in an incident report, explaining that they performed the frisk "for officer safety." Although the officers provided no information that suggested the individuals were armed or dangerous, BPD supervisors signed off on the report. Our review of incident reports and interviews with several hundred community members indicate that the unconstitutional frisk practice is widespread. We were unable to precisely quantify the scope of these unconstitutional frisks, however, because BPD does not reliably record when officers conduct a frisk.

BPD's misapplication of the *Terry* frisk standard subjects Baltimore residents to embarrassing invasions of privacy and needlessly escalates encounters with law enforcement. In one typical case, a BPD officer unlawfully frisked an African-American man after a traffic stop for driving with headlights off. Because the driver "looked nervous" as the officer approached, the officer ordered the driver and his passenger to exit the vehicle and stand on the side of the road. The officer then frisked the passenger, which included a public pat down of the passenger's groin. The officer identified no basis for frisking the passenger other than the *driver's* "nervous" appearance—far short of the required showing of particularized facts pointing to the presence of a weapon. *See Powell*, 666 F.3d at 183, 185, 187 (no reasonable suspicion to frisk man during a vehicle stop for a burned out light even where officers had information that the man had prior arrests for armed robbery). In another incident, an officer approached an African-American man walking on a sidewalk in November 2010 in an area the officer stated was "known for violent crime and narcotics distribution." When the officer "attempted to interview him about his activities," the man fled. According to the report the officer filed the day of the incident, he chased the man and deployed his taser because the man "refused to comply with my orders to stop." The taser prongs hit the man on the back but failed to stop him. As the chase continued, the officer reloaded his taser cartridge and again fired probes into the fleeing man's back. After catching up with the man, the officer used his taser yet again—this time in drive stun mode—detained the man for investigation, and conducted a weapons frisk. The report provides no reason to believe the man was armed.[45] The frisk and investigation found no weapon or other evidence of wrongdoing. The man—after being tased multiple times, taken to the ground, and frisked—was released without charges.

---

[45] More than a month later, the officer filed a supplemental report claiming that he "decided to frisk [the man] based on my suspicion that he was armed," citing the man's presence in a high crime area, his loose clothing, the fact that he "looked back over his shoulder," and that the man ran past a dumpster where he could have theoretically discarded a weapon or narcotics.

Even where BPD officers properly initiate a frisk based on reasonable suspicion that a person is armed or dangerous, we found instances in which the scope of those frisks exceeded the brief pat down of the "outer layers of the suspect's clothing" that *Terry* prescribes. *See, e.g., Holmes*, 376 F.3d at 275. While "[a]n officer is not justified in conducting a general exploratory search for evidence under the guise of a stop-and-frisk," *United States v. Brown*, 188 F.3d 860, 866 (7th Cir. 1999) (citing *Dickerson*, 508 U.S. at 378), BPD officers commonly frisk individuals in a way that seems intended to find small packages of narcotics rather than weapons. In cases reviewed by the Justice Department, officers reached inside of subjects' clothing, asked subjects to remove articles of clothing, and squeezed pockets to detect small bags that may contain illegal drugs.

ii.   BPD Conducts Unconstitutional Strip Searches

In addition to impermissible *Terry* frisks, our investigation found many instances in which BPD officers strip-searched individuals without justification—often in public areas— subjecting them to humiliation and violating the Constitution. Strip searches are "fairly understood" as "degrading" and, under the Fourth Amendment, are reasonable only in narrow circumstances. *Safford Unified Sch. Dist. #1 v. Redding*, 557 U.S. 364, 375 (2009). Strip searches are never permissible as part of a pre-arrest weapons frisk. *See Holmes*, 376 F.3d at 275 (weapons frisks must be limited to the outer layers of a suspect's clothing). Following a lawful arrest, the reasonableness of a strip search turns on "the scope of the particular intrusion, the manner in which it is conducted, the justification for initiating it, and the place in which it is conducted." *Bell v. Wolfish*, 441 U.S. 520, 559 (1979). Absent specific facts indicating that an arrestee is concealing a weapon or contraband, officers may not strip search a person incident to arrest for an offense that is not "commonly associated by its very nature with the possession of weapons or contraband." *Logan v. Shealy*, 660 F.2d 1007, 1013 (4th Cir. 1981). Moreover, courts have "repeatedly emphasized the necessity of conducting a strip search in private." *Amaechi v. West*, 237 F.3d 356, 364 (4th Cir. 2001) (finding strip search unreasonable where it was conducted in public view). BPD policy likewise recognizes that strip searches should be conducted only "under very limited and controlled circumstances" and that "strip searching . . . [] suspects in public view or on a public thoroughfare is forbidden."

Nevertheless, our investigation found that BPD officers frequently ignore these requirements and strip-search individuals prior to arrest, in public view, or both. Numerous Baltimore residents interviewed by the Justice Department recounted stories of BPD officers "jumping out" of police vehicles and strip-searching individuals on public streets. BPD has long been on notice of such allegations: in the last five years BPD has faced multiple lawsuits and more than 60 complaints alleging unlawful strip searches. In one of these incidents— memorialized in a complaint that the Department sustained—officers in BPD's Eastern District publicly strip-searched a woman following a routine traffic stop for a missing headlight. Officers ordered the woman to exit her vehicle, remove her clothes, and stand on the sidewalk to be searched. The woman asked the male officer in charge "I really gotta take all my clothes off?" The male officer replied "yeah" and ordered a female officer to strip search the woman. The female officer then put on purple latex gloves, pulled up the woman's shirt and searched around her bra. Finding no weapons or contraband around the woman's chest, the officer then pulled down the woman's underwear and searched her anal cavity. This search again found no evidence of wrongdoing and the officers released the woman without charges. Indeed, the woman received only a repair order for her headlight. The search occurred in full view of the street, although the supervising male officer claimed he "turned away" and did not watch the woman disrobe. After the woman filed a complaint, BPD investigators corroborated the woman's story with testimony from several witnesses and by recovering the female officer's latex gloves from the search location. Officers conducted this highly invasive search despite lacking any indication that the woman had committed a criminal offense or possessed concealed contraband. The male officer who ordered the search received only a "simple reprimand" and an instruction that he could not serve as an officer in charge until he was "properly trained."

An African-American teenager recounted a similar story to Justice Department investigators that involved two public strip searches in the winter of 2016 by the same officer. According to the teenager, he was stopped in January 2016 while walking on a street near his home by two officers who were looking for the teenager's older brother, whom the officers suspected of dealing narcotics. One of the officers pushed the teenager up against a wall and frisked him. This search did not yield contraband. The officer then stripped off the teenager's jacket and sweatshirt and frisked him again in front of his teenage girlfriend. When this search likewise found no contraband, the officer ordered the teenager to "give your girl your phone, I'm checking you right now." The officer then pulled down the teenager's pants and boxer shorts and strip-searched him in full view of the street and his girlfriend. The officers' report of the incident disputes this account, claiming that they did not conduct a strip search and instead recovered narcotics from the teenager during a consensual pat down. No narcotics were ever produced to the teenager's public defender, however, and the State's Attorney's Office dismissed the drug charges for lack of evidence. The teenager filed a lengthy complaint with BPD describing the incident and identifying multiple witnesses. The teenager recounted to us that, shortly after filing the complaint, the same officer approached him near a McDonald's restaurant in his neighborhood, pushed the teenager against a wall, pulled down his pants, and grabbed his genitals. The officer filed no charges against the teenager in the second incident, which the teenager believes was done in retaliation for filing a complaint about the first strip search.

Other complaints describe similar incidents in which BPD officers conduct public strip searches of individuals who have not been arrested. For example, in September 2014, a man filed a complaint stating that an officer in the Central District searched him several days in a row, including "undoing his pants" and searching his "hindquarters" on a public street. When the strip search did not find contraband, the officer told the man to leave the area and warned that the officer would search him again every time he returned. The man then filed a complaint with Internal Affairs and identified the officer who conducted the strip search by name. When Internal Affairs investigators pressed the man to provide a detailed description of the officer, the man recalled that the officer "had red patches with sergeant stripes" on his uniform. The investigator recognized this description as patches worn by the officer in charge of a shift and confirmed that the officer named by the man was working as an officer in charge in the Central District on the dates the man alleged he was strip-searched. Internal Affairs nonetheless deemed the complaint "not sustained" without further explanation.

Deficient oversight and accountability has helped perpetuate BPD's use of unlawful strip searches. Although the Department's policy limits strip searches to specific, narrow circumstances following an arrest, BPD supervisors have failed to ensure that officers comply with this policy and internal affairs officials have not adequately investigated frequent complaints that officers violate it.

BPD does not separately categorize or track complaints alleging unlawful strip searches. But our manual review of BPD's Internal Affairs database revealed more than 60 such complaints in the last six years—only one of which was sustained. In response to dozens of other strip search complaints, IA has deemed them "administratively closed," classified them solely for "administrative tracking," or found them not sustained – after minimal, if any, investigation. For example, in 2015 an African American man filed a complaint stating that he was strip-searched by an officer whom BPD eventually fired in 2016 after numerous allegations of misconduct. The man stated that the officer ordered him out of his vehicle during a traffic stop and searched the vehicle without the man's consent. When the stop of the vehicle did not uncover contraband, the officer pulled down the man's pants and underwear, exposing his genitals on the side of a public street, and then strip-searched him. The officer seized marijuana and cash during the strip search and allegedly told the man that the officer would return his money and drugs if the man provided information about more serious crimes. The complaint stated that when the man did not provide this information, the officer arrested him and turned over only part of the confiscated money, keeping more than $500. Despite the serious charges in this complaint and the officer's lengthy record of alleged misconduct, IA deemed it "administratively closed" without interviewing the complainant. This type of inadequate oversight has allowed BPD's unlawful strip search practice to continue.

3. BPD Makes Unconstitutional Arrests

Our investigation likewise found reasonable cause to believe that BPD's approach to street-level crime suppression has contributed to officers making thousands of unlawful arrests over the past five years. This pattern has three main components: (1) warrantless arrests made without probable cause in violation of the Fourth Amendment; (2) arrests for minor offenses, such as failure to obey and trespassing, in circumstances that violate the Due Process Clause's requirement to provide fair notice of prohibited conduct; and (3) investigative detentions that exceed the limits of *Terry* and constitute arrests.

a. BPD Arrests Individuals Without Probable Cause

The Fourth Amendment requires that arrests be supported by probable cause. *See, e.g.,* *Dunaway v. New York*, 442 U.S. 200, 207–13 (1979); U.S. CONST. AM. IV. Probable cause requires "a probability or substantial chance of criminal activity" and is evaluated by examining "the totality of the circumstances." *Illinois v. Gates*, 462 U.S. 213, 243 n.13 (1983). It "require[s] . . . the kind of fair probability on which reasonable and prudent people, not legal technicians, act." *Florida v. Harris*, 133 S. Ct. 1050, 1055 (2013) (internal quotations omitted). Police may satisfy the probable cause requirement by obtaining a warrant prior to arrest or determining that probable cause exists in the field. *Gerstein v. Pugh*, 420 U.S. 103, 113–14 (1975). Our investigation determined that, when BPD officers make arrests in the field without a warrant, they often do so without probable cause.

Data maintained by the State of Maryland shows that, from November 2010–July 2015, BPD made thousands of arrests that reviewing officials declined to charge. The State's data records information about each person arrested, the arresting agency, all charges levied, and whether reviewing officials found that the charges were adequately supported. This data captures several stages of review of officers' justification for each arrest. When a BPD officer makes a warrantless arrest and brings the arrestee to Central Booking, a supervisor at booking determines whether to commit the arrestee into jail; release the arrestee on bond, on their own recognizance, or with a citation; or to nullify the arrest and release the arrestee without charge. For all cases except where an arrestee is released without charge, a representative from the State's Attorney's Office then conducts an initial review of the charging documents to ensure that they recite probable cause. This review usually occurs the same day as the arrest and looks only at the officer's stated justification for the arrest, not evidence from any other source. In some cases, the State's Attorney's review finds that an arrest lacks probable cause or otherwise should not result in filed charges.

Analysis of this data reveals that, from November 2010–July 2015, supervisors at Central Booking released 6,736 arrestees without charge. Prosecutors from the State's Attorney's Office declined to charge an additional 3,427 cases, explicitly finding that 1,983 of the underlying arrests lacked probable cause. In sum, BPD officers made 10,163 arrests that authorities immediately determined did not merit prosecution—an average of roughly 200 arrests per month.

BPD's pattern of making arrests without probable cause is most pronounced with non-felony offenses that stem from street encounters between officers and residents. For example, during the last five years prosecutors and booking supervisors rejected 1,350 disorderly conduct charges—20 percent of the total. Arrests for other highly discretionary, non-violent offenses were nullified at even higher rates. Officials rejected 24 percent of disturbing the peace charges, 23 percent of failure to obey charges, and 24 percent of hindering charges. Officials likewise rejected 156 trespassing charges, comprising roughly 5 percent of the total. And these numbers almost certainly understate the extent of BPD's problematic arrests, as they reflect only cases dismissed during preliminary review based on facial deficiencies in officers' reports, not arrests later shown to be invalid during pretrial hearings or at trial.

Indeed, our review of a random sample of 150 incident reports describing the probable cause for these discretionary arrests found that officers frequently recite facially inadequate justifications. In particular, these reports reveal that officers often arrest individuals for "trespassing" where the person arrested was standing on a public street that bordered property owned by the City or a private party. Such conduct is not criminal. "[I]ndividuals in this country have significant liberty interests in standing on sidewalks and in other public places." *City of Chicago v. Morales*, 527 U.S. 41, 54 n.19 (1999) (quoting Brief for the United States as Amicus Curiae 23).

Several examples highlight this pattern. In June 2011, an officer dispatched in response to suspected drug sales observed an African-American male fitting the basic description of one of the suspects. The officer wrote in his report that the suspect was standing on a public street "in front of" property owned by "the mayor and city council of Baltimore City." When the officer approached, the man "became nervous and could not provide a valid explanation for being at this location." Lacking any further evidence suggesting that the man was involved in narcotics sales or other criminal activity, the officer nonetheless transported the man to the Western District headquarters for "debriefing" and then to Central Booking, where the man was charged with trespassing. The man was not charged with any other offense, and the officer's account of the encounter furnishes no basis for the trespassing arrest. Rather, it shows that the man was merely standing lawfully on a public street. In January 2010, officers similarly approached a man who was "standing in front of 1524 Mount Mor Ct looking around" and who walked away when he saw officers. Officers stopped the man and arrested him when he "could not provide a valid explanation for *being in front of* 1524 Mount Mor Ct," a part of the Gilmore Homes public housing complex. In another case, an officer arrested an African-American man observed "standing in front of 578 Orchard St." The officer's report explained that when he approached, the man "began to walk east bound on Orchard St attempting to elude the officer." The officer stopped the man and asked him "why was he *standing in front of* 578 Orchard St and if he knew the resident" who resided there. When the man replied that he did not know the resident, the officer arrested him for trespassing. The officers' accounts of these and many similar incidents describe facially unlawful arrests for conduct that is not criminal.

b. BPD Arrests People Lawfully Present on Baltimore Streets in Violation of Due Process

BPD's application of city ordinances banning loitering, trespassing, and failing to obey an officer's order violates the Fourteenth Amendment. Citing these provisions, BPD frequently arrests people who are lawfully present on public sidewalks without providing the constitutionally required notice that they are engaging in prohibited conduct. These arrests are unconstitutional under the void-for-vagueness doctrine where they are made in circumstances that "fail to provide the kind of notice that will enable ordinary people to understand what conduct it prohibits." *Morales*, 527 U.S. at 56 (invalidating city ordinance that defined loitering as "to remain in one place with no apparent purpose."). Where conduct—like loitering—is generally lawful, police may make arrests only where the arrestees violated the ordinance knowingly. *See id.* at 57–58.[46]

Moreover, absent clear standards and an intent element, a "dispersal order itself is an unjustified impairment of liberty" and cannot form the basis of an arrest for failure to obey. *Id.* at 58. The Court of Special Appeals of Maryland has criticized BPD's application of the Baltimore's anti-loitering ordinance for precisely these reasons. *See Williams v. Maryland*, 780 A.2d 1210 (Md. Ct. App. 2001). The *Williams* court reversed a defendant's narcotics conviction after finding that the defendant's underlying arrest for loitering violated due process. The court noted that, although BPD officers claimed the man was part of a group that was impeding pedestrian traffic on a sidewalk, there was no "evidence even remotely supporting an inference of scienter" or that the defendant had notice that such conduct was illegal. *Id.* at 1217. Moreover, the court held that such notice must include a specific description of the prohibited conduct; officers could not provide sufficient notice by "[t]elling someone merely that he is 'loitering' and that if he does not move on he will be arrested." *Id.* at 1218.

The same vagueness problem exists in BPD's enforcement of trespassing statutes against individuals who are standing on sidewalks adjacent to public housing or private establishments. Indeed, a federal district court in Maryland has expressed concern about the type of highly discretionary trespassing arrests that BPD utilizes. *See Diggs v. Housing Authority*, 67 F. Supp. 2d 522, 532–35 (D. Md. 1999). There, the court enjoined enforcement of the City of Frederick's trespassing ordinance and noted that a "policy of issuing citations to persons with 'no apparent legitimate reason' for being on Housing Authority property may raise serious due process concerns in light of the Supreme Court's recent decision in *Chicago v. Morales.*" *Diggs*, 67 F. Supp. at 534 n.19.

---

[46] We do not address whether Baltimore City ordinances criminalizing loitering, failing to obey, and trespassing are facially unconstitutional.

BPD's arrests of "loiterers" for trespassing and failing to obey orders to disperse frequently fall short of these due process standards. BPD often arrests people standing on streets or sidewalks for "trespassing" when they cannot provide a reason for their presence that officers deem acceptable. Our review found numerous cases in which BPD officers arrested individuals on sidewalks near public housing complexes or private businesses simply because officers determined that the arrestees had "no legitimate purpose" or "no business" in the area—precisely the type of vague, subjective trespassing standard invalidated in *Morales*. *See* 527 U.S. at 56 (finding unconstitutionally vague a statute that permitted arrest of "loiterers" who lack an "apparent purpose"); *see also Diggs*, 67 F. Supp. 2d at 534 n.19 (questioning arrests premised on having 'no apparent legitimate reason' for being on Housing Authority property").

For example, in April 2010, BPD officers approached five African Americans sitting on a brick wall in front of a private business. Officers wrote in their report that they "approached the group to ascertain their purpose for sitting on the wall in front of this location." When the individuals responded that they "were 'just chillin,'" officers arrested them for trespassing because the men "could not give a valid purpose for being on [the property]." Officers provided no warning before arresting the men and did not charge them with any other offense. Later the same month, a different BPD officer approached "two males sitting on the steps of 110 North Fremont Ave," a street that borders a public housing complex. When the men "attempted to get up and walk away," the officer stopped them and "asked what they were doing on the property."[47] The men responded that they were "just talking." The officer then—without any warning—arrested the men for trespassing because "neither was able to provide any legitimate explanation for being on the Housing Authority property." In September 2011, a BPD officer similarly arrested a man "loitering directly beside the 2501 E. Preston Street Greater Missionary Baptist Church." The officer made the arrest after asking the man "why he was in the area" and learning that the man "had no business near the area of the [church's] steps." Each of these arrests violates constitutional due process requirements because the arrested individuals lacked notice that their apparently innocent behavior was unlawful.

We found evidence that BPD supervisors have explicitly condoned trespassing arrests that do not meet constitutional standards, and evidence suggesting that trespassing enforcement is focused on public housing developments. A shift commander for one of BPD's districts emailed a template for describing trespassing arrests to a sergeant and a patrol officer. The template provides a blueprint for arresting an individual standing on or near a public housing development who cannot give a "valid reason" for being there—a facially unconstitutional detention. Equally troubling is the fact that the template contains blanks to be filled in for details of the arrest, including the arrest data and location and the suspect's name and address, but does not include a prompt to fill in the race or gender of the arrestee. Rather, the words "black male" are automatically included in the description of the arrest. The supervisor's template thus presumes that individuals arrested for trespassing will be African American.

---

[47] Officers lacked reasonable suspicion to make the initial stop, as the men were observed only sitting on steps and then walking down a public sidewalk.

Trespassing Wording

ON **(Date)** AT APPROXIMATELY **(Time)** OFFICER JOHN DOE WAS WORKING IN A UNIFORM CAPACITY IN THE **(Address in Housing Location)** WHICH IS A HIGH DRUG TRAFFICKING AREA AND AN AREA KNOWN FOR VIOLENT CRIMES. OFFICER DOE OBSERVED A BLACK MALE LATER IDENTIFIED AS **(Name of Suspect)** (LOITERING, INVOLVED IN NARCOTIC ACTIVITY, ETC) IN THE **(Address)**. OFFICER DOE THEN APPROACHED **(Suspect)** AND ASKED HIM WAS HE A RESIDENT OF THE **(Name of Development)** PUBLIC HOUSING DEVELOPMENT, WHICH HAS SIGNS POSTED "NO TRESPASSING" PLACED IN A CONSPICUOUS MANNER THROUGHOUT THE DEVELOPMENT. **(Suspect)** ADVISED OFFICER DOE THAT HE WAS NOT A RESIDENT OF **(Development)** OFFICER DOE THEN ASKED **(Suspect)** WHAT WAS HIS REASON FOR BEING ON HOUSING PROPERTY, AT THIS POINT **(Suspect)** COULDN'T GIVE A VALID REASON FOR BEING ON HOUSING PROPERTY. **(Suspect)** WAS THEN PLACED UNDER ARREST AND TRANSPORTED TO CBIF FOR PROCESSING.

BPD likewise makes constitutionally deficient arrests of people who fail to obey officers' unlawful orders to disperse. BPD policy requires that, prior to making such an arrest, officers warn people allegedly loitering that their specific conduct is illegal. Yet our review found that officers frequently do not provide this warning or indicate only that a person must disperse because he or she is "loitering"—an instruction that is unconstitutionally vague. *See Williams*, 780 A.2d at 1218 (due process requires more than "telling someone merely that he is 'loitering' and that if he does not move on he will be arrested."). Instead, we found numerous "failure to obey" arrests made without the required warning and premised on an officer's subjective dissatisfaction with a person's stated reason for standing or sitting on a public sidewalk.

In October 2011, for example, an officer approached a group of African-American men standing on a sidewalk "within 100 feet of Amko liquor store." All but two of the men left when the officer approached. The officer stopped the two remaining men and warned them that they were "loitering" by blocking pedestrian traffic and that they were "trespassing near a liquor store." The officer then told the men "to leave the area, to stop loitering . . . and to stop trespassing near the liquor store." When one of the men replied, "I'm not leaving, I'm going to stay and finish talking to my brother," the officer arrested him for failing to obey. The order the man failed to obey—a general instruction not to "loiter" or trespass "near a liquor store"—falls far short of the notice required to support an arrest. Similarly, in July 2011 officers approached three males standing on the sidewalk in front of Crazy John's restaurant on East Baltimore Street because they were purportedly "obstructing pedestrian traffic in a public walkway." After several warnings, the officer ordered the men to leave the area and informed them that they would be arrested if they "returned." The three men then walked away and crossed the street, where they resumed "hang[ing] out." When the officer followed the men to their new location, the men walked farther down Baltimore Street, "taunted" the officer, and then ran away. Forty minutes later, the officer saw the men walking down an adjacent street while "attempting to come back on the 400 block of Baltimore Street" and arrested them for failure to obey the order not to "return." This arrest is premised on an unconstitutionally vague order not to return to a public street for an indeterminate time period.

These and similar arrests identified by our investigation reflect BPD officers exercising nearly unfettered discretion to criminalize the act of standing on public sidewalks. Absent clear warning about the specific types of conduct that will result in such arrests, this practice fails to provide notice required by the Due Process Clause and risks arbitrary and discriminatory enforcement. *See Kolender v. Lawson*, 461 U.S. 352, 357 (1983).[48] Accordingly, these arrests are unconstitutional.

c. BPD Unlawfully Detains Individuals for Investigation, Effectively Arresting Them Without Probable Cause

Our investigation further revealed that BPD officers unlawfully detain persons for extended periods of time—sometimes for at least several hours—without probable cause. These detentions constitute arrests and violate the Fourth Amendment. BPD does not process these detentions as arrests; instead officers use them to: (1) detain and question people suspected of crimes in hopes of uncovering evidence supporting an arrest; and (2) facilitate custodial interrogations of witnesses or other people with knowledge of suspected crimes. Neither purpose vitiates the requirement that officers must have probable cause to exceed the constitutional limits on investigative detentions.

"[D]etention for custodial interrogation—regardless of its label—intrudes so severely on interests protected by the Fourth Amendment as necessarily to trigger the traditional safeguards against illegal arrest." *Dunaway*, 442 U.S. at 216; *see also Brown v. Illinois*, 422 U.S. 590, 605 (1975) (detention in a police station without probable cause "for investigation or for questioning" violates the Fourth Amendment). The Fourth Amendment likewise prohibits officers extending detentions "for the purpose of gathering additional evidence to justify the arrest." *County of Riverside v. McLaughlin*, 500 U.S. 44, 56 (1991); *see also Brown*, 422 U.S. at 605 (station house detention and questioning "in the hope that something might turn up" requires probable cause). While *Terry* allows officers to detain individuals for brief investigation where officers have reasonable suspicion that criminal activity is afoot, *Terry* stops may not "resemble a traditional arrest." *Hiibel v. Sixth Judicial District Court*, 542 U.S. 177, 186 (2004). Courts have resisted putting precise limits on the permissible duration of *Terry* stops, but have found 90-minute detentions unconstitutional. *See United States v. Place*, 462 U.S. 696, 709–10 (1983); *accord United States v. Watson*, 703 F.3d 684 (4th Cir. 2012) (investigative detention for three hours without probable cause constituted an unlawful custodial arrest under the Fourth Amendment); *Zavala*, 541 F.3d at 579–80 (90-minute detention in which subject was transported to different location constituted "a de facto arrest"); *United States v. Chamberlin*, 644 F.2d 1262, 1266–67 (9th Cir. 1980) (placing a suspect in the back of a police car for twenty minutes while the officer pursued another suspect exceeded the limits of a *Terry* stop).

While BPD does not formally document investigative detentions, we found troubling indications that BPD officers use such detentions as a regular part of investigating people suspected of criminal activity. Local prosecutors described this practice to Justice Department officials as BPD officers making arrests without probable cause on the street, then hours later deciding to "un-arrest" when detention and questioning failed to uncover additional evidence. Our review of BPD documents confirmed that BPD uses these unlawful detentions.

---

[48] Indeed, as set forth in Section II(B), *infra*, these practices have resulted in highly discriminatory outcomes.

For example, in October 2010, an officer responded to a call for suspected burglary that indicated several African-American men were using a green truck to carry away a furnace. The officer arrived on the scene and approached three African-American men who were standing around a green truck with a furnace in the back. In response to the officer's questions, one of the men stated that he was helping the other men move the furnace, which had been found in a nearby alley. The officer detained the men while he conducted a canvass of the area, which did not find any property from which the furnace could have been removed. Despite failing to identify evidence suggesting the men were involved in a burglary, the officer nonetheless placed all three men in custody and transported them to the Western District headquarters "for further investigation." While the men were held at the station, the officer reviewed a CitiWatch camera that confirmed their explanation that they moved the furnace from an alley. After detaining the men for 1 hour and 40 minutes, the officer released them. BPD records contain no indication that the men consented to their detention, much less to being detained for nearly two hours. In other cases, BPD officers have likewise stopped individuals based on reasonable suspicion, transported them to precincts for fingerprinting and further investigation, then ultimately released them more than an hour later when the investigation failed to uncover probable cause to make an arrest. *See supra*, at 29. These custodial detentions violate the Fourth Amendment, which forbids extending *Terry* stops "for the purpose of gathering additional evidence to justify [an] arrest." *Riverside*, 500 U.S. at 56; *see also Brown*, 422 U.S. at 6025 (station house detention and questioning "in the hope that something might turn up" requires probable cause).

4. **BPD's Unconstitutional Stops, Searches, and Arrests Result from a Longstanding Practice of Overly Aggressive Street Enforcement with Deficient Oversight and Policy Guidance**

BPD's pattern of making unconstitutional stops, searches, and arrests arises from its longstanding reliance on "zero tolerance" street enforcement, which encourages officers to make large numbers of stops, searches, and arrests for minor, highly discretionary offenses. This approach to street-level enforcement magnifies the importance of providing officers with robust policies and training and overseeing officer activity with comprehensive accountability systems. Yet BPD failed to collect reliable data, conducted minimal oversight of enforcement activities, and forced officers to rely on policies that provide insufficient guidance or, in several important areas, facially misstate constitutional requirements. Taken together, these deficiencies contribute to widespread constitutional violations.

a. **Baltimore Leadership Prioritized "Zero Tolerance" Crime Suppression Tactics for Many Years**

Starting in the late 1990s, Baltimore City and BPD leadership expressly adopted a policing model that embraced the principles of "zero tolerance" street enforcement. According to City and BPD leaders past and present, as well as media reports, Baltimore City based its approach in part on tactics developed by the New York Police Department and brought in consultants from NYPD's program to oversee its implementation in Baltimore.[49] As we heard from BPD officers and leaders,

---

[49] *See, e.g.*, Gerard Shields, *O'Malley is wooing zero-tolerance gurus*, BALTIMORE SUN, Oct. 2, 1999, http://articles.baltimoresun.com/1999-10-02/news/9910020227_1_jack-maple-violent-crime-police-commissioner (last accessed Aug. 5, 2016).

as well as numerous community members, the strategy involved BPD officers making widespread use of pedestrian stops and searches in a purported effort to seize guns and narcotics and deter crime. BPD supervisors encouraged officers to issue citations and make arrests for low-level "quality of life" offenses, including loitering, trespassing, disorderly conduct, failure to obey, and disturbing the peace. As part of this strategy, BPD leadership pressured officers to increase the number of arrests and to "clear corners," whether or not the officers observed criminal activity. The result was a massive increase in the quantity of arrests—but a corresponding decline in quality. Of the 100,000 arrestees that BPD processed through Central Booking in 2004,[50] more than one in five were released without charge.[51] Although our investigation did not analyze data on the number of stops and searches that took place during the same time period, it is doubtless that they far exceeded the number of arrests.

From the beginning, some community members and policymakers questioned the value of the policy, arguing that it could lead to harassment of residents without an appreciable reduction in crime. Zero tolerance enforcement made police interaction a daily fact of life for some Baltimore residents and provoked widespread community disillusionment with BPD, as well as calls from activists, former police officers, and state officials to adopt new practices. The strategy also created disillusion within the Department. According to the police union president at the time, some officers referred to the stop-and-frisk program as a "VCR detail," standing for "violation of civil rights."[52]

In June 2006, the ACLU of Maryland and the NAACP filed a lawsuit alleging that BPD was illegally arresting thousands of residents every year. The complaint asserted that BPD had not properly trained officers on the legal standard necessary to make an arrest, and had placed pressure on supervisors to bolster numbers, leading to citizens being improperly detained without probable cause. Shortly after the suit was filed, BPD began to take steps to decrease its reliance on zero tolerance policing. In the late 2000s, under Baltimore Police Commissioner Frederick H. Bealefeld III, the number of arrests, and arrestees released without charge, began to decrease.[53] In 2010, BPD and the City entered into a settlement to resolve the ACLU lawsuit, with BPD agreeing to adopt policies rejecting its former zero tolerance strategy and make changes to existing policies and procedures. The settlement established an Independent Auditor to evaluate BPD's progress toward adopting stop and arrest practices consistent with the Constitution. In 2015, BPD published a number of amended policies, including one addressing the core legal elements of quality of life offenses, in which it cautioned that verbal warnings, counseling, and citations are preferable to arrest. The policy states that arrest should only take place where the quality of life violation was committed in the officer's presence, and the officer has an objectively reasonable belief that arrest is necessary under the facts and circumstances or to otherwise protect the officer and citizens of Baltimore.

---

[50] At the time, Baltimore City had a population of approximately 650,000 residents.

[51] JUSTICE POLICY INSTITUTE, BALTIMORE BEHIND BARS 10 (2010).

[52] Gus G. Sentementes, *Police step up frisking tactic*, BALTIMORE SUN, Nov. 13, 2005, http://articles.baltimoresun.com/2005-11-13/news/0511130098_1_frisking-deter-crime-police-officers (last accessed Aug. 5, 2016).

[53] JUSTICE POLICY INSTITUTE, BALTIMORE BEHIND BARS 10 (2010).

Current Baltimore Police Commissioner Kevin Davis and former Commissioner Anthony Batts have acknowledged that BPD's zero tolerance strategy damaged community relationships and created obstacles to effective policing. Both commissioners have publicly supported a more holistic policing model focused on rebuilding and leveraging community trust. Nevertheless, the practices of officers on the street have continued to reflect many of the problematic aspects of the previous strategy, resulting in a pattern of unconstitutional conduct. These problematic practices are reflected in our findings. BPD's failure to engage in meaningful change was also noted in the reports of the Independent Auditor established by the ACLU lawsuit settlement agreement. At the end of the four-year monitoring period, the Auditor determined that BPD had not reached full compliance on more than half of the conditions of the agreement. Failure to consistently and adequately report arrests and engage in meaningful oversight of street-level enforcement was, and remains, a recurring problem. All of the Auditor's reporting indicated that arrest reports for quality of life offenses did not meet the requirements of BPD departmental policies. The final report from 2014 noted that there was no systematic improvement in reporting for these offenses during the monitoring period.

One of the reasons that the intended move away from zero tolerance policing has not sufficiently curbed BPD's practice of unconstitutional street-level enforcement is a persistent perception among officers that their performance continues to be measured by the raw numbers of stops and arrests they make, particularly for gun and drug offenses. Many officers believe that the path to promotions and favorable treatment, as well as the best way to avoid discipline, is to increase their number of stops and make arrests for these offenses. By frequently stopping and searching people they believe might possess contraband, with or without requisite reasonable suspicion, officers aim to improve their statistical output, which will in turn reflect favorably in their performance reviews. During shifts observed by Justice Department investigators, patrol officers actively sought out corners to clear and indicated that they believed they were obligated to move groups of people standing on sidewalks, whether or not the individuals in the groups appeared to be engaged in criminal conduct. Several officers demonstrated a mistaken understanding of the law, expressing that a group standing in front of a business or a vacant lot was necessarily loitering or trespassing on the property.

These views are reinforced by BPD's mid-level supervisors, many of whom served in the Department during the height of the zero tolerance strategy and continue to embrace its principles. Some officers we interviewed expressed frustration with supervisory pressure to prioritize drug and gun arrests over community policing and longer, more intensive investigations. One officer acknowledged the futility of breaking up a crowd of "loiterers" because the crowd would simply relocate to a different store or corner. Yet supervisors still encourage officers to "clear corners" and engage in blanket enforcement of low-level offenses, as demonstrated by the incident discussed in Section II.A., *supra*, in which the officer's supervisor encouraged him to "make something up" in order to disperse residents who were gathered peaceably on a street corner. Other officers told us that they were denied the opportunity to work overtime because supervisors believed they did not make enough stops and arrests.

This pressure from supervisors not only contributes to constitutional violations, but can also result in poor tactical decision-making that imperils the lives of officers and innocent civilians. In one incident we reviewed, an officer observed a gathering of people talking, eating, and waiting for food outside a late-night restaurant after bars had closed. None of the people appeared to be committing any crimes. But rather than monitoring the group or calling for backup in case of trouble, the officer decided to attempt to disperse the gathering alone. The officer reported that he decided to do this because he believed his supervisor would not be happy if he saw the area had not been cleared. As a result of his decision to clear the corner, the officer ended up in a physical altercation with a man who refused to leave. Alone and surrounded by an unfriendly crowd, the officer fired his service weapon at a man he feared was about to kick him. The bullet struck two people, at least one of whom was not involved in the incident. Despite the officer's serious tactical mistakes, reviewing supervisors did not report any errors and concluded that the officer had acted appropriately.

b. Deficient Policies, Training, and Oversight

BPD exacerbates the risk that its aggressive street enforcement tactics will lead to constitutional violations by failing to use effective policies, training, oversight, and accountability systems. While these deficiencies are discussed in greater depth in Section III, *infra* at 128-54, several failings are particularly relevant to BPD's pattern or practice of making unlawful stops, searches, and arrests.

i. BPD Policies and Training Materials Do Not Equip Officers to Police Effectively and Constitutionally

Important BPD policies and training materials either misstate the law or are too vague to provide meaningful guidance to officers about operative constitutional standards. As a result, officers committed to constitutional policing are often not equipped to provide it.

For example, BPD's newly adopted order titled "Quality of Life Offenses—Core Legal Elements" from April 2015 does not accurately explain the legal requirements for making loitering arrests. The order includes a section discussing special considerations for a violation of the Baltimore City Code prohibiting loitering, but fails to mention the requirement that officers may not arrest individuals for loitering until they have been told what specific conduct is prohibited, warned that a violation of law is occurring, and still refuse to desist. As discussed above, BPD's stops policy likewise misstated the applicable legal standard until 2015 by not requiring officers to have suspicion that a person is armed and dangerous prior to conducting a weapons frisk. Other policies are insufficiently specific to provide effective guidance to officers. For example, General Order 4-94, "Strip Searches and Body Cavity Searches," requires officers to obtain a warrant in order to conduct a body cavity search "unless exigent circumstances exist to justify a warrantless search." However, the policy provides officers with no guidance about what would constitute sufficient exigent circumstances to justify an immediate, warrantless body cavity search.[54]

---

[54] Other policies related to searches and seizures, though not directly related to our findings, are similarly troubling. For example, BPD General Order J-7 (January 5, 2004), "Search and Seizure Warrants" states that "Immediate entry may be initiated if sounds, conversations or other activity coming from within the premises leads you to believe that activity is occurring which may indicate a potential threat of physical harm to police officers/occupants, evidence is being destroyed, or a suspect is escaping." However, this does not accord with constitutional requirements. Prior to "forcibly entering a residence, police officers 'must knock on the door and announce their identity and purpose.'" *Bellotte v. Edwards*, 629 F.3d 415, 419 (4th Cir. 2011) (quoting *Richards v. Wisconsin*, 520 U.S. 385, 387 (1997)). While it is true that exigent circumstances may sometimes justify a "no-knock" entry, "police must have a reasonable suspicion that knocking and announcing their presence, under the particular circumstances, would be dangerous or futile, or that it

Several key training materials likewise fail to provide officers with an understanding of relevant constitutional requirements. For example, a lesson plan from a 2009 stop and frisk training indicates that "Investigative contacts of citizens by members of this agency will be conducted with articulable reason." The confusing reference to "articulable reason" misstates the *Terry* standard requiring reasonable suspicion based on specific and articulable facts. The lesson plan later instructs that the member "must be able to articulate reasonable suspicion or belief a crime has been or will be committed to perform a stop & frisk." This similarly misstates the relevant law, as it indicates that the same standard of suspicion is required for both an investigatory stop and a subsequent frisk—contrary to the requirement that an officer possess separate reasonable suspicion that an individual is armed and dangerous prior to initiating a frisk. Throughout the training, and on the reporting form, stop and frisk are consistently mentioned together, suggesting to officers that frisks are a matter of course during any stop. The training likewise does not mention that weapons frisks must be limited to a pat down of a person's outer clothing.

BPD leadership recognized the deficiencies in its stop and frisk guidance and updated the Department's policy on field interviews, investigative stops, weapons pat-downs and searches in 2015 to reflect a more accurate statement of the law. The new policy also requires that commanding officers provide trainings and conduct audits to ensure members engage appropriately and within policy, and fulfill reporting requirements. However, trainings have yet to be administered to the majority of field officers, and supervisors have not consistently audited reports or held officers accountable for failing to comply with the updated policy.

ii. BPD Lacks Effective Oversight and Accountability of Stops, Searches, and Arrests

BPD fails to use effective measures to review stops, searches, and arrests to identify and correct constitutional violations or provide counseling and support to its officers. BPD conducts minimal substantive review of the justification for particular stops, searches, and arrests, and does not sufficiently collect and analyze data to identify problematic patterns in these activities. Consequently, BPD relies almost exclusively on its complaint system to identify constitutional violations. These practices are not sufficient to ensure constitutional policing.

Substantive review of stops, searches, and arrests: BPD supervisors conduct minimal substantive review of officers' justifications for stops, searches, and arrests. Although BPD policy

---

would inhibit the effective investigation of the crime by, for example, allowing the destruction of evidence." *Bellotte*, 629 F.3d at 420 (citation omitted). "Generic" threats and dangers "raised at the most general level" are not particularized enough to establish exigent circumstances. *Id.* at 424 n.2. Entry without knocking based on mere speculation is likewise not reasonable under the Fourth Amendment. *Id.* at 423. The BPD policy also permits immediate entry, even in the absence of exigent circumstances, where there has been no response within 20 seconds of knocking on the door. This is not in accord with applicable law. Although 15–20 seconds may be a sufficient amount of time to wait if officers have reason to believe the delay gives rise to exigent circumstances, "in a case with no reason to suspect an immediate risk of frustration or futility in waiting at all, the reasonable wait time may well be longer when police make a forced entry, since they ought to be more certain the occupant has had time to answer the door." *United States v. Banks*, 540 U.S. 31, 41 (2003); *see also Hudson v. Michigan*, 547 U.S. 586, 590 (2006) ("Our reasonable wait time standard is necessarily vague.") (internal quotation marks and citations omitted).

instructs officers to document all stops, frisks, and searches on a stop form, it lacks an effective means to identify and address unconstitutional behavior. For most of the period covered by our review, BPD officers recorded stops on a "Stop and Frisk" form that typically did not record an officer's reasons for making a stop or initiating a frisk. As a result, BPD officers did not document the facts justifying a stop or search except in cases that resulted in an arrest or use of force, for which officers were required to complete an incident report or use of force report. This information deficit precluded supervisory review for the large majority of stops that do not lead to arrests or citations—stops for which such review is imperative. BPD attempted to address this data collection issue through a policy change in 2015, when it began requiring officers to document the basis for *Terry* stops and frisks on a "Form 309" and instructing supervisors to review these justifications. But this process has not generated robust review. While supervisors usually review stop reports, they almost universally sign off on the bases for stops and searches—even where officers describe facially unlawful activity. Indeed, BPD supervisors told us they view their role as merely "documenting" officer activity, not reviewing it for compliance with policy and law. Moreover, our ride-alongs and officer interviews revealed that many officers who make *Terry* stops that do not lead to arrest report that they conducted only a voluntary "field interview"—or no stop at all—to avoid the new documentation requirements. And BPD has not audited its field reports or CAD data to root out this practice.

We found similar deficiencies throughout BPD's review of officers' justifications for arrests. As with stops and frisks, BPD front line supervisors consistently sign off on incident reports describing the basis for warrantless arrests, even where the reports describe egregious constitutional violations. Indeed, our review did not identify a single arrest questioned by a front line supervisor. And as with stops, BPD supervisors told us that they see their role as documenting officer activity, not reviewing to ensure it conforms to constitutional standards.

Data collection and pattern analysis: BPD likewise fails to collect and analyze data to identify patterns in officers' stops, searches, and arrests. Despite a long record of public outcry and numerous complaints regarding illegal stops, searches, and arrests for low level offenses, BPD has never consistently collected and analyzed data regarding the number, type, and nature of its investigatory stops. BPD enters certain information from stop forms into an electronic database, but the limited types of data and inconsistent data entry practices preclude analysis. Indeed, BPD does not conduct any statistical analysis of its stops or searches using these data, nor are the data entered into BPD's early intervention system to help identify officers whose activities may warrant further scrutiny. This lack of meaningful data analysis hinders BPD's ability to manage its officers effectively.

The inability to analyze data keeps BPD from identifying important trends, curbing unlawful practices, and assisting officers or units that may benefit from additional training or support. For example, BPD's data systems cannot identify whether specific officers or units bear a disproportionate share of responsibility for illegal stops and searches. During the course of our investigation, we received a large number of anecdotes specifically identifying plainclothes officers enforcing violent crime and vice offenses (the names and organization of the units have changed multiple times over the years covered by the investigation) as particularly aggressive and unrestrained in their practice of stopping individuals without cause and performing public, humiliating searches. A disproportionate share of complaints likewise accuse plainclothes officers of misconduct. Yet much of BPD's stop data does not even identify the unit of the officers involved in the stop, making unit-level analysis impossible. Indeed, BPD's data on roughly half of the 300,000 stops recorded from 2010–2014 contain no information about the units of the officers who made the stop.

BPD similarly fails to track data on arrests made by officers. Although BPD enters information on arrests in a basic database, the Department conducts no analysis to identify trends in the type, frequency, or quality of arrests made by particular officers or units. For example, one measure that could be used to assess whether individual officers or units are engaged in a pattern of illegal arrests would be to monitor arrest outcomes to determine if prosecutors filed or dismissed charges in cases stemming from arrests by certain officers, units, or supervisors. Doing so would identify officers who make arrests that cannot be prosecuted due to lack of probable cause, failure to collect evidence in a constitutional manner, or other improprieties. Tracking arrest outcomes is an important tool for imposing accountability as well as identifying officers who would benefit from additional training, guidance, or other early intervention. Yet BPD does not take any steps to track or identify officers or units who make arrests that cannot be prosecuted, or to identify supervisors who sign off on such arrests.

Even where prosecutors have provided BPD with specific information on problematic officers who routinely make improper arrests, searches, or seizures, the Department has failed to meaningfully investigate the information or take appropriate action. For several years, the State's Attorney's Office maintained a "Do Not Call" list of officers that prosecutors should not subpoena to testify because prosecutors determined that the officers did not testify credibly about their enforcement actions. Although the State's Attorney's Office regularly shared this list with BPD, the Department rarely used the information to identify officers who may need support or discipline. As a result, problematic officers remain on the street, detaining, searching, and arresting people even though the State's Attorney's Office has determined that it cannot prosecute a crime based on the officers' testimony. The State's Attorney's Office no longer maintains a written "Do Not Call" list, but prosecutors informally maintain a registry of problematic BPD officers who cannot be used to support criminal prosecutions. In recent years, the State's Attorney's Office has contacted BPD leadership on several occasions to identify officers that prosecutors determined can no longer testify credibly due to misconduct. In most of these cases, BPD leadership took no action against the identified problem officers.

B. BPD Discriminates Against African Americans in its Enforcement Activities

We find reasonable cause to believe that BPD engages in a pattern or practice of discriminatory policing against African Americans. Statistical evidence shows that the Department intrudes disproportionately upon the lives of African Americans at every stage of its enforcement activities. BPD officers disproportionately stop African Americans; search them more frequently during these stops; and arrest them at rates that significantly exceed relevant benchmarks for criminal activity. African Americans are likewise subjected more often to false arrests. Indeed, for each misdemeanor street offense that we examined, local prosecutors and booking officials dismissed a higher proportion of African-American arrests upon initial review compared to arrests of people from other racial backgrounds. BPD officers also disproportionately use force—including constitutionally excessive force—against African-American subjects. Nearly 90 percent of the excessive force incidents identified by the Justice Department review involve force used against African Americans.

In the early 2000s, BPD began a "zero tolerance" enforcement strategy that encouraged officers to make frequent stops, searches, and arrests for misdemeanor offenses. This strategy overwhelmingly impacted the City's African-American residents and predominantly African-American neighborhoods. BPD has had notice of concerns about its policing of African-American communities for many years, yet it has failed to take adequate steps to ensure that its enforcement activities are non-discriminatory. The Department did not implement a "Fair and Impartial Policing" policy until 2015 and conducted virtually no analysis of its own data to assess the impact of its enforcement activities on African-American communities. BPD likewise has failed to effectively investigate complaints alleging racial bias—often misclassifying complaints to preclude any meaningful investigation. In some cases, BPD supervisors have ordered their subordinates to target African Americans specifically for heightened enforcement. We also found numerous examples of BPD officers using racial slurs or making other statements that exhibit bias against African Americans without being held accountable by the Department. These racial disparities and indications of intentional discrimination erode community trust that is a critical component of effective law enforcement. We heard repeatedly from community members who believed they were treated disrespectfully or singled out for enforcement because of their race. BPD leadership acknowledges that its legacy of zero tolerance enforcement in certain neighborhoods has damaged community partnerships and has taken steps to begin improving the Department's relationship with African-American communities. While we applaud these steps, significant work remains.

In addition to harming its relationship with the broader community, BPD's racially disparate enforcement violates the Safe Streets Act and Title VI of the Civil Rights Act of 1964. These statutes prohibit law enforcement practices that disparately impact African Americans unless the practices are necessary to achieve non-discriminatory objectives. *Cf. Gallagher v. Magner*, 619 F.3d 823, 837 (8th Cir. 2010) (in the related context of Fair Housing Act litigation, an official action that causes racially disparate impact may be justified only by showing that the action "has a manifest relationship to legitimate, non-discriminatory objectives"); *Albemarle Paper Co. v. Moody*, 422 U.S. 405, 425 (1975) (finding in the Title VII employment discrimination context that an employer may rebut prima facie showing of disproportionate impact by proving that the requirement causing disparate impact has a "manifest relationship to the employment in question"). Title VI provides that no person shall "be excluded from participating in, be denied the benefits of, or be subjected to discrimination under any program or activity receiving [f]ederal financial assistance" based on race. 42 U.S.C. § 2000d. The Title VI implementing regulations ban recipients of federal funds from using "criteria or methods of administration" that have an unnecessary disparate impact based on race. 28 C.F.R. § 42.104(b)(2). The Safe Streets Act likewise proscribes law enforcement practices that cause disparate impact based on race except where such impact is necessary to achieve nondiscriminatory objectives. *See* 28 C.F.R. § 42.203.

1. BPD's Enforcement Activities Disproportionately Impact African Americans

There is overwhelming statistical evidence of racial disparities in BPD's stops, searches, and arrests. This evidence demonstrates a discriminatory impact on African Americans under Title VI and the Safe Streets Act. *See Chavez v. Illinois State Police*, 251 F.3d 612, 637 (7th Cir. 2001) ("The Supreme Court has long noted the importance of statistical analysis in cases in which the existence of discrimination is a disputed issue.") (internal citation omitted); *Bradley v. United States*, 299 F.3d 197, 206 n.11 (3d Cir. 2002) ("In profiling cases . . . statistical evidence of discrimination may be the only means of proving a discriminatory effect"); *Floyd v. City of New York*, 959 F. Supp. 2d 540, 661–62 (S.D.N.Y. 2013) (statistical evidence of racial and ethnic disparities in police stop and frisk practices, including post-stop outcomes, proved adverse impact under the Equal Protection Clause); *Melendres v. Arpaio*, No. CV-97092513, 2013 WL 2297173 (D. Ariz. May 24, 2013) (statistical evidence proved that certain patrol operations at a sheriff's office disparately impacted Latinos); *Maryland NAACP v. Maryland State Police*, 454 F. Supp. 2d 339, 349 (D. Md. 2006) (disparities in stops and searches of African Americans constituted "powerful circumstantial evidence of racial profiling"). Here, statistical evidence highlights racial disparities at all levels of BPD's street enforcement, from the initial decision to stop pedestrians or vehicles to conducting searches and making arrests. We also found troubling trends in the sample of use of force reports we reviewed, suggesting that force may be used disproportionately against African Americans.

a. Racial Disparities in Stops and Searches

BPD officers subject African Americans to a disproportionate number of pedestrian and vehicle stops on Baltimore streets and search African Americans disproportionately during these stops.

i. Stops

BPD disproportionately stops African Americans standing, walking, or driving on Baltimore streets. The Department's data on all pedestrian stops from January 2010 to June 2015 shows that African Americans account for 84 percent of stops[55] despite comprising only 63 percent of the City's population. Expressed differently, BPD officers made 520 stops for every 1,000 black residents in Baltimore, but only 180 stops for every 1,000 Caucasian residents.

---

[55] Stops for which officers did not record the subject's race are excluded from this analysis.

Figure 1 – BPD Pedestrian Stops Per 1,000 Residents, 2010-2015

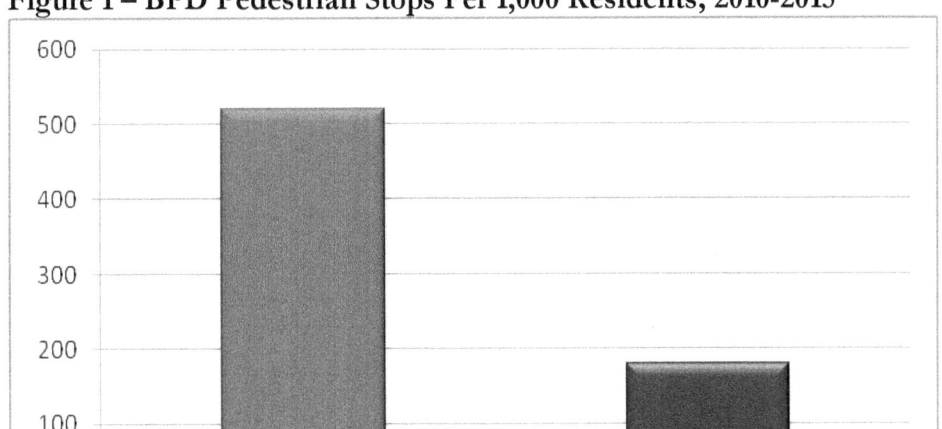

The high rate of stopping African Americans persists across the City, even in districts where African Americans make up a small share of the population. Indeed, the proportion of African-American stops exceeds the share of African-American population in each of BPD's nine police districts, despite significant variation in the districts' racial, socioeconomic, and geographic composition.[56] For example, African Americans accounted for: 83 percent of stops in the Central District (compared to 57 percent of the population), which contains the City's downtown business area; over 93 percent of stops in the Eastern District (compared to 90 percent of the population), which includes predominantly low-income, urban neighborhoods; and 83 percent of stops in the Northern District (compared to 41 percent of the population), which includes many affluent, suburban neighborhoods. Even in the Southeast District—with an African-American population of only 23 percent—two out of three BPD stops involved African-American subjects. Figure 2 illustrates this pattern.

---

[56] The proportion of African American pedestrian stops and population was virtually identical in the Western District, where both figures are approximately 96 percent.

Figure 2 –Pedestrian Stops Compared to Population, by BPD District, 2010-2015

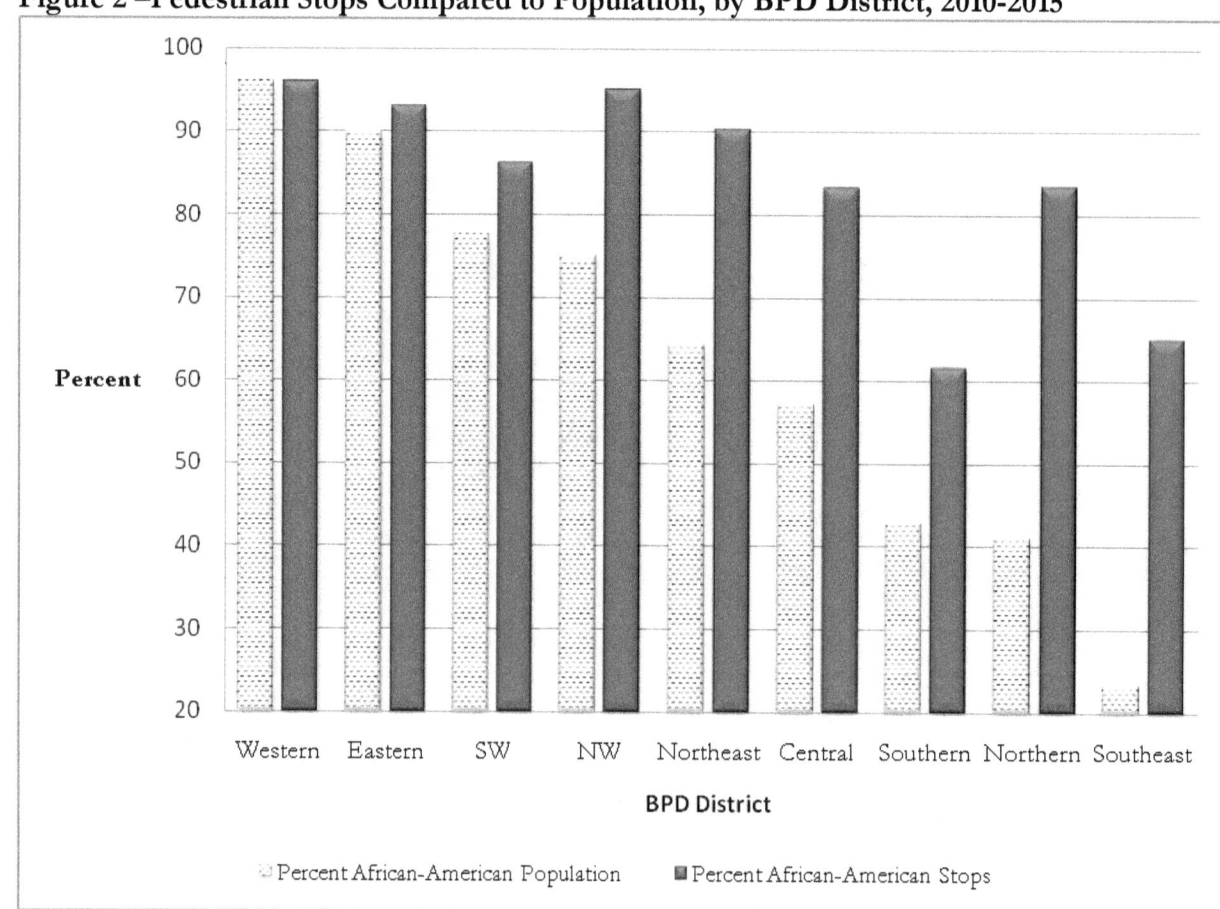

Closer analysis highlights the impact of these racial disparities. Individual African Americans are far more likely to be subjected to multiple stops within relatively short periods of time. African Americans accounted for 95 percent of the 410 individuals stopped at least ten times by BPD officers from 2010–2015. During this period, BPD stopped 34 African Americans at least 20 times and seven other African Americans at least *30 times*.[57] No person of any other race was stopped more than 12 times. One African-American man in his mid-fifties was stopped 30 times in less than four years. The only reasons provided for these stops were officers' suspicion that the man was "loitering" or "trespassing," or as part of a "CDS investigation." On at least 15 occasions, officers detained the man while they checked to see if he had outstanding warrants. Despite these repeated intrusions, none of the 30 stops resulted in a citation or criminal charge. The map on the following page shows the concentration of stops in African-American neighborhoods.

---

[57] As explained in Section II.A.1, there is strong evidence that BPD under-reports its pedestrian stops. Thus, the true number of African Americans who hit these—or higher—stop thresholds may be significantly larger.

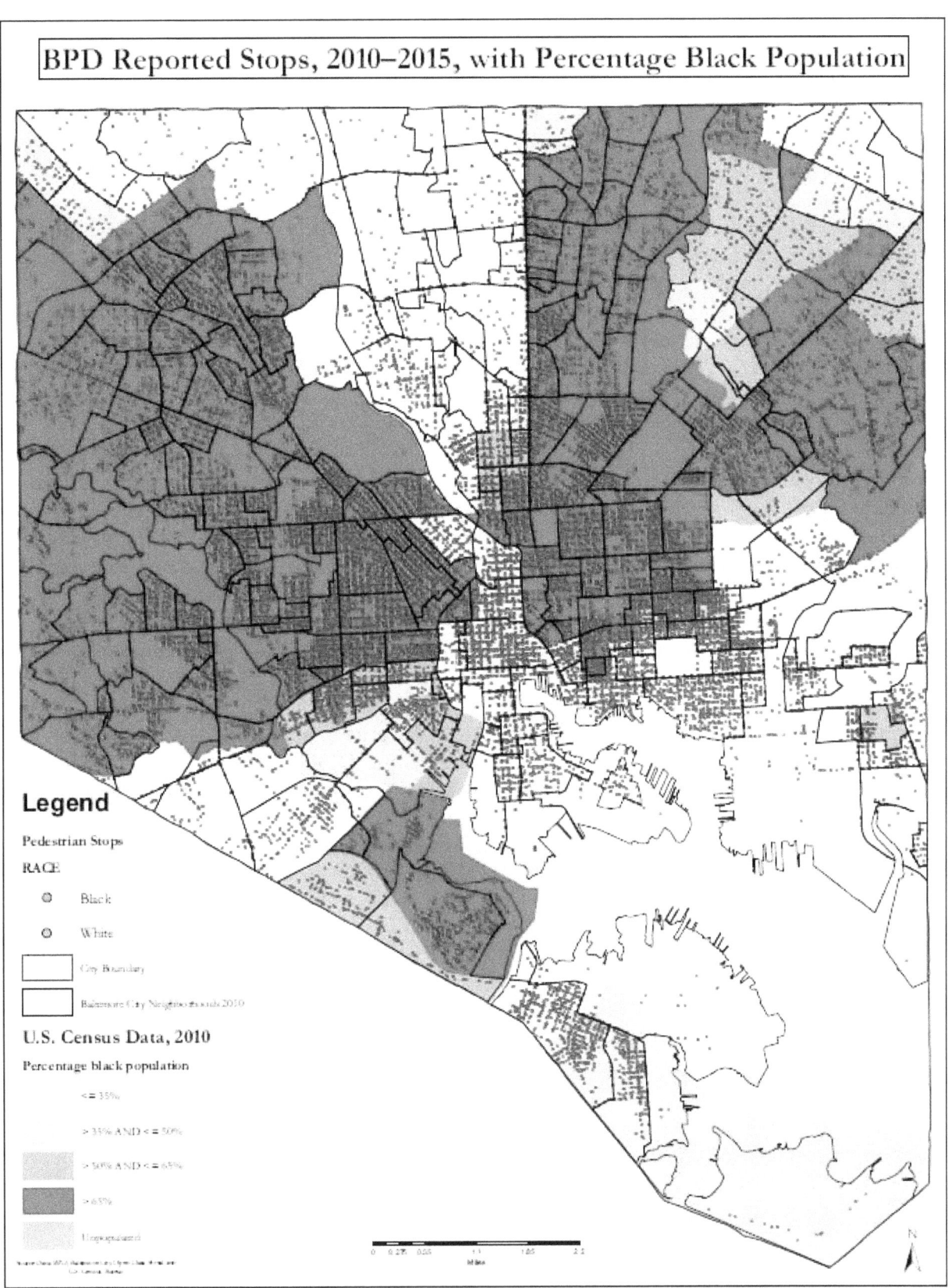

BPD Reported Stops, 2010–2015, with Percentage Black Population

Legend

Pedestrian Stops

RACE

○ Black

○ White

City Boundary

Baltimore City Neighborhoods 2010

U.S. Census Data, 2010

Percentage black population

< = 35%

> 35% AND < = 50%

> 50% AND < = 65%

> 65%

Unpopulated

BPD likewise stops African-American drivers at disproportionate rates. From 2010–2015, African Americans made up 82 percent of people stopped by BPD officers for traffic violations, compared to only 60 percent of the City's driving age population. As with pedestrian stops, BPD stopped a higher rate of African American drivers in each of the City's districts, despite large differences in those districts' demographic profiles and traffic patterns. For example, African Americans accounted for 80 percent of vehicle stops in the Northern District despite making up only 41 percent of the district's population, and made up 56 percent of stops in the Southeast District compared to only 23 percent of the population living there.

While there are limitations on using population data to benchmark vehicle stops because the proportion of drivers on roadways does not necessarily match the population living in a particular area, there are strong indications that BPD's high rate of stopping African-American drivers is discriminatory. Indeed, the proportion of African-American drivers on Baltimore roadways is almost certainly less than their 60 percent share of the City's driving age population. Baltimore's traffic patterns are influenced by commuters and visitors from surrounding areas with significantly smaller African-American populations than the City's. BPD's data confirms that 25 percent of the Department's traffic stops involve drivers who live outside the City, overwhelmingly in towns and suburbs within the Baltimore metropolitan area. The presence of these individuals on Baltimore roads lowers the proportion of African-American drivers, as African Americans account for only 27.6 percent of the driving age population in the Baltimore metropolitan area. Moreover, basic population data is likely to overstate the portion of African-American drivers on Baltimore roadways because African Americans are less likely than other City residents to have access to vehicles.[58] Nationally, 19 percent of African Americans live in households that do not have access to automobiles, compared to 4.6 percent of Caucasians, a disparity that "follows directly from sharp racial differences in household income and poverty." Berube, Deakin, & Raphael, SOCIOECONOMIC DIFFERENCES IN HOUSEHOLD AUTOMOBILE OWNERSHIP RATES 203 (2008). This trend is pronounced in Baltimore, where over 100,000 African Americans live in poverty, constituting an outsized share of the City's low-income residents.[59] Consequently, African Americans almost certainly comprise less than 60 percent of Baltimore drivers, but account for 82 percent of BPD's traffic stops.

ii. Searches

We also found evidence of bias in BPD's searches during pedestrian and vehicle stops, although our analysis is limited by significant shortcomings in BPD's data collection. We first examined spreadsheets provided by BPD that purportedly reflect the Department's data on all vehicle and pedestrian stops from 2010–2015, including whether officers conducted a search during each stop. Although these spreadsheets typically record the race of the person stopped and the district in which the stop occurred, they do not appear to reflect complete information about searches. BPD's data record that officers conducted searches in only 1.3 percent of pedestrian stops

---

[58] According to the U.S. Census Bureau's American Community Survey 2010–2013, 30 percent of Baltimore residents do not have access to automobiles.

[59] African Americans account for more than 76 percent of Baltimoreans living below the poverty line despite making up only 63 percent of the City's population. U.S. Census Bureau, American Community Survey 2014 One-Year Estimate.

and 0.5 percent of vehicle stops—rates that are implausibly low. Interviews with BPD personnel responsible for entering data from officers' stop reports into the spreadsheets confirmed that information on searches is frequently not captured. Other relevant data—such as the reason for the stop, officers' unit assignments, etc.—also appear to be recorded inconsistently. In an attempt to address this under-reporting and facilitate more comprehensive analysis of searches, experts retained by the Justice Department drew a sample of nearly 14,000 hard copy BPD stop reports, manually coded them, and created a new database containing all of the information recorded on the reports. Within this sample, officers conducted searches in 13 percent of pedestrian stops and 8.2 percent of vehicle stops—far higher rates than reflected in the data BPD captured in its data entry.

The database we created from hard copy stop reports reveals that BPD officers search African Americans at disproportionate rates. During pedestrian stops, officers searched 13 percent of African Americans compared to only 9.5 percent of other people—making African Americans 37 percent more likely to be searched when stopped than other residents. Similarly, officers were 23 percent more likely to search African Americans during vehicle stops. These differences are significant beyond conventional levels of statistical significance.[60] Justice Department experts found that racial disparities in search rates persisted after using regression techniques to control for relevant variables, including the area in which a stop occurred and the assignment and experience level of the officers involved.

These racial disparities suggest that BPD's search practices discriminate against African Americans. Search rate differences do not alone establish disproportionate impact based on race, however, because it is possible that differential search rates are driven by race-neutral explanations. For that reason, the best measure of racial patterns in searches is a comparison of the rates at which officers find contraband during searches, or "hit rates." *See, e.g.*, John Knowles, Nicola Persico & Petra Todd, *Racial Bias in Motor Vehicle Searches: Theory and Evidence*, 109 JOURNAL OF POLITICAL ECONOMY 203 (2001). A lower hit rate for searches of a particular demographic group is evidence that officers apply a lower threshold of suspicion when deciding to search members of that group compared to others.

To the extent that BPD collects hit rate data, it suggests that officers' search decisions are biased against African Americans. Indeed, BPD's data on all stops from 2010–2015 shows that searches of African Americans have significantly lower hit rates than other searches. During vehicle stops, BPD officers reported finding some type of contraband less than half as often when searching African Americans—in only 3.9 percent of searches of African Americans, compared to 8.5 percent of other searches. Search hit rates during pedestrian stops also exhibited large disparities, with officers finding contraband in only 2.6 percent of African American searches compared to 3.9 percent for other searches—a 50 percent difference.[61] These results are statistically significant.

---

[60] In the fields of statistics and criminology, results are generally considered statistically significant if they would occur by chance no more than 5 times out of 100.

[61] This analysis is based on all 3,863 searches that BPD recorded for pedestrian stops and 1,495 searches recorded for vehicle stops from 2010–2015. As discussed above, these data likely fail to capture a significant number of searches that BPD officers actually conducted during this period. The *hit rates* from these searches are nonetheless indicative of bias, however, because there is no reason to believe that there are systematic differences in how BPD records search outcomes based on the race of the person searched. In other words, BPD officers sometimes fail to record their searches at all. But when searches are recorded, there is no indication that officers change how they record the fruits of the search based on the race of the person searched. Nor does it appear that officers disproportionately record searches

Figure 3 – Search Hit Rates, 2010-2015

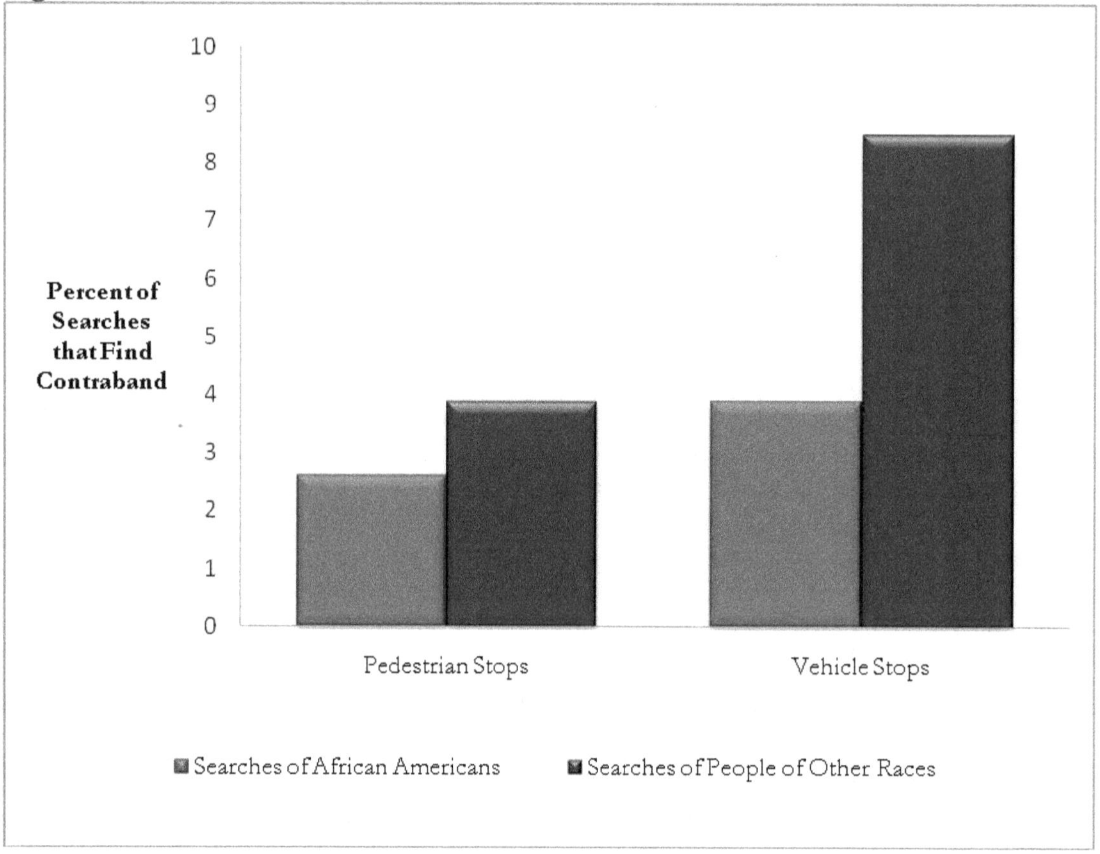

In short, BPD's pedestrian and vehicle stops disproportionately impact African Americans. The large racial disparities in stops persist throughout the City, subjecting African Americans to heightened intrusion from the police in their lives. Officers also search African Americans at higher rates during these stops, even though searches of African Americans are less likely to find contraband than searches of people from other racial backgrounds. These differential search rates are not justified by characteristics of the people searched.

Our analysis of racial patterns in BPD's searches was challenging because of the Department's deficient data collection. BPD's failure to record consistent search information not only inhibits our analysis here, it limits the Department's ability to root out discriminatory conduct by its officers. Moving forward, BPD must reform its data collection and analysis systems to ensure that robust search data is tracked and analyzed to prevent and correct discriminatory practices.

in certain parts of the City. To the contrary, the proportion of searches recorded in each district roughly tracks the number of stops in those districts. In sum, BPD's data showing that searches of African Americans are less likely to find contraband than other searches is reliable evidence of disproportionate impact.

b. Racial Disparities in Arrests

The racial disparities in BPD's stops and searches are further reflected in BPD's arrest practices. From November 2010–July 2015, BPD charged African Americans with 280,850 criminal offenses, constituting over 86 percent of all charges filed for which the race of the offender is known.[62] Expressed a different way, African Americans in Baltimore were charged with one offense for every 1.4 residents, while individuals of other races were charged with only one offense per 5.1 residents. This discriminatory pattern is particularly apparent in two categories of BPD's enforcement: (1) warrantless arrests for discretionary misdemeanor offenses such as disorderly conduct and failing to obey an officer's order; and (2) arrests for drug possession. In both cases, officers arrest African Americans at rates far higher than relevant benchmarks.

i. Racial Disparities in Misdemeanor Street Arrests

BPD's warrantless arrests for discretionary misdemeanor offenses exhibit substantial racial disparities. Our analysis of these arrests is based on data the State of Maryland tracks for all criminal charges made by law enforcement officers. For each charged offense, this data captures the agency making the arrest, the race and gender of the person arrested, and the arrest's disposition. As explained in Section II.A, *supra*, the disposition data records whether each arrestee was committed into jail, issued a criminal or civil citation, released without charges, or released because of mistaken identity. For arrests that do not result in immediate release, the data also record whether reviewing officials at the State's Attorney's Office found that the arrest lacked probable cause or otherwise declined to charge the offense. Analysis of this data reveals that African Americans account for the overwhelming majority of BPD's discretionary misdemeanor arrests, and that reviewing officials are more likely to dismiss charges against African Americans—indicating that officers apply a lower standard when making them.

As an initial matter, BPD officers arrest African Americans for several common misdemeanor offenses at high rates. Although they make up only 63 percent of Baltimore's population, African Americans accounted for: 87 percent of the 3,400 charges for resisting arrest; 89 percent of 1,350 charges for making a false statement to an officer; 84 percent of the 4,000 charges for failing to obey an order; 86 percent of the more than 1,000 charges for hindering or obstruction; 83 percent of the roughly 6,500 arrests for disorderly conduct; and 88 percent of the nearly 3,500 arrests for trespassing on posted property. Figure 4 highlights the magnitude of these disparities by expressing the number of arrests for these offenses per 1,000 Baltimore residents.

---

[62] After removing duplicates from data provided by the State of Maryland, we found that BPD filed 331,764 criminal charges during this period. Of these charges, 5,641 were excluded from analysis because the arrestee's race was not recorded.

Figure 4 – Misdemeanor Charges Per 1,000 Residents, 2010-2015

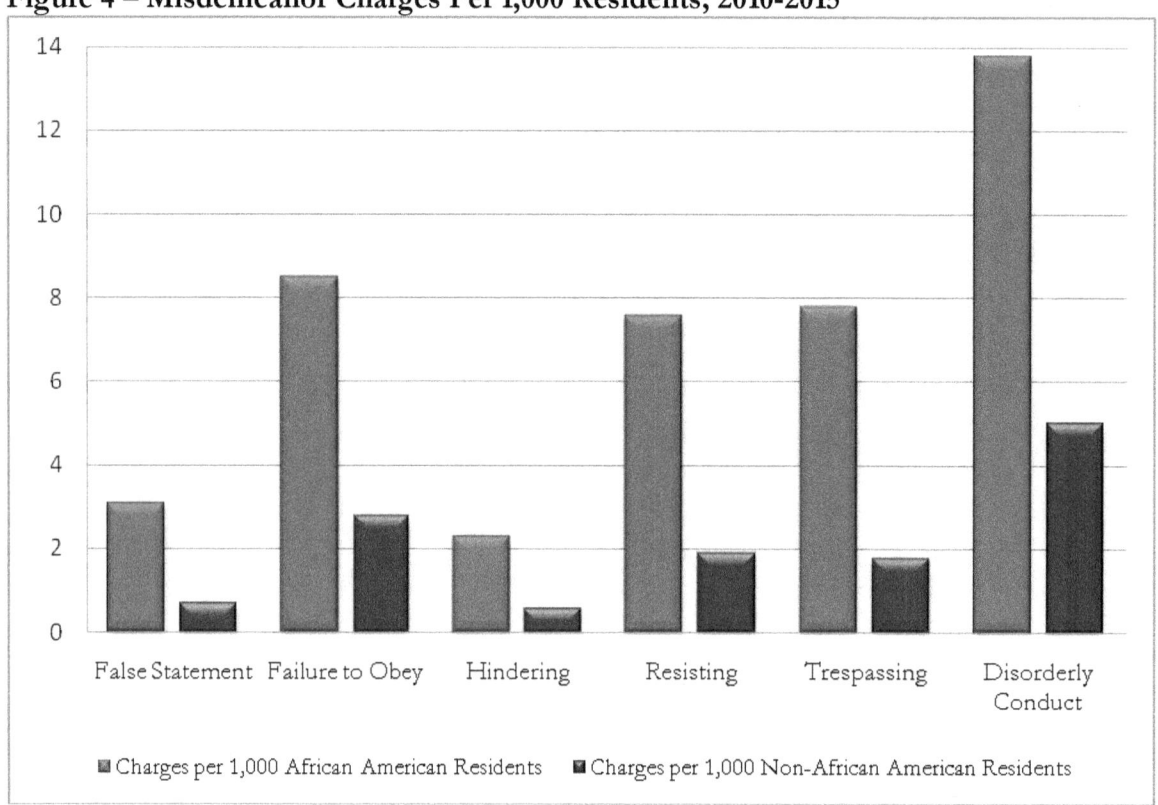

■ Charges per 1,000 African American Residents   ■ Charges per 1,000 Non-African American Residents

These disparities are even more pronounced where officers arrest individuals solely for a misdemeanor street offense, unconnected to a more serious charge. In such cases, African Americans comprise 91 percent of trespassing charges; 91 percent of failure to obey charges; 88 percent of hindering charges; and 84 percent of disorderly conduct charges. BPD also charged 79 people solely with "resisting arrest," despite not arresting them for any other crime. African Americans accounted for 90 percent of these charges.

In addition to these common misdemeanor offenses, BPD enforces other minor charges almost exclusively against African Americans. For example, BPD charged 657 people with "gaming" or playing "cards or dice," of whom 652—over 99 percent—were African Americans. Although we are not aware of any data tracking the precise rate at which people of different races play cards or dice, it is extremely unlikely that African Americans comprise 99 percent of those doing so. Notably, in some cases, BPD has expended significant resources to enforce these minor offenses against African Americans. For example, BPD has used a helicopter unit known as "Foxtrot," which typically coordinates officers' response to shootings and other serious crimes, to enforce misdemeanor gambling offenses against African Americans. In early 2016, a Foxtrot unit alerted patrol officers that a group of young African-American men were playing dice on a street corner. Officers on the ground responded to this intelligence by confronting the group and arresting one of the men, who was charged solely with "playing dice."

The differential rates at which BPD supervisors release without charges or local prosecutors decline to charge BPD's misdemeanor arrests underscore their discriminatory nature. To arrest for a misdemeanor offense, BPD officers must have probable cause that an offense occurred. As explained above, in some cases reviewing officials at booking or the State's Attorney's Office disagree with officers' probable cause determinations and decline to charge arrestees. If officers apply a consistent, unbiased standard when making arrests, the rate of such declinations should be roughly equivalent across racial groups for arrests on any particular offense. However, our outcome analysis shows large racial disparities: misdemeanor arrests of African Americans are dismissed or declined at significantly higher rates than other arrests.

During their initial review of arrest documents, booking officers and prosecutors dismissed charges against African Americans at significantly higher rates than arrests of other people. This disparity exists for every common misdemeanor offense we examined, as evident in Figure 5 below. Officials dismissed charges against African Americans for trespassing at a rate 52 percent higher than the rate at which they dismissed other trespassing arrests; dismissed African American resisting arrest charges at a 57 percent higher rate; failure to obey charges at a 33 percent higher rate; false statement charges at a 231 percent higher rate; disorderly conduct charges at a 17 percent higher rate; and disturbing the peace charges at a 370 percent higher rate. These disparities are statistically significant. Notably, the racial disparities in outcomes for these highly discretionary, non-violent offenses are not present for less discretionary felony offenses. We found that reviewing officials' initial review resulted in dismissal of charges for first degree assault, burglary, and robbery at nearly identical rates across racial groups. The implication of these findings is that there are no underlying conditions that cause officials to dismiss African-American charges at higher rates. Instead, the large racial differences in the proportion of dismissed charges for misdemeanor street offenses demonstrate that, where officers have wider discretion to make arrests, they exercise it in a discriminatory manner.

Figure 5 – Percent of Charges Dismissed Upon Initial Review, 2010-2015

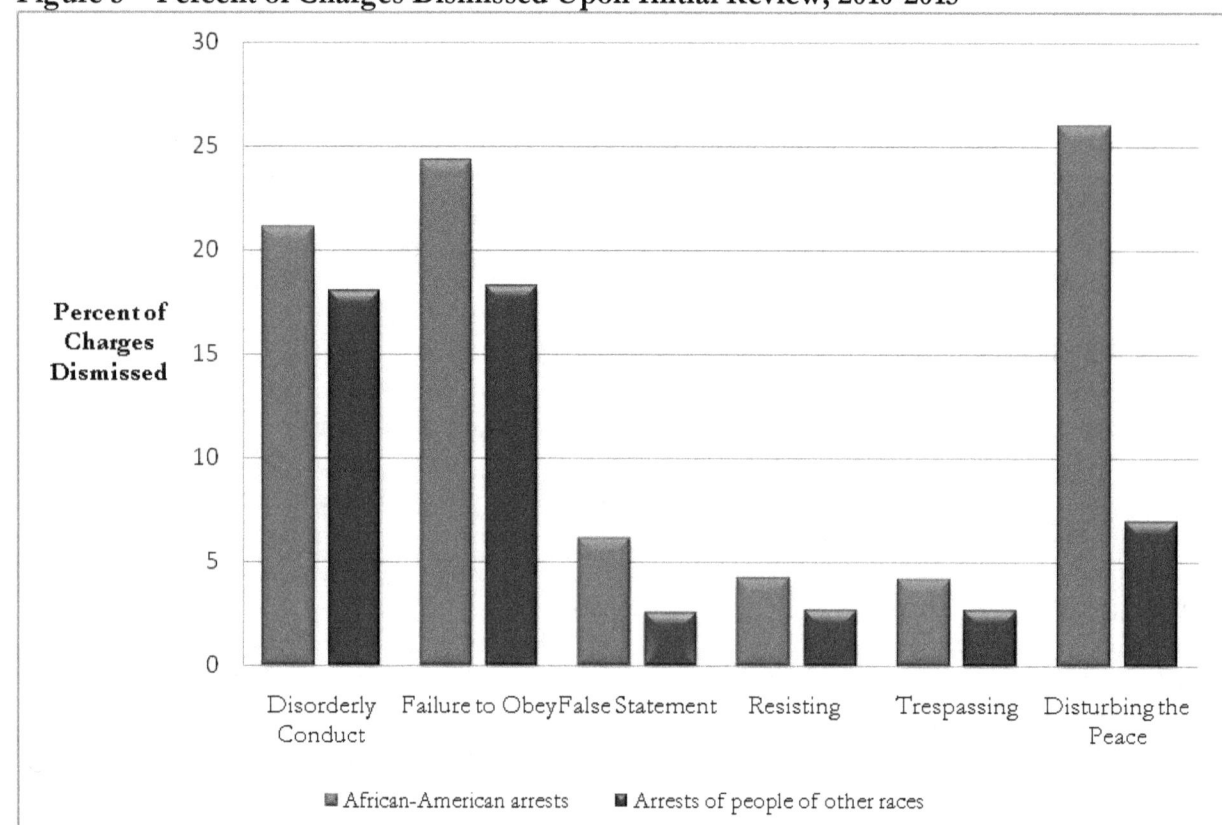

In sum, BPD disproportionately arrests African Americans for common misdemeanor street offenses. The proportion of African Americans arrested for these offenses is far higher than their share of Baltimore's population, and reviewing officials determined that arrests of African Americans for these offenses are significantly more likely to lack probable cause or otherwise not merit prosecution. Taken together, these facts demonstrate that BPD arrests African Americans for misdemeanor offenses based on lower evidentiary thresholds than it uses when arresting people from other racial backgrounds.

ii.   Disproportionate Arrests for Drug Possession

There are large racial disparities in BPD's enforcement of laws criminalizing possession of controlled substances. We analyzed drug possession charges for several reasons: such charges make up more than one third of all BPD arrests; stakeholders and community members we interviewed frequently expressed their belief that BPD focuses on African Americans for heightened drug enforcement; and data on the drug arrests can be compared to relevant benchmarks on drug usage to assess whether BPD enforces drug laws disproportionately. For this analysis, we compared BPD's drug arrests to: (1) survey data on drug usage; and (2) the rates of drug arrests in jurisdictions similar to Baltimore. We find that BPD arrests far more African Americans for drug offenses than would be expected based on drug usage and population data, and that this disparity is not attributable to any legitimate law enforcement objective. Indeed, BPD's rate of African-American drug arrests is significantly higher than the rate of such arrests by law enforcement agencies in cities with similar demographic profiles and socioeconomic challenges. These analyses reveal that BPD's drug enforcement disproportionately impacts African Americans.

BPD arrests African Americans for drug possession offenses at rates far exceeding their drug usage: To assess the racial impact of BPD's drug arrests, we first aggregated all drug possession offenses[63] for which BPD made at least 3,000 charges from November 2010–June 2015. BPD charged approximately 100,000 people for drug possession under these offenses. Eighty-nine percent of those charged were African American.[64] BPD made 254 drug arrests for every 1,000 African-American Baltimore residents while making only 52 drug arrests per 1,000 residents of other races.[65] African Americans were thus five times more likely than others to be arrested for drug offenses.

Figure 6 – Drug Possession Charges Per 1,000 Residents, 2010-2015

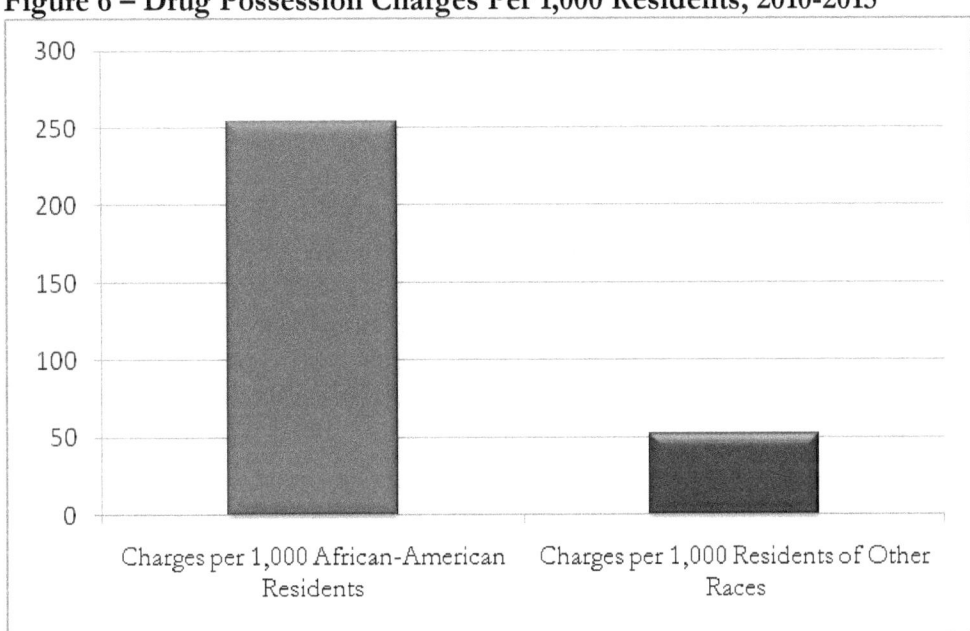

The racial disparities in BPD's enforcement are far higher than any demographic differences in the rates at which individuals use drugs. While the observed prevalence of illicit drug use varies somewhat by data source, most comprehensive surveys indicate that African Americans use drugs at rates that, at most, only modestly exceed other population groups. The Center for Disease Control's (CDC) National Survey on Drug Use and Health found that, in 2013, 8.7 percent of African Americans over age 12 had used drugs within the past month, compared to 7.7 percent of Caucasians. The 2012 survey reported similar figures, with 9.1 percent of African Americans and 7.4

---

[63] Some criminologists believe that, when comparing drug arrests to survey data on drug usage, the most accurate comparison includes police arrests for drug possession and drug distribution because law enforcement officers may charge individuals possessing controlled substances with intent to distribute them. Accordingly, we also compared BPD's rate of charging individuals for all drug possession *and distribution* offenses to data on drug usage. This comparison yielded nearly identical results. African Americans account for 90 percent of possession and distribution offenses charged by BPD, compared to 88.5 percent of possession charges alone.

[64] We excluded a small number of charges for which the race of the arrestee was not recorded.

[65] These figures include only drug offenses for which BPD made at least 3,000 charges from 2010–2015. The total number of all drug arrests is higher, as indicated in the analysis of Bureau of Justice Statistics data discussed below.

percent of Caucasians reporting drug use.[66] In other words, the CDC survey found that African Americans were between 1.1 and 1.2 times more likely to use drugs than Caucasians, yet BPD arrests African Americans for drug possession 5 times as often as others.[67]

BPD's disparate rate of arresting African Americans for drug crimes cannot be explained by differences in drug usage within Baltimore as compared to the nation as a whole. To the contrary, drug use in Baltimore appears broadly similar to national averages. For example, data maintained by the Substance Abuse and Mental Health Services Administration (SAMHSA) shows that the rate of marijuana use from 2010–2012 averaged 8.2 percent in Baltimore, compared to a national average of 7.0 percent. For drugs other than marijuana, SAMHSA surveys show that usage in Baltimore averaged 3.3 percent during this period, compared to a national average of 3.4 percent.

BPD arrests African Americans for drug possession offenses at higher rates than similar cities: A second measure of BPD's disproportionate drug enforcement is the agency's high rate of arresting African Americans for drug possession offenses compared to law enforcement agencies in cities with comparable demographic profiles, crime rates, and economic profiles. Expert criminologists retained for our investigation identified five cities most comparable to Baltimore for purposes of this analysis: Atlanta, Cleveland, Detroit, Memphis, and Milwaukee. These cities reported overall drug usage rates in line with Baltimore's 8.2 percent, including: 9.0 percent in Milwaukee; 13.6 percent in Detroit; and 6.5 percent in Atlanta.[68] The comparison cities likewise reported usage rates similar to Baltimore's 3.3 percent for drugs other than marijuana. Cleveland reported 3.5 percent non-marijuana usage, Atlanta 3.1 percent, and Detroit 3.7 percent.[69] Despites these similarities in rates of drug *use*, however, we found that BPD makes far more drug *arrests* than agencies in Baltimore's peer cities.

To make this comparison, we collected data from the Bureau of Justice Statistics (BJS) on drug arrests in Baltimore and the five comparison cities. The most recent period for which BJS data is available is 2010–2012. We used the 2010–2012 BJS data for all cities—including Baltimore—to standardize how arrests are categorized and reported.[70] We then controlled for population differences among these cities by measuring arrest rates based on the number of drug arrests per 1,000 residents in each racial category. The results show that BPD's rate of arresting African Americans for drug crimes dramatically exceeds the rate of such arrests by agencies in the comparison cities. Indeed, for each of the three years we examined, Baltimore drug arrests of

---

[66] *See* National Survey on Drug Use and Heath, CENTER FOR DISEASE CONTROL (Aug. 4, 2016), http://www.cdc.gov/nchs/data.

[67] Ninety-nine percent of BPD's arrestees for drug possession were either African American or Caucasian.

[68] *National Survey on Drug Use and Health Table 5*, SUBSTANCE ABUSE AND MENTAL HEALTH SERVICES ADMINISTRATION (August 4, 2016), http://www.samhsa.gov/data/sites/default/files/NSDUHsubstateChangeTabs2012/NSDUHsubstateChangeTabs2012.htm.

[69] *Id.*

[70] The BJS data on drug arrests in Baltimore differs slightly from the data BPD provided to us during the investigation, but the small differences do not impact our analysis. Indeed, for all three years we examined, the BPD data show that the agency arrested an even larger number of African Americans than the data reported to BJS. The analysis presented here thus may slightly understate the magnitude of BPD's disparate drug arrests of African Americans when compared to agencies in other cities.

African Americans were between *200 and 500 percent higher* than the comparison cities.[71]

Figure 7 – Drug Possession Arrests Per 1,000 African-American Residents, 2010-2012

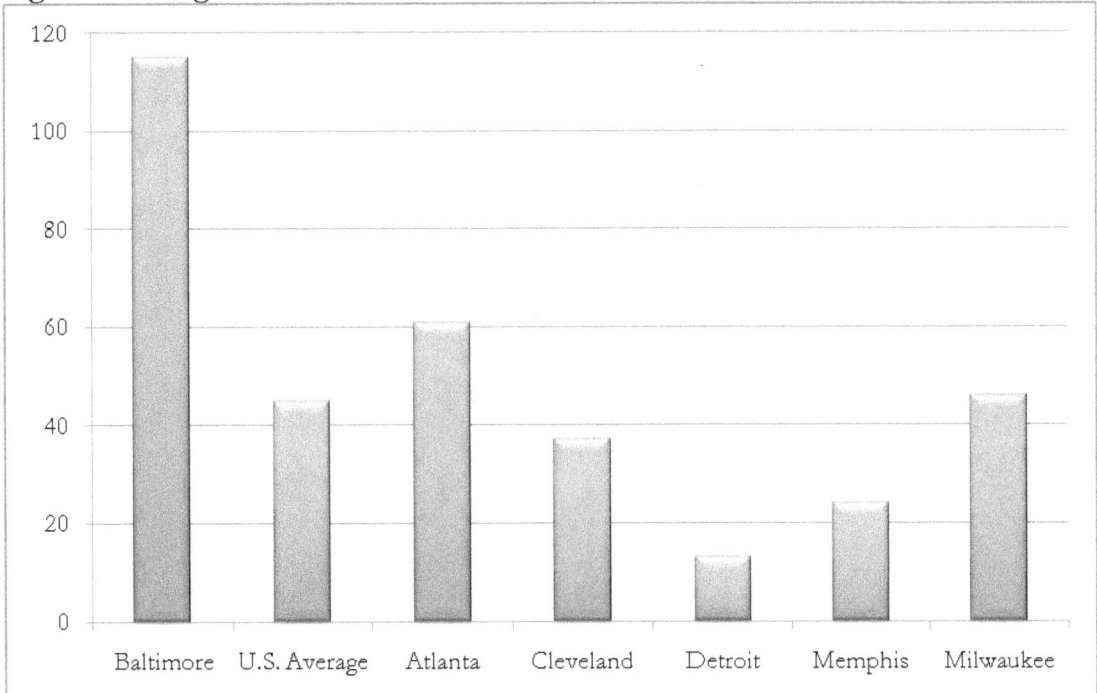

c. Use of Force

The consequence of the large racial disparities in stops, searches, and arrests may also manifest itself in what may be disproportionate use of force against African Americans by BPD. We found that African Americans accounted for roughly 88 percent of the subjects of non-deadly force used by BPD officers in a random sample of over 800 cases we reviewed. This trend is consistent across different types of non-deadly force, including tasers, the most common weapon used by BPD officers. While these patterns merit attention, we draw no firm conclusions about their relative impact on African Americans because we did not compare the rates of force to any "benchmark" of encounters in which force is warranted. Nevertheless, this rate of force is significantly higher than the proportion of African Americans in Baltimore's population, heightening our concerns.

*   *   *

In sum, we find large racial disparities in BPD's pedestrian stops, vehicle stops, searches, and arrests. We further identified troubling indications that BPD officers disproportionately use force during encounters with African Americans on Baltimore streets. As explained further below, BPD's disparate stops, searches, and arrests of African Americans are not part of a calibrated,

---

[71] BPD also arrests non-African Americans for drug possession offenses at somewhat higher rates than the national average and the comparison cities. As explained above, however, the *proportion* of BPD drug arrests of African Americans is far higher than would be expected based on drug usage data and population statistics. The comparison to law enforcement agencies in similar cities demonstrates that these disparities are not driven by legitimate responses to socioeconomic conditions. Rather, BPD's discriminatory drug enforcement renders it a significant outlier.

proportionate strategy for responding to criminal activity. These disparities establish disproportionate impact under the Constitution and the nondiscrimination provisions of Title VI and the Safe Streets Act. Title VI and the Safe Streets Act prohibit law enforcement agencies that receive federal financial assistance from engaging in practices that have an unnecessary disparate impact based on race. Because BPD's disparate stops, searches, and arrest are not done in a manner necessary to achieve BPD's legitimate public safety goals, they violate Title VI and the Safe Streets Act.

2. Racial Disparities in BPD's Enforcement, Along with Evidence Suggesting Intentional Discrimination Against African Americans, Exacerbates Community Distrust

The policing practices that cause the racial disparities in BPD's stops, searches, and arrests, along with evidence suggesting intentional discrimination against African Americans, undermine the community trust that is central to effective policing. Indeed, we heard from many community members who were reluctant to engage with BPD officers because of their belief that the Department treats African Americans unfairly. *See also* Jack Glaser, *Suspect Race: Causes and Consequence of Racial Profiling* 96–126 (2015) (racial profiling has a "high risk" of undermining efforts to control crime and promote public safety). These concerns were acknowledged by BPD leadership and officers, who explained that the lack of trust—particularly in many of Baltimore's African-American communities—inhibited officers' efforts to build relationships that are a key component of effective policing.

Starting in the early 2000s, BPD implemented a "zero tolerance" policing strategy. This strategy encouraged officers to take discretionary enforcement actions, including stops, searches, and arrests for misdemeanor offenses like loitering and disorderly conduct. As described above, this enforcement strategy focused on African Americans and predominantly African American neighborhoods for discretionary enforcement actions, and it led to officers frequently stopping, searching, and arresting individuals without the required constitutional justification. We also found evidence of officers using racial slurs or making other statements exhibiting bias while taking enforcement actions against African Americans.

The Department has had notice of concerns about the impact of its zero tolerance strategy on African Americans and predominantly African-American neighborhoods for many years, but for many years it failed to take adequate steps to ensure that its policing efforts are non-discriminatory. BPD did not institute a "Fair and Impartial Policing" policy until 2015, leaving officers without critical guidance on how to lawfully perform their duties. We likewise found no evidence that BPD has performed any analysis to determine if its enforcement strategies and activities disparately impact African Americans, even though it has collected the basic data to perform such assessments for years. Indeed, every analysis we include in this report is based on BPD's own data, but BPD never developed systems to conduct this analysis. We also found that BPD repeatedly fails to investigate complaints of racial bias. In the approximately six years of complaint data we received from BPD, we found only one complaint that BPD classified as a racial slur. This is implausible. By manually reviewing and performing text searches on BPD's complaint data, we found 60 more complaints that alleged that BPD officers used just one racial slur—"n****r"—but all these complaints were misclassified as a lesser offense.

Recently, City and BPD leaders have acknowledged that the zero tolerance policing strategy has harmed the City's predominantly African-American communities. *See supra* at 17-18. During our investigation, one of BPD's top officials told us that "stop and frisk killed the hopes and dreams of entire communities." The City's and BPD's recognition that its zero tolerance policing strategy has had a significant, unwarranted impact on Baltimore's African-American communities has led to recent changes in the Department, including implementing the "Fair and Impartial Policing" policy in 2015, and efforts to improve its collection of data on its enforcement activities. We commend the City and BPD for these efforts.

Still, many BPD supervisors continue to reinforce zero tolerance enforcement. Officers patrolling predominantly African-American neighborhoods routinely receive orders to "clear corners" by stopping or arresting African-American youth standing on sidewalks. This practice has continued despite concerns raised by officers themselves, who have told BPD leadership that these actions lack legal justification, are time-consuming, and counterproductive. In some cases, supervisors have issued explicitly discriminatory orders, such as directing a shift to arrest "all the black hoodies" in a neighborhood. And when officers have expressed concerns about such directives, the Department has failed to take corrective action. To restore the community's confidence in BPD and ensure that its policing services are being provided equitably, BPD must continue to improve its policies, training, data collection and analysis, and accountability systems.

The assessment of discriminatory intent focuses on "circumstantial and direct evidence of intent as may be available." *See Vill. of Arlington Heights v. Metro. Hous. Dev. Corp.*, 429 U.S. 252, 266 (1977). "The impact of the official action . . . may provide an important starting point" for assessing discriminatory intent. *Id.; see also Williams v. Hansen*, 326 F.3d 569, 585 (4th Cir. 2003). In addition to evidence of disparate impact, other factors include: direct statements that exhibit bias; an agency's departures from its own procedures and accepted practices in the field; and the relevant historical context. *Arlington Heights*, 429 U.S. at 266–68; *Sylvia Dev. Corp. v. Calvert County*, 48 F.3d 810, 819 (4th Cir. 1995).

a. BPD's Enforcement Activities Disproportionately Impact African Americans

The magnitude of the racial differences in BPD's stops, searches, and arrests are evidence that BPD's disproportionate enforcement may constitute intentional discrimination. We found consistent racial disparities in BPD's stops, searches, and arrests that are not attributable to population patterns, crime rates, or other race-neutral factors.

- BPD stops African Americans disproportionately in each of its nine police districts, despite significant variation in the districts' demographic characteristics and crime rates. Moreover, BPD has used pedestrian stops as a regular part of its discretionary enforcement— documenting over 300,000 stops in five years—despite their demonstrated ineffectiveness for ferreting out crime. Only 3.7 percent of pedestrian stops uncovered evidence of criminal activity—and the rate of criminal activity found during stops of African Americans was lower than stops of others. *Supra* at 28.

- Racial disparities in BPD's search rates persisted after controlling for the area in which a search occurred and numerous other factors, including the unit assignment and experience level of the officers involved. And searches of African Americans were less likely to find contraband compared to searches of people from other racial backgrounds, indicating that officers apply a lower threshold of suspicion when deciding to search African Americans. *Supra* at 53.

- There is also substantial evidence that the large racial disparities in BPD's enforcement of drug possession statutes are not explained by rates of drug usage. While survey data on drug usage shows that African Americans use banned substances at rates similar to or slightly higher than other population groups, BPD arrested African Americans for drug possession offenses at five times the rate at which it arrested others. BPD also arrested African Americans for drug possession offenses several times more often than law enforcement agencies in cities with similar crime rates and demographic and economic characteristics. *Supra* at Section II.B.1

- The consistent racial disparities in outcomes from BPD's misdemeanor arrests also do not appear to be attributable to non-racial factors. For every misdemeanor offense we examined, supervisors at Central Booking and prosecutors dismissed a significantly larger share of charges brought against African Americans than others. This consistent pattern suggests that, for these highly discretionary offenses, BPD is disproportionately likely to arrest African Americans based on insufficient evidence. *See supra* at Section II.B.1.

Together, these findings provide substantial evidence that BPD's disparate stops, searches, and misdemeanor arrests of African Americans are not part of a calibrated, proportionate strategy for responding to criminal activity.

In addition, BPD's disproportionate enforcement against African Americans is suggestive of intentional discrimination because the racial disparities are greatest for enforcement activities that involve higher degrees of officer discretion. In the five years of arrest data we reviewed, African Americans accounted for a larger share of charges for highly discretionary misdemeanor offenses than for other offenses, including: 91 percent of those charged solely with trespassing, 91 percent of charges for failing to obey an officer's orders, 88 percent of those arrested solely for "impeding" and 84 percent of people charged with disorderly conduct. As noted above, booking supervisors and prosecutors dismissed a significantly higher portion of charges made against African Americans for each of these charges. This pattern indicates that, where BPD officers have more discretion to make arrests, they exercise that discretion to arrest African Americans disproportionately. Moreover, the racial disparities in dismissal rates exist only for highly discretionary misdemeanor arrests, not felony arrests. That is, booking officials and prosecutors dismissed charges at nearly identical rates across racial groups for felony charges like first degree assault, burglary, and robbery for which there is little officer discretion about whether to arrest suspects. For every discretionary misdemeanor offense that we examined, however, officials dismissed charges against African Americans at significantly higher rates—indicating that officers apply a lower standard when arresting African Americans for these offenses.

b. BPD's "Zero Tolerance" Strategy Focused on African-American Neighborhoods

In addition to this statistical evidence of disparate impact, we also have evidence that racial disparities occurred, at least in part, because of BPD's reliance on "zero tolerance" enforcement tactics in predominantly African-American neighborhoods. BPD employed these tactics without adequate oversight, training, or analysis, despite frequent community concerns about their impact. We also found evidence of direct orders that encourage discriminatory treatment.

Zero tolerance tactics in African-American neighborhoods prioritized officers making large numbers of stops and arrests for minor offenses, despite knowing the potential impact of these practices. For example, in the approximately five and half years of data we examined, BPD recorded nearly 55,000 pedestrian stops in its smallest police district—the Western District, with a population of a little more than 37,000 people that is 97 percent African American—while making only 21,000 stops in the predominantly white Northern District, with a population of approximately 91,000.[72] Expressed differently, BPD made 146 stops for every 100 residents in the predominantly African American Western District while making only 22.5 stops per 100 residents in the predominantly white Northern District—a more than 6 to 1 disparity. We found that disparities in BPD's stops of African Americans persist across all of BPD's nine police districts.

We heard concerns from numerous officers that zero tolerance tactics have resulted in unconstitutional stops and arrests, and that they are counterproductive. The Fraternal Order of Police's 2012 *Blueprint for Improved Policing* noted how zero tolerance tactics are counterproductive:

> Comstat numbers drive everything in BPD, which has led to misplaced priorities . . . As a result, officers in the BPD feel pressure to achieve numbers for perception's sake," and "[t]he focus on assigning blame for less-than-satisfactory numbers during Comstat, rather than problem-solving, is completely unproductive and weakens the collective morale of the BPD."

The *Blueprint* concluded that BPD "must discontinue the practice of rewarding statistically driven arrests."

Nevertheless, many BPD supervisors continue to encourage patrol officers to use zero tolerance tactics. Based on our observations during numerous ride-alongs and conversations with BPD officers, instructions to "clear corners" remain a regular feature of patrolling certain predominantly African-American neighborhoods. These activities frequently lack any legal basis. One officer informed us that she stops and disperses youth standing on sidewalks because "it looks bad." The same officer, while responding to a call about a gang fight, stopped to engage an African American man and his four-year-old son who were sitting on a fence by a playground where the young boy had been playing. The officer told them that they "couldn't just stand around" and "needed to move." A second officer, after explaining to his supervisor that he had no legal basis to clear a corner, was told to "make something up." BPD has continued this practice despite its impact on African-American residents and its lack of effectiveness for fighting crime. Indeed, we found

---

[72] These stops also fell disproportionately on African Americans. Despite making up only 41 percent of the Northern District's population, African Americans accounted for 83 percent of stops in the district.

that BPD's pedestrian stops—and searches conducted during these stops—uncover criminal activity at extremely low rates. *See supra* at Section II.A.2. And the rate of finding criminal activity when stopping and searching African Americans is lower still. *Id.*

In some cases, BPD supervisors have instructed their subordinates to specifically target African Americans for enforcement. A sergeant told us that in 2011 her lieutenant—a commander in charge of setting enforcement priorities for an entire police district during the shift—ordered the sergeant to instruct officers under her command to "lock up all the black hoodies" in her district. When the sergeant objected and refused to follow this order, she received an "unsatisfactory" performance evaluation and was transferred to a different unit. The sergeant filed a successful complaint about her performance evaluation with BPD's Equal Opportunity and Diversity Section, but BPD never took action against the lieutenant for giving the order to target "black hoodies" for enforcement. Similarly, as described above, in 2012 a BPD lieutenant provided officers under his command with a template for trespassing arrests that suggested officers would arrest exclusively African-American men for that offense. As in the first example, this directive is especially concerning because it came from a shift commander. *See supra* at 63. These statements targeting African Americans for enforcement reinforce the statistical disparities in enforcement outcomes that we measured. The enforcement activities ordered by the BPD commanders—arresting African Americans for trespassing and finding any possible basis to arrest "black hoodies"—are consistent with the racial disparities we found in BPD's discretionary stops, searches, and misdemeanor arrests.

c. Statements Exhibiting Bias Against African Americans

We also found numerous examples of BPD officers using racial slurs or other statements that exhibit bias. Officers' use of racial language was a recurrent theme during the hundreds of interviews we conducted with members of the Baltimore community. The frequency of this conduct is difficult to quantify, however, because BPD erects many formal obstacles to filing complaints, community members often do not file complaints because they believe doing so would be fruitless, and BPD fails to properly document and classify allegations that are made. *See infra* at 139. Even when individuals successfully make a complaint alleging racial bias, BPD supervisors almost universally misclassify the complaint as minor misconduct—such as discourtesy—that does not reflect its racial elements.

Indeed, BPD's internal affairs records contain only one complaint that officers categorized as a racial slur allegation in the six years of data we examined. Our interviews with hundreds of Baltimore residents, along with other complaints we have received from the Baltimore community, demonstrates that this number is implausibly low. Because of this, we manually reviewed the narrative descriptions of a subset of the complaints that were not classified as alleging racial bias, and we identified more than one hundred examples of officers allegedly using racial epithets, slurs, and making threats when interacting with African Americans in that subset. Indeed, we found 60 separate allegations between 2010 and 2016 that officers used the word "n****r" that were not classified as complaints alleging use of racial slurs or other racial bias.[73] As explained further below,

---

[73] Use of "racial epithets undoubtedly demonstrate racial animus." *Jones v. Robinson Prop. Group*, 427 F.3d 987, 993 (5th Cir. 2005). Many courts have recognized that particular slurs are extremely probative of racial animus. *See Spriggs v. Diamond Auto Glass*, 242 F.3d 179, 185 (4th Cir. 2001) ("Far more than a 'mere offensive utterance,' the word 'n****r is pure anathema to African-Americans."); *Brown v. E. Miss. Elec. Power Ass'n*, 989 F.2d 858, 861 (5th Cir. 1993) ("the term

BPD misclassifies and fails to investigate complaints of racial slurs and racial bias, allowing a culture of bias against African Americans to persist. Several examples highlight the types of statements we found that exhibit bias towards African Americans:

- The City paid $95,000 in 2012 to settle a lawsuit brought by an 87-year-old African-American grandmother who alleged that she was shoved against a wall after she refused to allow an officer to enter her basement to conduct a warrantless search. After shoving the woman to the floor, the officer allegedly stood over her and said, "Bitch, you ain't no better than any of the other old black bitches I have locked up."

- In 2014, a middle-aged African-American man alleged that a sergeant in Southeast Baltimore stopped him near Patterson Park and strip-searched him in public. When the man protested and said he would contact a lawyer, the sergeant allegedly told him, "Get your n****r ass out of here." BPD found the complaint "not sustained" without interviewing any of the involved parties.

- One Baltimore firefighter and an emergency medical technician told us that, prior to a march led by a prominent African-American pastor in 2015, a BPD officer told the firefighters "they're going marching and there's going to be a problem. What y'all should do is turn them hoses on them."

- In 2013 a white male BPD officer made a racially-charged threat to an African-American teenager while booking the youth into Baltimore's juvenile facility on a failure to appear charge. The incident stemmed from an argument about George Zimmerman, who had been acquitted of murdering Trayvon Martin four days earlier. In response to the teenager referring to the officers present as "Zimmermans," a white officer threatened the juvenile by referring to the outfit Martin wore at the time he was killed: "Put a hoodie on and come to my neighborhood, you will see." The officer also threatened the youth by stating, "If you come to my neighborhood I'll throw you in the water and feed you to the crabs. I will then let the crabs get fat off you and then sell them to your family." When BPD investigated the incident, the officer admitted to "talking about the crabs and throwing him in the river," but claimed to internal affairs investigators that he "could not recall" whether he made the remark about the hoodie. BPD sustained a complaint against the officer for "misconduct" and making an "inappropriate comment," but the investigative file contains no record of discipline. The officer remains employed at BPD.

- In a complaint from August 2011, an African-American man alleged that during a vehicle stop, an officer warned a second officer to "be careful" because the occupants of the car "might do voodoo on you"—an apparent reference to their heritage and accents. A second officer made monkey noises throughout the encounter. BPD closed the complaint without making an investigative finding.

'n****r is a universally recognized opprobrium, stigmatizing African-Americans because of their race."); *Boyer-Liberto v. Fontainebleau Corp.*, 786 F.3d 264, 280 (4th Cir. 2015) (use of the slur "porch monkey" is about as odious as the use of the word n****r).

- An African-American man told us that, while out walking in April 2015, officers stopped him, accused him of looting, and called him a "low life n****r."

The use of racial slurs and other racially charged statements described above, as well as others we uncovered during our investigation, typically occurred while officers were conducting stops or searches of African Americans. This is consistent with the areas in which we found large statistical disparities in BPD's enforcement.

d. BPD Misclassifies Complaints of Racial Bias and Fails to Investigate Racial Bias Allegations

BPD fails to record complaints of racial bias or affirmatively misclassifies complaints to mask their racial components. BPD also fails to investigate allegations of biased enforcement.[74] By not using its own procedures to deter and correct biased conduct, BPD exacerbates relationships with Baltimore's African-American communities. Numerous individuals told us that BPD either refused to accept complaints—even for egregious, racially-motivated misconduct—or did not take their complaints seriously. Many community members thus feel that BPD is biased against African Americans and does not respond their concerns.

i. BPD's defective procedures for recording and classifying complaints of racial bias

BPD's internal affairs database reflects only five complaints from 2010–2016 that BPD supervisors classified as alleging use of a racial slur or other racial bias.[75] The absence of such records stems from at least two procedural deficiencies. As discussed above, BPD erects significant obstacles to filing complaints. And even when community members succeed in filing a complaint of racial bias according to BPD's requirements, supervisory officers almost universally misclassify those complaints to mask their racial elements. As a result, BPD does not investigate the frequent allegations of race-related misconduct made against its officers and has no mechanism to track such allegations to correct discriminatory policing where it occurs.

Most notably, BPD supervisors affirmatively misclassify complaints of racial bias, precluding the Department from investigating or tracking bias allegations. A commander at BPD's Internal Investigation Division told us BPD requires all complaints claiming officers used a racial epithet to be categorized as "racial slur" complaints, and BPD's disciplinary matrix makes clear that "conduct relating to a person's race" is a serious offense that may result in termination. Yet in nearly every case in which an officer allegedly used a racial slur, BPD officials categorized the allegation merely as "discourtesy" or using "inappropriate language." For the complaints in which our manual review found that BPD recorded allegations that officers used the word n****r, supervisors failed to classify the complaint as a racial slur or other allegation of racial bias 98 percent of the time.

---

[74] Prior to enacting its "Fair and Impartial Policing" policy in 2015, BPD only had a general prohibition against discrimination, which did not provide sufficient guidance to officers on how to conduct their policing activities in a non-discriminatory manner, although it did provide a basis for BPD to discipline officers.

[75] We refer in this section only to complaints alleging bias by BPD officers towards members of the African American community in Baltimore.

BPD similarly misclassified nearly all of the complaints we identified that alleged other types of racial discrimination in BPD's enforcement. Out of the dozens of complaints that our manual review found to allege "racial profiling" or "racial discrimination," BPD supervisors classified only four as alleging any type of racial bias. And even those complaints triggered no meaningful review. BPD referred two of the complaints to command investigation units tasked with addressing only minor allegations, and closed a third complaint seven minutes after opening an internal affairs "investigation." Although we found that BPD routinely misclassifies other complaints due to systemic deficiencies in its practices, *see infra* at 138, we did not find anything approaching the level of systematic misclassification of complaints we found relating to alleged racial discrimination, such as the 98 percent misclassification of use of the word n****r. Moreover, the complaints that are misclassified allege racial discrimination on their face, such as the use of a racial epithet. Failing to recognize the potential for racial discrimination in the use of a racial epithet is difficult to attribute to a lack of training, policy guidance, or other systemic deficiency. This systematic misclassification of complaints, particularly when the classification is not difficult, indicates that the misclassification is because of the racial nature of the complaint.

BPD's practice of obscuring racial elements of misconduct impedes any significant disciplinary action, even in cases where an officer admitted to using a racial epithet. Several examples highlight this practice. In a case from 2010, an officer admitted that he said "you know, you're acting like a real n****r right now" during an encounter with a young African-American male he had stopped for "loitering." The officer's partner, who was African American, filed the complaint after witnessing the incident. The complaint was initially categorized as a "racial slur" complaint. Before issuing an investigative finding sustaining the allegation, however, the lead BPD investigator changed the categorization in BPD's internal affairs database from "racial slur" to "inappropriate comments, profanity, or gestures to a departmental member." This change in classification, shortly before the allegation was sustained, indicates an intent to disguise and excuse the racial motivation for the enforcement action. The incident resulted in minimal discipline against the offending officer.[76] Other aspects of the investigation are equally troubling. The detective who downgraded the complaint also expanded his review of the incident to investigate the officer who reported the racial slur for "neglect of duty," ostensibly based on the officer's failure to provide the African-American man with a citizen contact receipt. We are concerned that the expanded investigation may have been done in retaliation for reporting a fellow officer's racial bias. Despite the complaint's clear misclassification in violation of Department policy, BPD supervisors signed off throughout the chain of command.

In another incident from 2010, an African-American man stated that he witnessed officers use excessive force during an arrest and punch a fourteen-year-old boy who attempted to film the arrest on his cell phone. The African-American man recounted that the officers used "the word 'n****r' frequently" and asked him if he "take[s] it up the ass by Allah." When the man went to the district headquarters to report the misconduct, he was met by the same officers who told him, "what brings your black ass back here?" and "you can take your black ass down to Kirk Avenue[77] before

---

[76] The officer was not fired or suspended. Instead, he received a letter of reprimand, was required to attend sensitivity training, and forfeited thirty days of his leave.

[77] Kirk Avenue refers to the location of BPD's Internal Investigation Division, or "IID." Under BPD policy, members of the public should be able to file external complaints of officer misconduct both at district headquarters, and also at the IID.

the bus leaves because you know how you black people like the bus." Despite the seriousness of the allegations and the fact that the complaint identified two witnesses, BPD never investigated the incident's alleged racial motivation. Instead, detectives categorized the allegations as "misconduct," "excessive force," and "unwarranted action," and administratively closed[78] the case without conducting a single interview.

ii.   BPD fails to investigate racial bias allegations

BPD further impedes accountability for discriminatory policing by departing from its procedures for investigating biased conduct. BPD supervisors repeatedly fail to seek evidence that could corroborate bias allegations and result in officer discipline. For example, a 2011 complaint described an incident in which two white officers told an African-American man who had double-parked his car and was blocking the street to "move this car, n****r!" The man was double parked in order to assist his aunt into her home in Northeast Baltimore and was not charged with any offense. The man's complaint—the *one* complaint BPD correctly categorized as a "racial slur" in the more than six years of data we examined—was assigned to be investigated at the command level[79] and administratively closed six months later. The file BPD provided has no record of the investigation or any attempt to identify the officers involved.

BPD conducted a similarly inadequate investigation in a 2010 case that also alleged race-motivated misconduct. There, an African-American man alleged that while being held in a cell at the Southwest District, several officers called him a "monkey" and a "n****r" while beating him. The investigative file, which consisted solely of a few summary paragraphs about the incident, revealed that the investigating officer administratively closed the case without even reading a related incident report because "it was locked in the report box at the time of my investigation."

In another example, BPD failed to adequately investigate a complaint that an officer called an African-American woman a "black b***h." BPD never interviewed the officer accused of using the offensive term. Instead, he was asked only to complete a written questionnaire that omitted the racial component of the woman's allegation. The questionnaire asked whether the officer "at any time call[ed] or refer[red] to [the woman] as a bitch?" BPD found the allegation not sustained based on the officer's written denial. The omission of the racial component of the woman's allegation indicates that BPD investigators intended to conceal the racial nature of the interaction and avoid determining whether the heightened discipline required for using a racial slur should be imposed.

e.   Baltimore's History of Residential Segregation

BPD's "zero tolerance" policing strategy has focused on predominantly African-American neighborhoods that have been segregated for generations due to government policies that systematically prevented African Americans from acquiring wealth, and obstructed their ability to move into neighborhoods with better jobs or schools.

---

[78] As discussed further in Section III.C.1, *infra*, internal investigations should be issued one of four possible findings: sustained, not sustained, unfounded or exonerated. We found that BPD frequently disposed of cases with minimal or no investigation by labeling them as "administratively closed."

[79] As described further in Section III.C, *infra*, under BPD policy, "minor" misconduct can be investigated and handled at the command level by "command investigations units."

Starting in the early 20th Century, the City sponsored residential segregation programs that forced the large number of African Americans who settled in Baltimore during the "Great Migration" to live in economically depressed neighborhoods. Baltimore was the ninth most segregated city in the country when the Great Migration ended in 1970,[80] and the most recent U.S. Census Bureau data shows that the City remains extremely segregated.[81] In its lawsuit against Wells Fargo for discriminatory lending practices, the City of Baltimore itself acknowledged that its minority communities have been "victimized by traditional redlining practices," and that the city itself remains highly segregated:

> [E]ven though Baltimore is 64% African-American and 32% white, many neighborhoods have a much higher concentration of one racial group or the other. For example, the African-American population exceeds 90% in East Baltimore, Pimlico/Arlington/Hilltop, Dorchester/Ashburton, Southern Park Heights, Greater Rosemont, Sandtown-Winchester/Harlem Park, and Greater Govans. It exceeds 75% in Waverly and Belair Edison. At the same time, the white population of Greater Roland Park/Poplar, Medfield/Hampden/Woodberry, and South Baltimore exceeds 80%, and the white population of Cross-Country/Cheswolde, Mt. Washington/Coldspring, and North Baltimore/Guilford/Homeland exceeds 70%.

City of Baltimore v. Wells Fargo, No. 1:08-cv-00062-JFM (D. Md. Oct. 21, 2010).

City leadership encouraged and supported this segregation by passing the country's first block-by-block segregation ordinance, which made it a crime for African Americans to move to majority white blocks, and vice versa. At the time of the ordinance's enactment in 1910, the *New York Times* described it as "the most pronounced 'Jim Crow' measure on record" and noted that "[n]othing like it can be found in any statute book or ordinance record of this country."[82] The Supreme Court later struck down a similar ordinance in *Buchanan v. Warley*, 245 U.S. 60 (1917), but the effect in Baltimore was minimal. White property owners, with support from City leadership, continued to enforce the rule informally by requiring homeowners in certain white neighborhoods, like the affluent Roland Park area in North Baltimore, to sign covenants barring African Africans from owning or renting their property. The mayor directed City building and housing inspectors to institute a practice of citing for code violations anyone who rented or sold property to African-Americans in those neighborhoods. *See* Antero Pietila, NOT IN MY NEIGHBORHOOD 35, 53–54 (2010).

---

[80] *See* Douglas S. Massey and Nancy A. Denton, *Hypersegregation in U.S. Metropolitan Areas: Black and Hispanic Segregation Along Five Dimensions*, 26 Demography 3, 1989. The Great Migration refers to a mass relocation of African Americans between 1910 and 1970 when six million African Americans migrated from rural Southern states to settle across the country. When the Great Migration ended around 1970, nearly half of all black Americans were living outside the South, compared to ten percent when the Migration began. Baltimore is affected by "hyper-segregation," a term sociologists use to refer to the nearly complete division of races following the Great Migration. *See* Isabel Wilkerson, THE WARMTH OF OTHER SUNS 8–10, 398 (2010).

[81] According to the 2010 census, the dissimilarity index for Baltimore is 71.8, which indicates the percentage of African Americans that would need to move to less segregated areas for the population to be distributed equally with whites.

[82] *Baltimore Tries Drastic Plan of Race Segregation*, N.Y. Times, Dec. 25, 1910, at 34, 43, http://timesmachine.nytimes.com/timesmachine/1910/12/25/105900067.html?pageNumber=34.

The federal government also contributed to Baltimore's segregation by instituting policies that further isolated African Americans. During the Great Depression, the government's Home Owners' Loan Corporation (HOLC) created maps of 239 cities, including Baltimore, to rate residential areas for market value and risk. Baltimore's neighborhoods with large African-American populations were colored red on the map to signify HOLC's conclusion that these neighborhoods were "hazardous," leading to the term "red-lining." *See* HOLC 1937 map (following page).[83] After the Great Depression, the Federal Housing Administration (FHA) carried on HOLC's legacy well into the 1960s. The FHA promoted home-ownership in white suburban neighborhoods, and tolerated further red-lining by private banks and insurance companies. *Id.* at 61–74.

The legacy of this government-sanctioned discrimination continues to impact the African-American community in Baltimore today. The City remains highly segregated, and African-American residents live disproportionately in neighborhoods with social and economic challenges. More than 100,000 African-Americans residents live in poverty, constituting more than three-fourths of Baltimoreans who do so.

BPD leadership is acutely aware of the challenges posed by this backdrop. Former Commissioner Batts explained that when he was appointed to lead BPD in 2012 "it was like going back a little bit in time. It's about black and white racism in [Baltimore]. It's all the things you dealt with in the 1960s."[84] Commissioner Davis has also recognized the challenges officers face in addressing racism and poverty, among other social problems: "when cops hear that they have the burden to address racism and poverty and education and homelessness . . . I think cops misinterpret that message with, 'how do you expect me to do that?'"[85] Recently, BPD has taken several commendable steps towards addressing these concerns, including issuing a "Fair and Impartial Policing" policy and launching an educational program for officers that addresses some of the racial dynamics in the City's history.

Nevertheless, many challenges remain. BPD needs to ensure that it employs law enforcement strategies that do not discriminate against African Americans and predominantly African-American neighborhoods. Working together with the community will promote proactive, constitutional, and effective policing.

*   *   *

In sum, BPD's stops, searches, and arrests disproportionately impact African Americans and predominantly African-American neighborhoods and cannot be explained by population patterns, crime rates, or other race-neutral factors. This disparate impact violates Title VI and the Safe Streets

---

[83] HOLC devised a system of rating neighborhoods based on their perceived suitability to receive home mortgage loans, ranging from the ostensibly most suitable "A" areas to the least suitable "D" areas. HOLC classified the "A" areas, colored green on the map, as most "in demand" for home mortgage loans. The "B" areas, colored blue on the map, were rated as "still desirable." The yellow-coded "C" areas were rated as "definitely declining." The red "D" areas were rated as too "hazardous" for general lending practices. Baltimore residents living in the D areas were generally unable to obtain mortgages. *See Not in My Neighborhood*, at 67-70.

[84] *Q&A C-SPAN: Anthony Batts* (C-SPAN television broadcast Jan. 20, 2015), https://www.c-span.org/video/?323886-1/qa-anthony-batts.

[85] http://www.baltimoresun.com/news/maryland/bs-md-davis-challenges-20150711-story.html.

Act. We also found evidence suggesting intentional discrimination against African Americans. This racial discrimination undermines community trust in BPD.

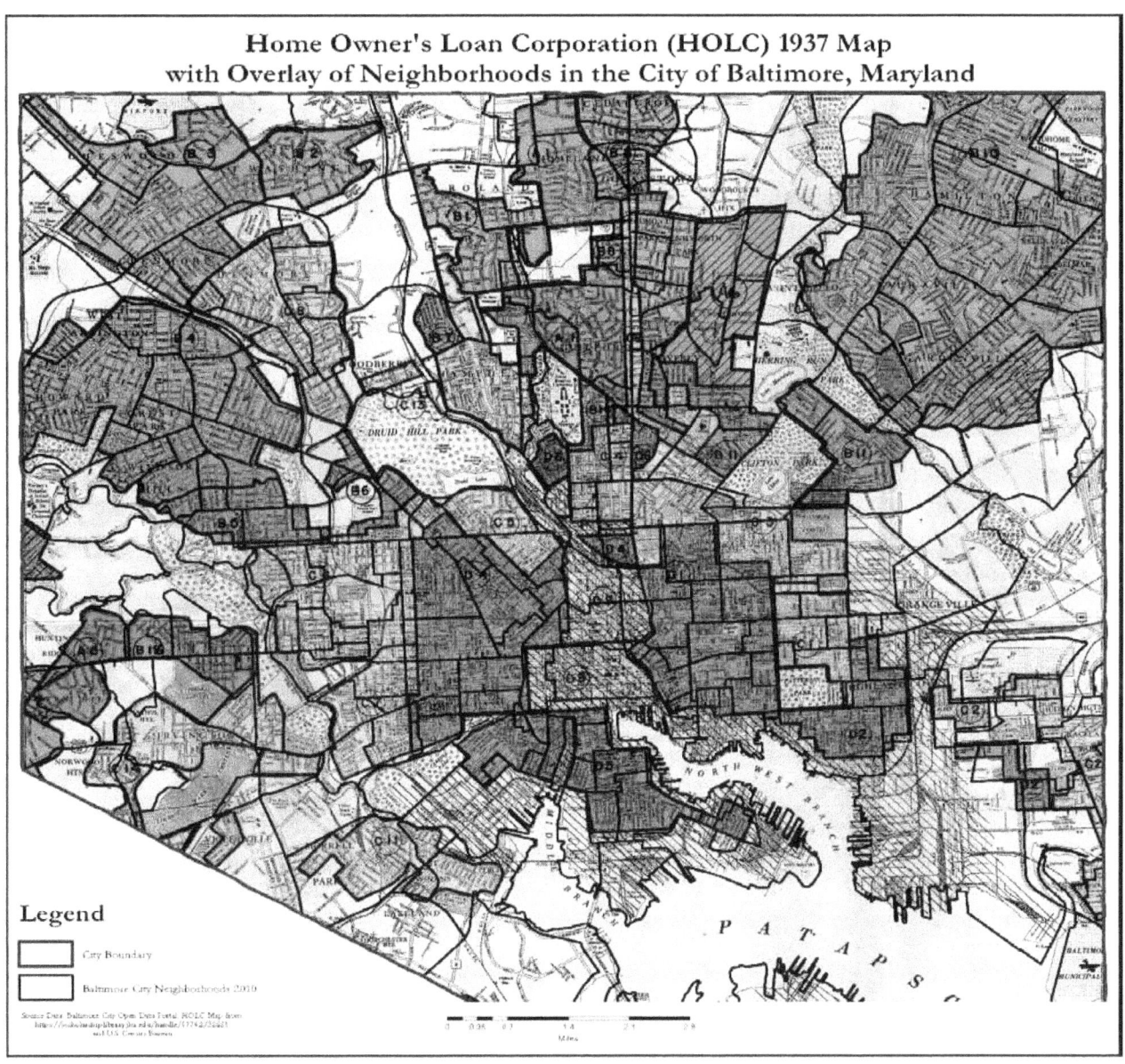

Home Owner's Loan Corporation (HOLC) 1937 Map with Overlay of Neighborhoods in the City of Baltimore, Maryland

C. BPD USES UNREASONABLE FORCE

Based on our review of nearly a thousand of BPD's own investigative files of its officers' uses of force, we find reasonable cause to believe that BPD officers use unreasonable force[86] in violation of the Fourth Amendment, and fail to make reasonable modifications necessary to avoid discrimination in violation of Title II of the Americans with Disabilities Act, contributing to the pattern or practice of conduct that violates the constitution and federal law. BPD's unreasonable force is not limited to officers' use of any specific weapon; we found it throughout the use of force files we reviewed.

The Fourth Amendment guarantees the "right of the people to be secure in their persons, houses, papers, and effects, against unreasonable searches and seizures." U.S. CONST. amend. IV. This protection from "unreasonable" seizures prohibits an officer from using excessive force when making a seizure. "Determining whether the force used to effect a particular seizure is 'reasonable' under the Fourth Amendment requires a careful balancing of the nature and quality of the intrusion on the individual's Fourth Amendment interests against the countervailing governmental interests at stake." *Graham v. Conner*, 490 U.S. 386, 396 (1989) (internal quotation marks omitted). The determination must be made while viewing the incident "from the perspective of a reasonable officer on the scene, rather than with the 20/20 vision of hindsight." *Id.* at 396, 399.

To determine whether force used by a law enforcement officer is reasonable, we look to (1) "the severity of the crime at issue;" (2) "the extent to which the suspect poses an immediate threat to the safety of the officers or others;" and (3) "whether [the suspect] is actively resisting arrest or attempting to evade arrest by flight." *Estate of Armstrong v. Vill. of Pinehurst*, 810 F.3d 892, 899 (4th Cir. 2016) (alteration in original) (internal quotation marks omitted). "To properly consider the reasonableness of the force employed we must view it in full context, with an eye toward the proportionality of the force in light of all the circumstances." *Id.* at 899 (internal quotation marks omitted). "[O]fficers using unnecessary, gratuitous, and disproportionate force to seize a secured, unarmed citizen, do not act in an objectively reasonable manner. . . ." *Meyers v. Baltimore County*, 713 F.3d 723, 734 (4th Cir. 2013) (internal quotation marks omitted).

Our evaluation of BPD's use of force was informed by many sources, including: (1) interviews with hundreds of individuals who have had encounters with officers or witnessed those encounters; (2) interviews of the Department's officers, supervisors, and command staff; (3) an extensive review of nearly one thousand of the Department's reports and investigations of officers' uses of force; (4) the Department's policies and training materials; and (5) analysis by our expert police consultants.

The nearly one thousand force cases we reviewed included a randomly selected, statistically significant sample from all use of force incidents by BPD officers occurring between January 1, 2010, and June 19, 2015. The sample of 814 cases was identified by our statistical experts from the universe of all 2,818 incidents of force, including both deadly force and less-lethal force, identified

---

[86] Throughout this letter, we use the terms "unreasonable" and "excessive" interchangeably; both terms refer to force that exceeds constitutional limits, or in other words, is disproportional in light of the severity of the crime suspected, threat posed to officers or others, and level of resistance. When using the term "unnecessary," we mean that force was used when the incident could have been resolved without resorting to any force at all.

by BPD. The sample size accounted for a number of factors, including the type of weapon used by officers and whether the force was used against people with mental health disabilities or in crisis.

Because of their critical nature, we also attempted to review all uses of deadly force by BPD occurring from January 1, 2010, through the duration of our investigation, and we reviewed what was provided to us through May 1, 2016. However, though we identified for BPD on multiple occasions additional deadly force cases that we had not received, BPD was never able to find and produce case files for all deadly force investigations from this time period. The Department informed us that it is unable to locate the files for twenty firearms discharges from the time period that we requested. Because of this lack of documentation, we were unable to conclusively determine the number of deadly force incidents that occurred during the time period we reviewed. This failure is quite concerning. The Department's inability to maintain the files for officers' firearms discharges reflects a serious deficiency in the oversight of officers' uses of deadly force. For a number of other shooting cases, BPD provided us with supplemental information nearly a year after we initially requested the complete files. In the end, we were able to review over one hundred investigations of BPD's uses of deadly force. We carefully reviewed each of the force files we were provided, both deadly force and less-lethal force, to determine whether each use of force was justified under applicable legal standards. Our review of individual use of force reports and investigations informed our determination of whether a pattern or practice of excessive force exists within BPD.

We note that, in a number of cases—of both deadly and less-lethal force—the reports and reviews of force provided too little information about the circumstances surrounding the use of force to allow our team and experts to determine whether the force was reasonable. This is troubling because, despite the lack of adequate information to determine whether these uses of force were reasonable, BPD supervisors still approved all but a handful of these uses of force. This systematic failure to provide adequate oversight of use of force requires correction. Even given the significant number of cases in which we were unable to make a decision, however, we were nevertheless able to make determinations in a sufficient number of cases to conclude that there is a pattern or practice of excessive force at BPD.

While reviewing BPD's force investigations, we noted a number of trends. First, in a significant number of cases, officers use aggressive tactics that escalate encounters and stifle public cooperation, leading to the use of physical force when it is not necessary to resolve an incident. Officers approach incidents involving mere quality of life violations in a confrontational manner and fail to use basic conflict resolution skills, creating conflict where it did not exist before. BPD trains officers to be aggressive, inculcating an adversarial mindset in its recruits and teaching them to, for example, point a weapon at unarmed and innocent civilians to control a scene. Tactics such as these unnecessarily escalate encounters, increase tensions and lead to unnecessary force.

Second, officers use excessive force against individuals with mental health disabilities or in crisis. When families in Baltimore confront a family member experiencing a mental health issue, they often call 911 to request an officer to safely escort their family member to a hospital for a mental health evaluation and, if necessary, commitment. In too many of these calls, officers arrive at the homes of families, knowing they are being called to assist with a mental health incident, without a plan to account for the mental health issue. Because of their lack of planning and proper tactics, they end up in violent confrontations with individuals with mental health disabilities or in crisis and use force, sometimes deadly, against these vulnerable individuals.

Third, officers use unreasonable force against juveniles. It is apparent that officers have not received guidance nor have been trained on well-established best practices for police interactions with juveniles that account for their developmental stage and prevent the unnecessary criminalization of overwhelmingly minority youth. The lack of policy and training for these interactions results in excessive force being used against youths.

Finally, officers use unreasonable force against people who present little or no threat to them or others. One such group includes individuals who are already restrained and under officers' control. Another group is individuals who are fleeing away from officers. Officers in Baltimore engage in a high number of foot pursuits, a tactic with a number of attendant risks, including endangering officers and community members. Due to the risks inherent in foot pursuits, agencies must exercise careful oversight over foot pursuits and provide proper guidance and training on when it is appropriate to engage in foot pursuits and how to do so safely. BPD fails to do so. In some cases, the people who officers pursue have not committed serious crimes and present no threat to officers or community members, but these pursuits end with BPD officers using significant force. Additionally, in some cases when individuals flee in vehicles, officers use unreasonable force after any potential threat to them has subsided.

The Department's failure to provide officers with the necessary guidance, skills, and oversight to resolve incidents in a way that keeps them and community members safe underlies officers' constitutional violations. The Department fails to provide proper policy guidance on how and when it is appropriate to use force. It also fails to properly train officers on how to operationalize its policies and, in some cases, has improperly trained its officers by teaching incorrect legal standards or improper tactics that lead to officers' unreasonable force. Finally, the Department fails to exercise proper oversight to address potentially unreasonable force and remedy bad tactics when they occur. These failures have led to the systemic use of unreasonable force that we observed in our investigation.

1. **BPD's Overly Aggressive Tactics Unnecessarily Escalate Encounters and Result in Excessive Force**

BPD officers' aggressive tactics in their encounters with civilians unnecessarily escalate situations and contribute to officers' systemic use of unreasonable force. Officers use aggressive tactics in encounters that begin consensually or in cases where officers stop individuals for low-level and highly discretionary violations such as "loitering," as well as violations that officers charge based on civilians' conduct during the encounter, such as "failure to obey," "resistance" or "disorderly conduct," as discussed *supra* at Section II(A). In these encounters, officers issue commands without explanation rather than communicating respectfully, explaining the purpose for their approach and providing subjects an opportunity to voice their concerns.[87] When subjects do not immediately comply with officers' commands, rather than attempt to problem-solve or use conflict-resolution skills, officers resort too quickly to physical force even if individuals do not present a threat to them or others. Even where force is justified, officers frequently use a high level of force when only a low

---

[87] Citizens who do not understand why they are being stopped and feel they are being treated unfairly and disrespectfully are less likely to comply with officers' orders. *See* Tom R. Tyler, *Procedural Justice, Legitimacy, and the Effective Rule of Law*, 30 Crime & Justice 283, 350–51 (2003) ("When people judge that legal authorities and institutions are making their decisions fairly, they view those authorities as more legitimate and more willingly defer to and cooperate with them in personal encounters and in their everyday law-related behaviors.").

level of force is objectively reasonable. Officers use these tactics against individuals with mental health disabilities or in crisis, who have committed no crime, and also on juveniles. The force used by officers in these situations is often unnecessary and disproportional to the suspected violation, threat, and resistance posed by civilians under *Graham*. *See Armstrong*, 810 F.3d at 900 (internal quotation marks omitted) ("The problems posed by, and thus the tactics to be employed against, an unarmed, emotionally distraught individual who is creating a disturbance or resisting arrest are ordinarily different from those involved in law enforcement efforts to subdue an armed and dangerous criminal who has recently committed a serious offense."). *Cf. Waterman v. Batton*, 393 F.3d 471, 477 (4th Cir. 2005) ("[T]he reasonableness of the officer's actions in creating the dangerous situation is not relevant to the Fourth Amendment analysis."). In addition to contributing to officers' unconstitutional conduct, these tactics greatly undermine BPD's efforts to repair its damaged relationship with some segments of Baltimore's community.

For example, in a 2014 incident, an officer informed a young man, Matthew,[88] that he could not smoke inside a public market and asked him to leave. Matthew left and the officer followed him outside. Once outside, the officer asked him for identification to issue a civil citation. According to the Department's use of force report, the Matthew "became agitated and started to argue" with the officer, attracting a crowd. The young man refused to provide identification and moved backward. The officer grabbed the young man by his jacket, at which point he pulled away and fled. Two officers pursued Matthew for blocks and when they eventually caught up with him, "used arrest and control techniques" to tackle him and "stop him from further fleeing." "While trying to control him on the ground and place him in handcuffs," he "sustained abrasions to the left and right side of his face and a cut to his upper lip," requiring two stitches. The officer arrested Matthew for being "disorderly," but according to the arrest database that BPD provided, the State's Attorney's Office declined to formally charge the young man.

The officer repeatedly escalated this encounter, using unnecessarily aggressive tactics against a young man who had not committed a crime, resulting in the man being subjected to excessive force. The decision to grab the man by his jacket, after he had obeyed the officer's warning by leaving the market, escalated the encounter and led to the man resisting the officer's force by pulling away. The officer's decision to then pursue the young man, for a mere civil citation, also escalated the encounter. Other than calling off the pursuit (which would have been appropriate), as discussed in more detail *infra* at page 91, the most likely way to end the pursuit was by using force. Tackling, and using control and arrest techniques resulting in two stitches and abrasions to his face, was disproportionate in light of the civil violation the young man had committed, and where he posed no threat to officers or anyone else. *See Graham*, 490 U.S. at 396.

In another example, in a 2010 incident, a major who was patrolling in uniform in an unmarked police vehicle "observed several people on the steps of an apartment building." He asked the group "if everyone lived there." One of the group, a young 5'6", 147-pound African-American man, Daniel, asked the major "what the problem was." The major "told the suspect there was no problem and he can go back to his steps." The major reported that Daniel "walked in front of [the major's] vehicle acting in a [sic] agitated state wearing and adjusting some type of athletic gloves and taking his shoes off." An older African-American man "was instructing [the young man] to 'stop

---

[88] We use pseudonyms for individuals who were the subject of force with BPD officers to protect against disclosing personally-identifying information. We also do not identify BPD personnel by name, as the purpose of these illustrations is not to assess individual liability but to support and illustrate the findings of a pattern or practice.

acting like this.'" Daniel began "yelling at this older male in a threatening manner and challenging him." The major called for backup, withdrew his taser,[89] and ordered Daniel to "sit on the curb." A lieutenant arrived as backup. The major reportedly told the lieutenant that the young man "was warned to desist but to no avail and is ready to fight . . . he needs to be arrested before he hurts someone." The investigating sergeant reported that the subject moved to one side of the street and sat on the curb. The major informed the lieutenant that Daniel "was the aggressor and he continued to be a threat." There is no indication in the report that Daniel stood up from his seated position on the curb. Nevertheless, the lieutenant "immediately pushed [Daniel] to the ground with [a] left foot kick to the chest." Daniel had committed no crime, was seated on a curb and obeying officer's commands at the time the lieutenant unnecessarily and unreasonably kicked him in the chest. This incident, involving a lieutenant and a major, was investigated by a lower-ranked sergeant, undermining the credibility of the investigation. The major, who was involved in the incident, ultimately approved the sergeant's investigation, though the major lacked the independence to objectively determine whether the force used was appropriate.

Officers also use heavy-handed tactics when civilians simply refuse to obey their commands and escalate encounters by resorting to force too quickly, including against individuals who are not being arrested for any crime, with mental health disabilities or in crisis.[90] We determined that approximately 20 percent of use of force files BPD provided involved individuals with mental health disabilities or in crisis. In one of many such incidents we reviewed, in 2013, three officers and one sergeant responded to a call to transport an individual to a hospital for a mental health evaluation. According to their report, the officers arrived at the back of a house and found a woman, "Ashley," the subject of the petition, sitting on the ground with a clenched hand. Ashley reportedly had a "small" build and was yelling "don't shoot me." One officer asked her to empty her hands and she refused, stating, "you have to shoot me first I am not giving it up [sic]." There is no indication that the officers attempted to verbally persuade Ashley in any way to open her hands or calm her down. Rather, the officers physically attempted to force her hands open. Ashley resisted the officers' physical attempts and began to "kick[] and swing[]" at them. According to the report, one officer used a taser in drive-stun mode "to try to calm [her] down." Because drive-stunning an individual causes great pain, it did not calm her. The technique also carries a heightened risk of serious harm or injury when used on individuals with mental health disabilities or in crisis. *See* Police Exec. Research Forum & Cmty. Oriented Policing Servs., *2011 Electronic Control Weapon Guidelines* 14 (2001) (hereinafter "PERF & COPS, *2011 Electronic Control Weapon Guidelines*"). Ashley continued to resist. In response, the officer drive-stunned her two more times, with similar results. The officers were

---

[89] A "taser," or an "Electronic Control Weapon" (ECW) is a weapon that "'can be used either in 'probe' mode or in 'stun' mode. In probe mode, two probes are fired from a distance, attached to thin electrical wires, to lodge in the skin of the subject. The [t]aser then delivers a fixed five-second cycle of electricity designed to cause electro-muscular disruption, effectively freezing the subject's muscles and thereby temporarily disabling him. In stun mode, the probe cartridge is removed and the [t]aser's electrodes are applied directly to the subject. The [t]aser operator can then deliver a painful electric shock, the duration of which is completely within [the operator's] control. In stun mode, the [t]aser does not cause muscular disruption or incapacitation, but rather functions only as a 'pain compliance' tool.'" *Meyers*, 713 F.3d at 728 n.3 (alterations in original) (quoting *Meyers*, 814 F. Supp. 2d 552, 555 n.3 (D. Md. 2011)).

[90] A "crisis" incident is one in which someone experiences or displays intense feelings of personal distress (*e.g.*, anxiety, depression, anger, fear, panic, hopelessness); a thought disorder (*e.g.*, visual or auditory hallucinations, delusions, sensory impairment, or cognitive impairment); obvious changes in functioning (*e.g.*, neglect of personal hygiene); or catastrophic life events (*e.g.*, disruptions in personal relationships, support systems or living arrangements, loss of autonomy or parental rights, victimization, or natural disasters). This could be a result of mental illness (including substance use disorders), an intellectual disability, a personal crisis, or the effects of drugs or alcohol.

eventually able to physically pry open Ashley's hands, which held two vials, the contents of which emptied onto the ground. Ashley was transported to the hospital for a psychiatric evaluation. Use of the taser in drive-stun mode three times against a woman experiencing crisis, who was unarmed, posed no serious threat to the officers or others, and was not being arrested for any crime, was unnecessary and unreasonable. Problematically, it appears the only investigation of this incident was conducted by the sergeant who was at the scene. A sergeant who participated in the incident lacks the necessary objectivity and independence to fairly assess whether officers on the scene acted appropriately. Having an involved sergeant investigate the force undermines the integrity of the investigation.

Aggressive and violent police interactions, such as those described above, have left some Baltimore residents with the belief that encounters with BPD officers will result in their being subjected to unnecessary force. Community members told us in interviews that even when they believe they have done nothing wrong, they flee from interactions with officers, believing that it is better to run at the sight of an officer rather than take the risk that an interaction with the officer will result in unnecessary and excessive force being used against them.[91] Indeed, officers' unnecessary and unreasonable force during arrests for highly discretionary charges such as "loitering," "disorderly conduct," "resisting" or "failure to obey" an officer's commands, confirm these community members' fears.

The fault for officers' systemic use of these heavy-handed tactics lies with BPD as an agency. Through training used for many years—some of which is still ongoing—BPD teaches officers to use aggressive tactics. We reviewed a number of training materials, such as BPD's Academy-Level training on Use of Force, Defensive Tactics, and BPD's in-service training on "Characteristics of an Armed Person." We also observed in person BPD's training on foot patrols and interactions with people with mental illness.[92] Through its Defensive Tactics training, for example, BPD instructs officers to point their firearm at individuals when they need to control a scene. In the cases we reviewed, and in media reports, we saw this troubling tactic in operation. BPD groups this tactic on par with "command presence," "verbal commands," and using a "firm grip." Pointing a gun at an individual for general control is an inappropriate use of a firearm and is a threat of deadly force where the underlying offense, if any, does not justify deadly force being used. *See Holland v. Harrington*, 268 F.3d 1179, 1192 (10th Cir. 2001) (explaining that an officer's pointing of a firearm "involves the immediate threat of deadly force" and thus "should be predicated on at least a perceived risk of injury or danger to the officers or others, based upon what the officers know at that time"). Pointing firearms directly at individuals is also dangerous because it can lead to accidental discharges; limit officers' ability to use other, more appropriate force when one hand is occupied with holding a firearm; and lead to unnecessary use of deadly force. During our review, we saw instances in which officers drew and pointed their firearms at individuals when the use of deadly force did not appear to be justified, including an incident that resulted in an accidental discharge that fortunately did not strike anyone. In part through aggressive tactics such as these, BPD's trainings fuel an "us vs. them" mentality we saw some officers display towards community members, alienating the civilians they are meant to serve.

---

[91] While flight in a high crime area may give officers reasonable suspicion to conduct a *Terry* stop under *Illinois v. Wardlow*, 528 U.S. 119, 124–25 (2000), flight alone does not provide a justification to use the amount of force we observed in many cases.

[92] Throughout this Report, the term "mental illness" includes substance use disorders.

Moreover, the Department has failed to equip officers with sufficient de-escalation skills and tactics. The Department had no comprehensive training on de-escalation techniques until 2015, when it added de-escalation training to the Academy's Use of Force curriculum for new recruits. We commend the Department for its efforts and desire to implement de-escalation training. Nevertheless, work remains to ensure that these de-escalation skills are sufficiently emphasized within the Academy's Use of Force curriculum. Even with the new Academy training, these skills must be constantly refreshed through in-service training for experienced officers after they leave the Academy. BPD does not sufficiently prioritize these skills in the in-service training courses it offers.

The other trends we identified below through BPD's own force investigations—using force against vulnerable groups and individuals who are not a threat—also reflect officers' aggressive tactics that result in unreasonable force.

2. BPD Uses Unreasonable Force Against Individuals with a Mental Health Disability and Those in Crisis and Fails to Make Reasonable Modifications When Interacting with Individuals with Mental Health Disabilities

BPD officers routinely use unreasonable force against individuals with mental health disabilities or those experiencing a crisis[93] in violation of the Fourth Amendment. Additionally, by routinely using unreasonable force against individuals with mental health disabilities, BPD officers repeatedly fail to make reasonable modifications necessary to avoid discrimination in violation of Title II of the Americans with Disabilities Act of 1990 (ADA), 42 U.S.C. §§ 12131–12134. Since 2004, BPD has provided some specialized training to its new officers on how to interact with individuals with disabilities and those in crisis. But this training has not been provided to all officers. Moreover, the Department does not have a protocol requiring that a person with this training be dispatched to a crisis call. The result is that BPD officers frequently fail to de-escalate encounters with unarmed individuals with mental health disabilities and those in crisis. Indeed, their tactics often escalate these encounters. Instead of requesting an officer trained in handling crisis events or a mobile crisis team made up of trained mental health professionals, officers handcuff and detain people with mental health disabilities and those in crisis and resort too quickly to force without understanding or accounting for the person's disability or crisis.

For example, BPD officers often are called to the scene to escort individuals likely to have disabilities to a hospital for a mental health evaluation (referred to as an "emergency petition" under Maryland law), and possible civil commitment. Frequently, these individuals have committed no crime and present no significant threat to officers or other members of the public. "Where a seizure's sole justification is preventing harm to the subject of the seizure, the government has little interest in using force to effect that seizure. Rather, using force likely to harm the subject is manifestly contrary to the government's interest in initiating that seizure." *Armstrong*, 810 F.3d at 901. In the course of engaging with these individuals, usually to transport them for medical treatment, BPD officers resort to using unreasonable force if individuals fail to comply with their commands.

Under the Fourth Amendment, "officers who encounter an unarmed and minimally threatening individual who is "exhibit[ing] conspicuous signs that he [i]s mentally unstable" must

---

[93] For a definition of "crisis," *see* note 90, *supra.*

"de-escalate the situation and adjust the application of force downward." *Id.* at 900. Similarly, the ADA, which applies to BPD's services, programs, and activities, including on-the-street encounters, arrests, and transportation to a hospital for mental health evaluation, *see* 42 U.S.C. § 12132; 28 C.F.R. § 35.130(a), requires BPD to "make reasonable modifications in policies, practices, or procedures when the modifications are necessary to avoid discrimination on the basis of disability." *See also* 28 C.F.R. 35.130(b)(7); *Title II Technical Assistance Manual* § II-3.6100, at 14.[94] BPD's obligations apply when officers respond to a scene where they know or reasonably should know that an individual has a mental health disability.[95] For example, BPD has knowledge of an individual's disability when BPD is called for an emergency petition, when a mother calls 911 and says her son has schizophrenia and is not eating, or when a person is exhibiting apparent signs of mental illness.

Training BPD officers on how to interact with individuals with mental health disabilities is a reasonable modification to policies, practices, and procedures to afford people with mental health disabilities the equal opportunity for a police intervention that is free from unreasonable force. *See Estate of Saylor v. Regal Cinemas, Inc.*, 54 F. Supp. 3d 409, 424 (D. Md. 2014) (holding that the failure to provide appropriate training for officers to interact with individuals with developmental disabilities, which resulted in the death of a 26-year-old man with Down Syndrome after officers attempted to force him to leave a movie theater, properly stated a claim under Title II of the ADA). Among other things, such training should result in officers employing appropriate de-escalation techniques or involving mental health professionals or specially trained crisis intervention officers.

Rather than employing such de-escalation tactics, we found that BPD officers often resort too quickly to using force against individuals with mental health disabilities or in crisis. We found that on many occasions, the officers' unreasonable use of force involved use of tasers in drive-stun mode. As the Fourth Circuit has recognized, "[d]eploying a taser is a serious use of force. The weapon is designed to cause . . . excruciating pain and application can burn a subject's flesh." *Armstrong*, 810 F.3d at 902 (internal quotation marks and citations omitted). The court noted that "using drive stun mode 'to achieve pain compliance may have limited effectiveness and, when used repeatedly, may even exacerbate the situation.'" *Id.* at 902 (quoting PERF & COPS, *2011 Electronic Control Weapon Guidelines*, at 14); *see also Armstrong*, 810 F.3d at 897 n.3 (internal quotation marks and citations omitted) ("Tasers generally have two modes. In dart mode, a taser shoots probes into a subject and overrides the central nervous system. Drive stun mode, on the other hand, does not cause an override of the victim's central nervous system; that mode is used as a pain compliance tool

---

[94] The ADA's obligation to make "reasonable modifications in policies, practices, or procedures" is not limitless. A modification is not required if it would "fundamentally alter the nature of the service, program, or activity." 28 C.F.R. § 35.130(b)(7). The requested modifications here would not "fundamentally alter" BPD's programs. As discussed in further detail in Section II(C)(5), *infra*, BPD already offers some policing services specifically tailored toward individuals in crisis, although significant work remains to fully develop this program. Additionally, the requested modifications are consistent with BPD's obligations under the Constitution. BPD would not have to make the requested modifications if the person requiring the modification poses a direct threat to the safety of an officer or others. *See* 28 C.F.R. § 35.139. A direct threat is "a significant risk to the health or safety of others that cannot be eliminated by a modification of policies, practices, or procedures, or by the provision of auxiliary aids or services." 28 C.F.R. § 35.104. In many of the incidents we reviewed involving individuals with mental health disabilities or in crisis, however, the person against whom force is used does not meet the definition of "direct threat" as that term is used in the ADA.

[95] Guidance on ADA Regulation on Nondiscrimination on the Basis of Disability in State and Local Government Services, 28 C.F.R. pt. 35, app. B, at 686 (2015) (Law enforcement agencies and officers are "required to make appropriate efforts to determine whether perceived strange or disruptive behavior . . . is the result of a disability"), *available at* https://www.gpo.gov/fdsys/pkg/CFR-2015-title28-vol1/pdf/CFR-2015-title28-vol1-part35-appB.pdf.

with limited threat reduction."). Even Taser International, the company that manufactures tasers, has cautioned against using the drive stun mode on "emotionally disturbed persons or others who may not respond to pain due to a mind-body disconnect." *Id.* at 903.

Nonetheless, BPD officers have repeatedly used drive-stuns while responding to people with mental health disabilities and those in crisis, causing unnecessary pain and suffering without any noticeable benefit. In fact, these uses have often, if anything, exacerbated the situation. In a 2011 incident we reviewed, several officers responded to a call about a domestic disturbance, at which point they were flagged down by "Michael," standing outside without shoes in January weather, smelling of alcohol. His wife, present on the scene, informed officers that she had not been assaulted, but that her husband was intoxicated and that she was packing things to leave for the night. Michael yelled profanities and stated that he wanted to die. Instead of using de-escalation techniques, calling for help from an officer trained in crisis intervention techniques or a mental health professional, or working to connect Michael with appropriate treatment services, the officers attempted to physically force Michael into handcuffs, and when he resisted, drive-stunned him with a Taser five to six times. One officer specifically noted in his report that "[t]he Taser seemed to have a minimal affect [sic] upon [Michael] possibly due to his level of alcoholic intoxication and mentally disturbed state." After handcuffing him, the officers took Michael to the hospital for stabilization. He was never charged with a crime. The force used by the officers was unreasonable because he had not committed a crime and did not appear to pose a threat to officers or his wife. It was also ineffective in rendering Michael compliant, and caused unneeded suffering without any appreciable benefit.

In another 2011 incident, nine officers responded to a call for service regarding a man, "Christopher," standing in the street with no clothing on. In this case, there is no documented attempt to have a specially-trained officer at the scene. When the officers encountered Christopher, they reported that he was speaking religious verses and arguing with himself. They believed he had a mental illness and decided to transport him to a hospital to be evaluated. There is no indication in the reports that the officers sought to have Christopher go with them voluntarily, and instead they sought to place him in handcuffs, even though he was not under arrest. In order to handcuff him, one officer held his left arm, a second officer held his right arm, and a third officer attempted to apply the handcuffs. Christopher reportedly "became aggressive and violent," attempting to grab and bite officers. The officers and Christopher fell onto the ground. From the officers' reports, it appears that six additional officers were on the scene and available to assist in bringing Christopher under control, but there is no indication that they attempted any control techniques on Christopher. There is also no indication that de-escalation techniques or other reasonable modifications were used, such as attempts to verbally calm Christopher, create distance or slow down the incident.

Instead, the transport van driver exited his van and promptly drive-stunned Christopher. Using a taser in drive-stun mode is to be avoided unless it is necessary to "creat[e] a safe distance between the officer and subject." PERF & COPS, 2011 Electronic Control Weapon Guidelines, at 14. BPD had no policy or training so limiting the use of drive-stuns, even against individuals with mental illness or in crisis, at this time. Thus, the van driver continued to drive-stun Christopher, an individual in crisis, "a few more times in his chest and back area"[96] until Christopher became compliant. As a result of the encounter, Christopher and two officers received minor injuries, and Christopher was transported to the emergency room for treatment. Before the officers' attempts to handcuff him, he had not committed any violent offense, and presented no immediate physical danger to the officers or the public at large. Christopher was never arrested or charged with a crime. In 2016, BPD issued new guidance limiting officers' uses of tasers, a positive step forward. Additional work remains, however, to ensure that officers abide by the new guidance.

In many incidents involving individuals in crisis, the use of force was precipitated by officers' perceived need to bring the individual into immediate custody at all costs, including handcuffing them and placing them into a police vehicle for transport in order to provide necessary mental health treatment. During this detention process, a number of uses of unreasonable force against individuals with mental illness and crisis have occurred when they had committed no crime at all— instead, BPD's interaction with the individual was precipitated by calls for help from a loved one, friend or concerned citizen. That a person has committed no crime "weighs heavily" against a finding that the use of force by law enforcement was reasonable. *Bailey v. Kennedy*, 349 F.3d 731, 744 (4th Cir. 2003) (finding that blows and kicks against a man resisting arrest for an unwarranted emergency medical evaluation were unreasonable). In many incidents, however, officers have failed to distinguish between people in crisis who are being escorted to the hospital for treatment, and people who have committed crimes and are being placed under arrest. From our review of BPD's force reports, it appears that officers make little, if any, effort to de-escalate or engage peaceably with the person in crisis, resorting to the use of force as a first option in order to transport the individual for treatment. If they do not submit to handcuffing or respond immediately to officers' commands, they are often subjected to uses of force in order to physically restrain them, rather than neutralize a threat. The only difference is that the final destination will be an emergency room, rather than jail.

In one such incident, in 2010, several officers responded to a call from the father of a man, "James," in mental health crisis. The father informed the officers that James was the subject of an emergency petition, had a history of mental illness and hospitalization, and was unarmed. The petition itself indicated that James was not taking his medication, wearing a winter coat in hot weather, and yelling at people on the street and his father. When they could not convince James to open the door, officers attempted to pry the door open with a crowbar, then sprayed two bursts of mace in an attempt to force him out of the apartment. Once inside, a lieutenant deployed his taser in probe mode, striking James, when he resisted being handcuffed. Despite the fact that James had committed no crime and there is no indication in the force report that he was a threat himself or the officers other than resisting handcuffing, the officers resorted to a high-level of force to detain the man. *See Armstrong*, 810 F.3d at 900 (internal quotation marks omitted) ("The problems posed by, and thus the tactics to be employed against, an unarmed, emotionally distraught individual who is creating a disturbance or resisting arrest are ordinarily different from those involved in law enforcement efforts to subdue an armed and dangerous criminal who has recently committed a serious offense."). Using effective de-escalation techniques and calling for assistance from a mental

---

[96] In an October 2009 Training Bulletin, Taser International recommended that its Tasers, the leading brand of ECWs, not be used on individuals' chests, to avoid controversy about whether such shots affect the human heart. *See* TASER Int'l, *Training Bulletin 15.0 Medical Research Update & Revised Warnings* (Oct. 15, 2009).

health provider or crisis intervention trained officer would have likely prevented the use of force against James.

In another incident, two officers encountered a "possible mental patient" inside a vacant dwelling. The man, "David," was "yelling incoherently" and would not come out of the building when ordered. The officers entered, and when David became louder and placed his hands in his pockets, one officer pointed a taser at him as a threat, purportedly to protect himself and to persuade David to comply with the order to exit the building. David told the police officers that tasers did not work on him. In response, the officer deployed one cycle of his taser in probe mode, striking the man "to eliminate the need for a fight." Without waiting to assess whether additional force was necessary, the officer used a second cycle. David was handcuffed and transported to the hospital. The only justification offered by the officer for the second taser cycle was that it was necessary "to gain his full compliance." For many people with mental health disabilities or in crisis, the appearance of officers pointing weapons may convey the impression that they are being threatened or arrested, rather than provided treatment that is intended to help them. The use of a taser against David in this context was unnecessary and unreasonable where it had the sole purpose of bringing him into the physical custody of the officers for treatment, and David presented no immediate threat to himself or others. Using effective de-escalation techniques and calling for assistance from a mental health provider or officer trained in crisis intervention techniques would have likely prevented the use of force against all of these individuals.

Tragically, some encounters with people with mental health disabilities or in crisis have resulted in uses of deadly force that may have been avoided had officers used tactics to account for the mental state of the individuals involved. For example, in a 2012 incident, a single officer was the first to arrive on the scene in response to a call by a man, Zachary, who informed the dispatcher that he had "a weapon" and was "about to do something crazy." After the officer was dispatched, another officer and sergeant stated over the air that they would respond as backup. The officer did not wait for backup to arrive, however, or request the presence of a specially trained crisis intervention officer, despite the fact that he had prior information that Zachary had a weapon and was in crisis. The officer also made no attempt to contact Zachary inside the house before approaching the door, or consider less-lethal options for intervention. Instead, the officer went up to the door, alone, and with his gun already drawn. When Zachary opened the door with a lit cigarette in one hand, and a knife in the other, the officer reportedly ordered the man three times to drop the knife, and when he did not comply, the officer fired, killing him. After radioing dispatch to inform that he had arrived on the scene, less than two minutes passed before he announced that Zachary had been shot two to three times. Although there is insufficient information to make a determination about the shooting itself, this incident shows how different tactics could have changed the outcome.

Officers' use of arrest techniques, including force, handcuffing and prisoner transport vans to detain people with mental health disabilities or in crisis for emergency petitions when they present no immediate threat to officers or the public, may cause people to perceive that they are being attacked or arrested, rather than transported for treatment. This perception may escalate the encounter, resulting in additional force.

In some cases, officers resort to arresting individuals with mental health disabilities or in crisis in situations where treatment—instead of jail—would more effectively serve the goals of public safety and welfare and could prevent the need for unnecessary force. For example, in one case, officers responded to a "mental case" and found a man, "Robert," speaking to his mother, who explained that her son had a mental illness and that she was afraid of him. The officers told Robert to leave and put a shirt on, which he did, and then returned. Officers then told Robert he had to leave, or would be arrested. When he refused, officers handcuffed him and sat him in a chair while waiting for a transport van to arrive. This decision to arrest and handcuff Robert, a person in crisis, led to unreasonable force. While waiting, Robert repeatedly stood up in what the officer believed was an attempt "to flee," and was "kicking his legs" to "create space around himself." After being told several times to stop standing and stop kicking, and that he would be struck in the leg with a baton if he did not comply, Robert refused to comply. He attempted to stand again, in what officers reportedly believed was another attempt to flee. One officer struck him in the right shin with his baton. This force used against Robert, while he was handcuffed, was unreasonable because he had not acted violently, did not present any evident threat to the officers or his mother, and the officers had been informed that he had a mental illness. This force could have been avoided by using de-escalation techniques before handcuffing Robert or by calling a mobile crisis team for assistance. In this incident, as with all of the above incidents involving individuals with mental health disabilities or in crisis, officers did not seem to understand that individuals' mental illness or intoxication might diminish their ability to comply with orders. Moreover, the officers in this incident believed—contrary to the Department's policy—that they could not emergency petition Robert because he had not displayed any signs of mental illness in their presence, despite his mother's call for assistance based on that mental condition and her explanation of his history of hospitalization. Instead, the officers arrested him and charged him with disorderly conduct, trespassing, resisting arrest, and failure to obey. All charges against him were subsequently dismissed.

BPD routinely uses unreasonable force against people with mental illness or in crisis, even when they have not committed any crimes and when the officers know or should know that the individual has a mental health disability. As a result, individuals are exposed to serious harm that exacerbates their disability and the crisis that precipitated the request for BPD assistance. This unreasonable use of force against individuals in crisis violates the Fourth Amendment. And BPD further violates Title II of the Americans with Disabilities Act by failing to make reasonable modifications to its policies, practices and procedures, such as training in de-escalation, effectively using specialized crisis intervention trained officers, and involving mental health professionals as necessary to avoid discrimination against individuals with disabilities.

3. BPD Uses Unreasonable Force Against Juveniles And Ignores Widely Accepted Strategies For Police Interactions With Youth

BPD officers frequently use unreasonable force against juveniles without implementing widely accepted techniques and tactics for engaging with youth. Courts have recognized that an individual's age can be a factor in whether the force used against them was reasonable. *See Graham*, 490 U.S. at 396 ("the test of reasonableness" . . . "requires careful attention to the facts and circumstances of each particular case. . . ."); *Doe ex rel. Doe v. Hawaii Dep't of Educ.*, 334 F.3d 906, 909–10 (9th Cir. 2003) (noting Plaintiff "was eight years old" in analysis under *Graham* of whether force was reasonable); *Ikerd v. Blair*, 101 F.3d 430 (5th Cir. 1996) (finding a reasonable jury could conclude a deputy used excessive force where "the appellants produced evidence that Deputy Varnado, a 300–pound man, violently jerked Laura, a ten-year-old child, out of her living room chair and dragged her into another room"). We found that BPD officers engage in unnecessary and excessive force with youth and fail to adjust their tactics to account for the age and developmental status of the youth they encounter.

For example, in a 2011 incident, an officer noticed a 5'2," 85 pound female youth standing with a male in a "known area for high drug trafficking." The officer in charge who investigated the force reported that the involved officer "was familiar with the female juvenile and her past history for selling CDS." The involved officer's incident report does not mention any history of selling drugs but states that she "suspected [the female was] a missing juvenile." Regardless of the basis for stopping the youth, the officer got out of her patrol vehicle "to identify" the female. When she did so, the youth and the male began to "walk away very quickly." The officer commanded the individuals to "stop" but they did not comply. The officer again commanded the two to stop. When they continued to not comply with her command, the officer discharged her taser in probe mode at the young 85-pound female, "which gave an electric shock." The youth "stopped and supported herself on [a] fence," and the officer "discontinued the electric discharge[]." When the officer discharged her taser, she did not have probable cause for an arrest. There is also no indication in BPD's own reports that the youth was threatening the officer or others; rather, she was simply walking away. Even assuming that there is reasonable suspicion for a stop, refusing to obey an officer's command to "stop," when the officer has no probable cause to arrest and there is no threat to the public or officer, does not justify the use of a taser. The officer's use of a taser was unnecessary and excessive.[97] The chain of command failed to identify any issues with the officer's use of force.

In another incident, in 2010, two officers approached a group of individuals who were standing on a sidewalk in a residential neighborhood and "verbally warned this small crowd to disperse." A juvenile, Brian, and his sister walked onto the steps of their home, remaining outside. When one of the officers approached Brian's sister to "warn her about loitering," she informed the officers, yelling and cursing, that she lived in the house. The officers did not appear to dispute her claim that she lived in the house. Their reports do not show that any effort was made to confirm whether it was her home. Nevertheless, the officers continued to "warn" her to leave and "cease causing a disturbance." They eventually attempted to arrest her for "non-compliance." One of the officers walked up the steps of the siblings' stoop to attempt to make the arrest. Brian attempted to block the officer, and the officer began to "struggle" with the juvenile. According to civilian witness statements that are summarized in the Department's reports, the officer punched Brian in the face. The officer also used oleoresin capsicum, or "OC" spray, against both siblings and arrested them for loitering, resisting arrest and assault on a police officer. All of the officer's uses of force against the siblings, who were standing on or in front of their own property, were unreasonable. These individuals were placed into the criminal justice system for standing on their own steps.

Allegations of BPD's unreasonable use of force against juveniles are not new. BPD has a history of problematic encounters with youth that pre-date the period of our review. For example, in 2007, officers arrested a seven-year old child for sitting on a dirt bike during an initiative to

---

[97] Behind where the youth and her male companion were stopped, officers found bags of "a green leaf substance suspected to be [m]arijuana." Additional bags of the green leaf substance fell out of the man's pants. The youth was arrested for a controlled substance violation and taken to a juvenile detention center.

confiscate dirt bikes. Allegedly, although the dirt bike was turned off, it was not "securely locked or otherwise immobilized" in violation of Baltimore City Code. According to Court documents filed by the family's attorney, officers attempted to confiscate the bike and "maliciously and unreasonably grabbed [the child] by his shirt collar and dragged [him] off the bike." According to the same documents, the child's mother informed officers that she intended to file a complaint, and the officers, in turn, arrested the child. The family alleged he was handcuffed to a bench at the district station for hours, and detained and questioned without his parents' consent. He was eventually released and never formally charged. This incident garnered widespread media attention in Baltimore and invoked a community outcry about BPD's aggressive tactics, particularly against a seven-year old child. Despite the outcry and widespread attention, BPD failed to create policy guidance or comprehensive training for officers' interactions with youth.

In addition, three officers were criminally charged this year for assaulting a youth who had been in crisis and was restrained in a 2015 incident. According to a complaint filed about the incident, when the child was admitted to the hospital for evaluation of a mental health condition, independent witnesses on the scene indicated that he had no injuries. In his hospital room, he was handcuffed with both hands behind his back but was being unruly—yelling and kicking his legs. One of the officers reportedly ordered hospital staff to leave the room and reportedly slapped or punched the youth in the face repeatedly. The nurses observed the officers being verbally abusive to the child and observed injuries to his face when they returned to the youth's room.

Research has established that adolescent development affects the manner in which juveniles comprehend, communicate, and behave. These unique realities of adolescent development warrant specific policies and tactics for officers' interactions with juveniles. The International Association of Chiefs of Police (IACP) has recognized this need and created guidance for officers' interactions with youth.[98] Specific strategies for officers include "[a]pproach[ing] youth with a calm demeanor, conveying that you are there to help them" because "[a]ggression may cause the youth to shut down and make the situation worse."[99] BPD officers are not provided guidance on the causes and unique qualities of youth behavior and communication or trained on the skills and tactics necessary for interacting with youth. Officers use the same overly aggressive tactics they use with adults, unnecessarily escalating encounters with youth. As the President's Task Force on 21st Century Policing notes, "[u]se of physical control equipment and techniques against vulnerable populations—including children . . . can undermine public trust and should be used as a last resort."[100]

We reviewed numerous other cases that also raised concerns about officers' interactions with juveniles. These cases demonstrate that BPD fails to adjust its tactics, even when dealing with youth. They also show that BPD needs to provide detailed and comprehensive policy guidance and training for interactions involving juveniles, and to hold officers accountable if they fail to abide by their training and guidelines.

---

[98] Int'l Assn. of Chiefs of Police, *The Effects of Adolescent Development on Policing* 2 (2015), available at http://www.iacp.org/teenbrain).

[99] *Id.* at 4.

[100] Final Report of the President's Task Force on 21st Century Policing 15 (May 2015).

4. BPD Uses Unreasonable Force Against People Who Are Not a Threat to Officers or the Public

a. BPD Uses Unreasonable Force Against People who Are Already Restrained

BPD uses unreasonable force against people who are already restrained and pose little or no threat to the officer or the public. In some instances, these individuals may continue to verbally resist or not submit to officer's demands, but this type of passive resistance or non-compliance does not justify using force. This practice contravenes well-settled law.

In *Meyers*, the Fourth Circuit determined that an officer's use of force was excessive and unreasonable where the officer repeatedly administered electrical shocks from a taser on an individual who was no longer armed, was no longer actively resisting arrest and was physically restrained by several other officers. 713 F.3d at 734. "We also have stated in forthright terms that 'officers using unnecessary, gratuitous, and disproportionate force to seize a secured, unarmed citizen do not act in an objectively reasonable manner.'" *Id.* (quoting *Bailey v. Kennedy*, 349 F.3d 731, 744–45 (4th Cir. 2003)); *see also Champion v. Outlook Nashville, Inc.*, 380 F.3d 893, 902 (6th Cir. 2004) (citing cases) ("We have consistently held that various types of force applied after the subduing of a suspect are unreasonable and a violation of a clearly established right."). The Court in *Meyers* also indicated that "any 'unnecessary, gratuitous, and disproportional force'" against unarmed and secured individuals was objectively unreasonable regardless of the type of weapon used, whether arising from a gun, a baton, a taser, or other weapon. 713 F.3d at 734–35 (quoting *Jones v. Buchanan*, 325 F.3d 520, 532 (4th Cir. 2003) (fists)) (citing *Park v. Shiflett*, 250 F.3d 843, 852–53 (4th Cir. 2001) (pepper spray)).

In Baltimore, BPD officers use excessive force against restrained individuals, often when those individuals are awaiting transport to Central Booking after being arrested for committing low-level street offenses. For example, in a 2011 incident, three BPD officers responded to an anonymous tip about persons using illegal drugs inside a pick-up truck. Arriving on scene, the officers located illegal drugs and drug paraphernalia in the truck's cab. The three occupants—two women and one man—were removed from the vehicle and arrested for controlled substance violations. While waiting for a prisoner transport vehicle, one of the women, "Sarah", began "moving around" in a perceived attempt to wander away or escape. Sarah attempted to get up on six occasions and "each attempt to rise was met with a verbal warning to stop" and an admonition that the next time she tried to "escape" the officer would use force to against her. Sarah again tried to stand up and the officer, already holding his police baton in his hand, struck Sarah in the leg and then "managed to maintain physical control over her." This baton strike appears to be used as punishment for failing to follow the officer's commands rather than necessary and reasonable force to control Sarah, who was not actively aggressive and was being detained for a minor drug offense. Sarah later told the investigating supervisor that she was not attempting to escape; rather she was trying to stand up because her knees were in pain from kneeling on the hard pavement for such a long time. In this situation, other less forceful techniques should have been employed—for instance an escort position, joint manipulation, or utilizing leg restraints if escape was truly a concern. Moreover, BPD specifically trains its officers that impact weapons should not be used when individuals are non-compliant or passively resisting. Rather, striking an individual with an impact weapon should only be used to stop an attacker who is actively attempting to inflict injury. Nevertheless, this strike against a restrained individual was summarily approved by the chain of command.

In a 2014 incident that we reviewed, a CitiWatch operator who was monitoring security cameras placed throughout Baltimore notified BPD patrol officers that he observed an unknown male, later identified as "Brandon," conduct a hand-to-hand exchange of suspected narcotics. An officer and a trainee responded to the scene and entered a local store to interview Brandon. After producing identification, the officers smelled an odor of marijuana emanating from Brandon, whom they then patted down for weapons, but found none. As they were exiting the store, BPD officers noticed a baggie containing a white powdery substance on the floor near the entrance where Brandon had been standing. According to their force reports, having seen no one else enter or leave the store, the officers determined that the baggie belonged to Brandon, handcuffed him and took him outside to wait for a transport wagon.

When a BPD sergeant arrived on scene, Brandon was sitting on the ground in handcuffs. The sergeant began speaking to Brandon and reportedly observed another small baggie containing a white powdery substance and a clear sandwich baggie containing green plant material under Brandon's tongue. According to the sergeant, he asked Brandon to spit out the baggies, but Brandon clenched his mouth "and attempted to destroy the narcotics/evidence by swallowing them." The sergeant placed his hand on Brandon's cheeks and, most troublingly, on his throat and then applied pressure—"not to restrict his breathing, but just to keep him from swallowing the illegal narcotics/evidence which could have also put [Brandon's] life at risk." When Brandon refused to spit out the suspected narcotics, the sergeant ordered the police officer trainee on the scene to tase Brandon, even though he was restrained. The trainee drive-stunned Brandon on his legs. When Brandon did not spit out the baggies, the sergeant ordered the trainee to drive-stun Brandon three additional times. Brandon spat out "several" small baggies and was transported to the district for processing.

The use of force on Brandon's neck—a handcuffed detainee who did not pose a threat to officer safety, and who was being arrested for what the officer's described in their own report as a "street level drug transaction"—was excessive and unreasonable. Although some force to prevent the destruction of evidence or to protect Brandon may be reasonable, the sergeant's application of pressure to Brandon's throat was a use of lethal force that was not justified by the possible destruction of evidence or even the potential threat to Brandon of swallowing the narcotics. If Brandon had actually swallowed the baggies, officers should have transported him to a hospital for treatment by trained medical professionals. The officer's use of his taser on Brandon was also highly questionable, if not excessive.

In a 2010 incident, two BPD officers and a lieutenant arrested a 5'6," 160-pound man for littering after observing him throw a cigar wrapper on the ground and then empty the tobacco contents from the cigar. The officers handcuffed and sat 19-year old "William" on a curb, and conducted a search incident to arrest. They removed William's shoes and recovered a blue Ziploc bag containing what they suspected was marijuana. According to the force reports, William began to yell profanities and accuse the officers of planting the drugs. One officer placed William against a wall while they waited for a transport vehicle. William continued to yell, then pushed off the wall and began to run. After only a few steps, an officer pushed William to the ground. According to the force report, William continued to flail and try to "strike the officers by head butting, kicking, shouldering and spitting." The officers attempted to gain control of William, but were unable. A crowd formed around the officers and William. Although William was in handcuffs and three officers were present to control the restrained man, the officers resorted to tasing the man in drive-stun mode "approximately six times." The lieutenant and one of the officers also reportedly kicked William several times either in an effort to get him to the ground or to keep him on the ground; the reports are unclear. When the drive-stuns were reportedly ineffective, and William reportedly pushed away the taser and continued to fight, the lieutenant ordered the officers to move away and deployed two bursts of pepper spray in William's face. The officers were then able to hold William on the ground and place him in a transport vehicle. The inability of three officers to control William is concerning and reflects insufficient training on arrest and control techniques. While we take no position on the reasonableness of much of the force used in this incident, the use of the taser on a handcuffed individual "approximately six times" was unreasonable. The use of taser on a restrained individual is rarely reasonable, and tasing the person in drive-stun mode six times is unreasonable and excessive in almost any case. A drive-stun is to be used only to create distance. William suffered abrasions on his knees, arm, back and a small fracture of left shoulder. He was charged only with littering and disorderly conduct.

BPD officers also use excessive force against restrained detainees who refuse to exit BPD transport vehicles, in some cases when being transported to the hospital for an emergency petition evaluation. In a 2010 case we reviewed, a BPD transport officer responded to a call about a person with possible mental illness in a wheelchair who was allegedly exposing himself to take him to a hospital for an evaluation. Although the incident report is vague, difficult to read, and lacks any follow-up investigation, it appears that the officer approached the man, "Timothy," who was "agitated and disorderly," and asked for identification. Timothy produced his identification and then jumped out of the wheelchair and kicked the patrol car. When the officer attempted to take Timothy into custody, Timothy began kicking, and the officer tased him and took him into custody. Timothy was transported to an area hospital for an emergency petition evaluation. Upon arriving at the hospital, Timothy refused to come out of the transport vehicle and kicked at the BPD transport officer. The transport officer gave Timothy several commands to stop kicking or he would be tased. A second officer stood outside witnessing the events, but there is no indication that he made any effort to intervene. After the transport officer gave Timothy a third command to stop kicking, the transport officer deployed his taser in drive-stun mode.

The reasonableness of the first taser incident cannot be determined because there were conflicting accounts of what occurred, there was no supervisory investigation, and the incident reports contain little detail. However, tasing Timothy the second time while he was restrained in the back of a transport vehicle was unreasonable. In *Orem v. Rephann*, 523 F.3d 442 (4th Cir. 2008), *abrogated on other grounds by Wilkins v. Gaddy*, 559 U.S. 34, 39 (2010), the Court of Appeals addressed whether the use of a taser against an arrestee who was being transported to jail in a police officer's car constituted excessive force. Because the subject was already in custody, the court analyzed the excessive force claim under the Fourteenth Amendment's standard of whether the officer "inflicted unnecessary and wanton pain and suffering." *Orem*, 523 F.3d at 446; *but see Kingsley v. Hendrickson*, 135 S. Ct. 2466 (2015) (holding that excessive force claims brought by pretrial detainees need only meet the *Graham* standard of objective unreasonableness). In doing so, the court held that the use of a taser on a detainee who was already in handcuffs and restrained in the back of a police car was clearly unlawful, despite the fact that the detainee was extremely unruly and uncooperative. *Orem*, 523 F.3d at 446–47; *Cf. Wernert v. Green*, 419 F. App'x 337, 342–43 (4th Cir. 2011). Here, Timothy was transported to an area hospital because BPD officers determined that he needed an emergency psychological evaluation. Timothy was in crisis and kicked at the transport officer, but he was restrained and was not currently a danger to himself or a threat to the officers. There was no urgent need to remove Timothy from the transport vehicle. Instead of having patience and attempting to de-escalate the situation—or asking for assistance from the other officer on scene or qualified medical personnel in the hospital—the transport officer resorted to a high level of force to gain compliance from a person in crisis who may not have understood his commands. The use of the taser in this instance, and in other similar BPD force files we reviewed, was punitive rather than necessary and reasonable.

Nevertheless, in determining that the officer's actions conformed to Departmental Guidelines, the supervisor justifying this use of force wrote: "The X26 Taser fills the action void with a force less than either espantoon[101] or deadly force to elicit compliance from individuals who are about to be arrested. It allows members to use a relative mild force and provides a safer option than suffering or inflicting serious injury." The supervisor's determination that drive-stunning a restrained, mentally ill person is "mild" and justified because it prevents suffering or serious injury illustrates a lack of appreciation for the seriousness of the force used and the possibility of harm that could result. *See Bryan v. MacPherson*, 630 F.3d 805, 825 (9th Cir. 2010) ("The physiological effects, the high levels of pain, and foreseeable risk of physical injury lead us to conclude that the X26 and similar [tasers] are a greater intrusion than other non-lethal methods of force we have confronted."). It also demonstrates an ignorance of applicable Fourth Circuit law that prohibits the use of a taser in these circumstances. *Orem*, 523 F.3d at 446–47.

In a strikingly similar 2014 incident, a BPD officer responded to a domestic violence call, took the subject into custody, and transported him to the district station. When officers ordered "Eric" to exit the transport wagon, he refused and stated "I want the police to shoot me. I have nothing to live for." The officers warned Eric several times that he would be tased, but when he refused to comply with their commands, the sergeant on the scene ordered one of the officers to tase Eric. The taser probes struck Eric in the arm and buttocks. Subsequently, the officers transported Eric to the hospital for an emergency petition. This use of force on a passively non-complaint person in crisis was unreasonable. The officers resorted to force simply to gain compliance from Eric, not because they needed to gain control over him. In doing so, BPD officers disregarded an individual's constitutional rights in favor of expediency. The sergeant who ordered the officer to tase Eric—and also investigated the use of force, despite the conflict of interest— justified the taser deployment by citing what appears to be a version of the Department's Training Guidelines titled "Electronic Shock Devices," that had been replaced in 2010, four years before the incident took place.

b. BPD Uses Unreasonable Force Against Persons who Are Fleeing from Them and Present Little or No Threat of Harm

A significant number of incidents we reviewed involved BPD officers using force against individuals who were fleeing from officers and presented little or no threat of harm to them or others. Many of these incidents involved officers who chased civilians on foot, often without suspicion that they had committed any serious crimes. Such foot pursuits increase the likelihood that officers will use force in order to stop an individual that is not reasonable in light of the threat

---

[101] An "espantoon" is one type of baton used by BPD officers.

posed or crime committed by the person. Foot pursuits of individuals for low-level offenses are also an unsafe tactic that unnecessarily endangers officers and community members.

Similarly, we found a number of cases in which officers shot at vehicles that were fleeing or moving away from them, after any threat of harm to them or others had subsided. Such shootings are unreasonable.

i. In Foot Pursuits, BPD Uses Excessive Force Against Individuals Who Are Fleeing From Them and Tactics That Endanger Themselves and Community Members

BPD officers used excessive force against individuals during foot pursuits. When officers encounter civilians who flee from them, officers nearly always give chase, without weighing the severity of any suspected crime, whether the person poses a threat, and any alternative, safer means to affect a stop or seizure. Once engaged in a foot pursuit, BPD officers then often used force to end the pursuit regardless of whether they had only reasonable suspicion to conduct a stop, or probable cause to make an arrest. *See Cortez v. McCauley*, 478 F.3d 1108, 1126 (10th Cir. 2007) ("[P]olice have historically been able to use more force in making an arrest than in effecting an investigative detention."); *see also Rabin v. Flynn*, 725 F.3d 628, 632–33 (7th Cir. 2013) ("When an officer's use of force during such a *Terry* stop becomes so disproportionate to the purpose of such a stop in light of the surrounding circumstances—and the purpose may include ensuring the safety of the officers or others—then the encounter becomes a formal arrest (which must then be justified by probable cause.")) (citations omitted). Often, the force officers used to end the pursuit was disproportional to the suspected crime and the threat posed by the civilian. *See Armstrong*, 810 F.3d at 899 (internal quotation marks omitted) ("To properly consider the reasonableness of the force employed we must view it in full context, with an eye toward the proportionality of the force in light of all the circumstances."). Based on the force reports we reviewed, the frequency with which officers engaged in foot pursuits, without considering the seriousness of the suspected crime, any alternative means to stop the individual, and risks to themselves, the suspect, and others is concerning.

Foot pursuits are generally a high-risk tactic and have civil rights implications. *See generally* IACP, *Protecting Civil Rights: A Leadership Guide for State, Local, and Tribal Law Enforcement*, p. 133. In particular, at the end of a foot pursuit, when officers seize an individual, they may experience an adrenaline rush; actions taken under such circumstances may impede an officer's ability to exercise proper judgment and appropriate restraint. For this reason, police departments should, and generally do, give careful consideration to foot pursuits in policy and training.

BPD has not engaged in the careful consideration that foot pursuits require as a policy and training matter. BPD has no policy on foot pursuits to guide, and hold accountable, its officers' conduct. An internal report in 2013 recommended that the Department issue a policy on these pursuits, and its internal documents indicate that it has intended to draft a policy to guide officers' conduct in pursuits for a number of years. However, to date, BPD has not issued any policy on this issue. BPD's training on foot pursuits for both new and experienced officers also is deficient. Only in 2015 did BPD create a specific training on foot pursuits for its recruits in the Academy. Previously, its training on this tactic was spread throughout several different courses, leaving it to officers to tie the lessons together. Additionally, the skills that officers learn in the Academy must be refreshed frequently throughout an officer's career through in-service training. For experienced officers, BPD provided in-service training on foot pursuits for the first time in 2015.

BPD officers resort to excessive force to end foot pursuits, or after a pursuit has occurred. For example, in the 2010 incident discussed *supra* on page 31, an officer reportedly in an area "known for violent crime and narcotics distribution" recognized an African-American man who had previously fled when the officer had attempted to conduct a field interview and again fled at the sight of the officer. The officer reportedly pursued the man because he believed he was "involved in criminal activity" though he did not identify any specific crime he suspected. He also reportedly believed he "may be armed with a concealed weapon" because of his "actions, loose clothing and the surroundings." Such generic and vague descriptions are insufficient to justify using serious force against a person. *Smith v. Ball State Univ.*, 295 F.3d 763, 771 (7th Cir. 2002) (applying *Graham* and finding force used in a Terry stop reasonable because it was "measured, brief, and appropriate to accomplish the purposes of the investigative stop."). Here, the officer pursued the man on foot for eight blocks. During the pursuit, the officer deployed his taser in probe mode two times on the man, and then finally used a drive-stun to stop the individual.[102] The officer then frisked the man and found he was not carrying any firearms. To strike the man with two deployments of a taser in probe mode and one in drive-stun was excessive in these circumstances. A lieutenant who arrived on the scene interviewed the man and asked why he had run from the officer. The man informed the lieutenant that "he was scared." Officers released the man without charging him with any crime.

Separate from the risk of excessive force, BPD officers also use unsafe tactics when they engage in foot pursuits, needlessly endangering themselves and community members. The risks of engaging in a foot pursuit may outweigh the benefits in a number of cases. Particularly when officers are acting alone, pursuits are not advised. Indeed, the International Association of Chiefs of Police (IACP) has also cautioned that "[n]ormally, conducting a foot pursuit alone is far too dangerous an undertaking to be permissible."[103] In our reviews of BPD's files, officers engage in solo foot pursuits frequently, even when, in some cases, they believe the person they are pursuing to be armed. Engaging in a solo pursuit of an armed person is dangerous to the officer, and may make it more likely that shots may be fired, increasing the danger to community members. BPD officers repeatedly fail to consider the risk factors inherent in foot pursuits. They too frequently employ tactics that are unsafe for officers, the individuals they pursue, and the community.

When officers decide to pursue a suspect, even though they must decide quickly whether to pursue, they should assess the seriousness of the suspected violation at issue, the dangerousness of the pursuit under the circumstances, whether the person they intend to pursue poses an immediate and serious threat or could be apprehended later or through other means. The need for the suspect's immediate apprehension must be weighed against the risks to officers and the public caused by engaging in a foot pursuit. If officers know the identity of the suspect, his or her immediate apprehension is likely unnecessary without exigent circumstances. However, if circumstances require that the suspect be immediately apprehended, officers should contain the suspect and establish a perimeter rather than engaging in a foot pursuit, particularly if officers believe the suspect may be armed. Officers may then conduct a sweep in a coordinated manner within the contained area to locate the suspect, with the assistance of surveillance if this is available. This recognizes that

---

[102] Striking a stationary individual with a taser in probe mode, if at a distance, can be difficult; striking a moving person while an officer is also running has a low likelihood of being effective.

[103] Int'l Ass'n of Chiefs of Police, *Foot Pursuits Concepts & Issues Paper* 2 (Feb. 2003).

the safety of the officers and community members is paramount when alternative tactics are available to resolve the incident. Containing a suspect and establishing a perimeter also slows the incident down, decreasing the need for rushed decisions or judgments made in adrenaline-filled circumstances, and decreases the need to use force to apprehend a suspect.

Officers should be encouraged and incentivized to choose safe and professional courses of conduct. Indeed, the IACP recommends that "[b]ecause of the inherent and demonstrated dangers involved in foot pursuits, it should be a matter of agency policy that officers should not be criticized or sanctioned for making a rational and professionally informed decision not to engage in or to terminate a foot pursuit." BPD, to the contrary, indirectly encourages foot pursuits by placing a heavy emphasis on officers' arrest numbers. As discussed above in Section II(A)(1) some supervisors still assess officers, at least in part, by the number of arrests they make, regardless of the severity of the underlying crime. This incentivizes officers to pursue individuals for even minor infractions to increase the number of arrests they make. Additionally, pressure from past City officials to lower the rate of violent crime also has encouraged officers to pursue and seize individuals who may be armed, in an attempt to seize and remove their guns from the street. This is a high-risk strategy that, if engaged in, must have strict controls and oversight to ensure that officers' actions are constitutional and that officers and the public are not exposed to unnecessary risk. Our investigation finds that such controls and oversight are not present, and that officers do not appear to be engaging in pursuits of individuals who they suspect are armed in a manner that keeps them and others safe.

For example, in a 2014 incident, a uniformed officer patrolling in an area allegedly known for drug trafficking and violence turned on his lights and sirens to respond to a call for service regarding "a silent alarm at a nearby block." As he did so, he noticed Andrew, "an unknown black male observe [his] marked uniform presence and flee on foot." The officer noted that Andrew was "holding his left side" which the officer believed to be "a characteristic of an armed person." The officer abandoned the call for service that he had been responding to and instead pursued Andrew, an unknown individual, alone, on foot. Andrew entered a residential home from the back porch and locked the door behind him. The officer, "[b]elieving that he might be armed, and fearing that the house he entered might not have been his, and also fearing that any evidence or contraband/weapons he may have on him would be destroyed/concealed," "forced entry into the house, damaging the door in the process."[104] If Andrew *had* been armed, the officer's choice of tactics—forcing entry without backup—could have resulted in the officer being shot. Andrew ran to the front door where the officer caught up to him and attempted to make an arrest—the officer did not specify the crime for which he was attempting to make the arrest. While the two were "struggl[ing]" at the front door, a pit bull charged at them from inside the house. The officer withdrew his service weapon "fearing" that he would "have to shoot the dog." Eventually, to avoid the dog, the officer let Andrew run out the front door and continued to pursue on foot. The officer then decided to tase Andrew because he believed Andrew "was involved in illegal activity," suspected he "had entered an unknown house," "might be armed," and "had already resisted all

---

[104] It is not clear that the officer had cause to enter the home without a warrant. *See Brigham City, Utah v. Stuart*, 547 U.S. 398, 403 (2006) (internal quotation marks omitted) ("It is a basic principle of Fourth Amendment law that searches and seizures inside a home without a warrant are presumptively unreasonable."). While officers in "hot pursuit" of a fleeing suspect are granted an exigency exception to the general principle prohibiting a search of a home without a warrant, it is not clear that this qualifies as a "hot pursuit" where the officer had insufficient basis to believe the man had committed a specific crime, or that any other exigency existed here permitting the officer to enter the home. *See id.*

attempts to apprehend him." The officer tased Andrew two times, as the first deployment was not effective. After taking him into custody, the officer discovered that Andrew was not armed, had no contraband, and was eventually determined, at a later, unknown time, to have an open warrant. The reason for the officer's force listed in his use of force report was that the "suspect refused to comply."

This officer repeatedly used unsafe tactics that endangered himself, the individual he pursued, and a homeowner, and damaged a homeowner's property. He chose to engage in a foot pursuit in an allegedly violent area, alone, while believing the person he was pursuing to be armed. There is no indication in the report that he called for backup or considered discontinuing the pursuit at any time. He forced entry into an unknown home, where the person he was pursuing was inside and at a tactical advantage to the officer. If Andrew had actually been armed, as the officer suspected he was, the officer could have been shot. The officer damaged a home by breaking the door, potentially increasing the danger to the homeowner he was trying to protect, and pointing his firearm at the homeowner's dog while struggling with a man, creating a risk of harm to the homeowner's property. The officer's use of force against Andrew was highly questionable, if not clearly unreasonable, particularly given the officer's own training on the likelihood that the individual was armed.

Like the officers in the above accounts, officers frequently cite factors learned in BPD's training on "Characteristics of an Armed Person" such as "grabbing one's waistband" or "wearing loose clothing." Officers appear to use these factors to justify the force they use during or following pursuits, asserting that they believe individuals who exhibit any one of these factors to be armed. BPD provides their training on "Characteristics of an Armed Person" to teach officers to identify when a person may be armed, which may provide reasonable suspicion for a stop. BPD training instructors warn students that there may be false positives, and informed us that they instruct students that *eighty percent* of individuals who show characteristics of an armed person—such as wearing loose or baggy clothing, or grabbing their waistbands while running—will *not* be armed.[105] Despite purportedly being trained on false positives, BPD officers nevertheless frequently engage in foot pursuits and use force on individuals based solely on factors such as "wearing loose clothing." We found that this results, at times, in the use of excessive force.

Some of the incidents we reviewed involved officers shooting at individuals who were fleeing from them and who officers suspected were armed. In a number of cases involving BPD officers' uses of deadly force, it was not clear that the individuals officers shot at had actually threatened the officer or others with serious or deadly harm. Without an immediate threat, simply being in possession of a firearm does not justify using deadly force. *Tennessee v. Garner*, 471 U.S. 1, 11 (1985); *Cooper v. Sheehan*, 735 F.3d 153, 159 (4th Cir. 2013) ("[T]he mere possession of a firearm by a suspect is not enough to permit the use of deadly force. Thus, an officer does not possess the unfettered authority to shoot a member of the public simply because that person is carrying a weapon. Instead, deadly force may only be used by a police officer when, based on a reasonable assessment, the officer or another person is threatened with the weapon.").

---

[105] It is highly unlikely that only eighty percent of individuals who are wearing loose or baggy clothing are unarmed. Nevertheless, this training gave officers clear notice that even a person who is displaying some of the characteristics of an armed person is most likely to be unarmed. BPD officers also appear to be relying too heavily on only a single characteristic of an armed person, rather than a set of characteristics that, when combined, together indicate that a person is armed.

However, because the investigations of these incidents were so incomplete, as further explained below in section II(C)(5), it is difficult to determine based on the information provided in BPD's investigative files whether officers faced any immediate threat before firing. For example, in a 2013 case, four officers traveling in two unmarked vehicles pursued a suspect after they heard gunshots. The suspect allegedly raised a firearm while running, then ran through the yard of a residence, though the officers' statements regarding the suspect's actions are inconsistent. The officers parked their vehicles and gave chase on foot. At some point during the foot pursuit, the suspect may have tossed his gun (one witnessing officer stated in his interview that the suspect tossed his gun when he "jumped on" a bush before the officer heard the next gunshot) which struck the suspect. When asked whether the potential gun toss occurred before or after he was shot, he stated he had not seen the actual gun toss. Another officer found a gun near a bush several feet from where the suspect lay after being shot. The interviewers did not thoroughly examine whether the potential gun toss occurred before or after the officer shot at the suspect. The four officers involved in this case were interviewed for only 5, 8, 8, and 14, minutes. During these cursory interviews, the interviewers made no efforts to probe the basis for the officer's initial statement that the suspect had tossed his gun, and did not question the other officers about whether and when the potential gun toss occurred.

Officers should have policy guidance and training on when and how to safely engage in foot pursuits, given the frequency with which officers conduct them in Baltimore, and the risks involved for both officers and the public. It is critical that BPD provide officers with policy guidance on how to assess whether circumstances warrant engaging in a foot pursuit, and sufficient training on how to conduct these pursuits safely, without needlessly endangering themselves, suspects, and the public.

ii.   BPD's Discharges of Firearms at Moving Vehicles Are Highly Dangerous, Ineffective, and May Be Constitutionally Impermissible

BPD officers shot at moving vehicles in eight cases during the time period we reviewed. Shooting at a vehicle that is fleeing away from officers is unreasonable except in rare circumstances. *See Waterman v. Batton*, 393 F.3d at 482 ("[O]nce Waterman's vehicle passed the officers, the threat to their safety was eliminated and thus could not justify the subsequent shots."); *cf. Plumhoff v. Rickard*, 134 S. Ct. 2012, 2021 (2014) (finding officers' use of deadly force against fleeing suspect reasonable where suspect engaged in "outrageously reckless driving," leading officers on a chase that exceeded 100 miles per hour and passing more than two dozen vehicles, several of which were forced to alter course). In some of these cases, although the factual descriptions were incomplete, it appeared officers may have fired shots at individuals in moving vehicles as the vehicle was fleeing away from them. At that point, the vehicle itself no longer posed a serious threat to the officers, and if it posed a threat to others, shooting at it likely increased the threat, rather than eliminating it. *See* Police Exec. Research Forum, *Guiding Principles on Use of Force* 44 (Mar. 2016) ("Shooting at vehicles must be prohibited. . . . unless someone in the vehicle is using or threatening deadly force by means other than the vehicle itself."); IACP Nat'l Law Enforcement Pol. Ctr., *Use of Force Concepts & Issues Paper* 5 (Rev. Feb. 2006). The investigations of these incidents often left critical questions unanswered, however, making it difficult to determine whether the officers faced an immediate threat of serious harm before discharging their weapons. Nevertheless, supervisors and investigators generally approved officers' decisions to fire shots at moving vehicles.

Additionally, shooting at a moving vehicle is a highly dangerous tactic and an ineffective way to stop the vehicle. Using firearms against a moving vehicle often creates greater risks than it

– 96 –

eliminates. If a driver is shot while a vehicle is in motion, the vehicle itself may become out of control and a danger, to officers and innocent bystanders in its path, rather than coming to a stop. Further, a moving vehicle is a difficult target to shoot with accuracy; shots fired may miss the intended target and hit bystanders or passengers in the vehicle. Thus, shooting at a moving vehicle should be permissible in only extreme circumstances. Since 2006, the IACP's model policy on Use of Force has accounted for these risks, requiring:

> Firearms shall not be discharged at a moving vehicle unless a person in the vehicle is immediately threatening the officer or another person with deadly force by means other than the vehicle. The moving vehicle itself shall not presumptively constitute a threat that justifies an officer's use of deadly force. An officer threatened by an oncoming vehicle shall move out of its path instead of discharging a firearm at it or any of its occupants.

Two illustrative incidents identify some of our concerns with BPD's use of firearms on fleeing vehicles, although we make no finding on whether the force used in either of these incidents was unreasonable. In one 2013 incident, an investigation into a possible drug transaction ended with an officer firing seven shots at the front, side and rear of a vehicle as it drove away. One of three officers on the scene observed what he suspected was a drug transaction in progress in a car parked near a gas pump and signaled to the other two officers to investigate. One officer approached to the driver's side door of the vehicle and the other to the passenger side. The officer at the driver's side, reportedly fearing the driver was reaching for a weapon, opened the driver's side door and reached inside while the car was still running; he does not appear to have ordered the driver to turn the engine off. Rather than reaching for a weapon, the driver had put the car into drive. With the officer's torso inside the vehicle, the driver hit the gas and the car sped forward. The officer, becoming caught halfway into the car, was dragged by the car. He reached for his weapon and fired one shot toward the driver of the car, missing both the driver and the officer standing on the other side of the vehicle. The officer's gunshot reportedly caused the driver to jerk the car, dislodging the officer from the car. The vehicle turned to exit the parking lot, driving towards the third officer who had observed the incident. According to BPD's documents, the third officer stepped out of the way of the oncoming vehicle and then fired seven rounds, two of which hit the front windshield, and five of which hit the right side passenger windows, and rear passenger door, shattering the rear windshield and hitting the rear roof of the car. The officer admitted—during a brief, 15 minute interview BPD investigators conducted 258 days after the incident—that he shot at the vehicle as it was fleeing away from him. It appeared he shot at the vehicle, which had fled the wrong way down a one-way street, to disable it, though BPD officers conducting his interview did not clarify this point. BPD determined all force in this incident to be reasonable.

In another incident from 2013, two officers were on foot, directing traffic near a crowded nightclub. A civilian car traveling the wrong direction struck the two officers from behind, knocking them to the pavement. The car then started to leave the scene. One of the two officers fired eight shots at the vehicle as it was fleeing away from him. In this case, investigators determined the discharges to be inappropriate. In our review, we observed additional incidents of firearms discharges at moving vehicles which, even if they were not unreasonable, endangered members of the public.

The disparate treatment of the officers in these two incidents may have resulted from the lack of clear policy guidance on when officers might be justified in shooting at moving vehicles. The

Department's 2001 "Use of Deadly Force Guidelines" instruct officers that they "may not shoot at vehicles moving away from them unless the vehicle turns around and attempts to injure them or someone else and adequate cover is not available." However, Guidelines function differently from policies—they are not binding on officers. The prohibition on shooting at vehicles moving away from officers was not made clear in policy until May 2016. The Department now prohibits shooting at moving vehicles unless confronted with a deadly threat, other than the vehicle itself. This new policy prohibiting shooting at moving vehicles, regardless of whether they are fleeing, is a positive step forward.

5.   **BPD's Deficient Policies, Training, Crisis Intervention Program, and Lack of Oversight Underlie The Pattern Or Practice Of Excessive Force and Violations of the Americans With Disabilities Act**

BPD's deficient policies, training, crisis intervention program, and failures in oversight over force incidents underlie the pattern or practice of unconstitutional force we observed. It is the Department's responsibility to articulate policies that provide sufficient guidance, both in quality and content, to officers on when and how it is appropriate and lawful to use force against members of the public. BPD's policies fail to provide this guidance. It is also the Department's responsibility to train officers to ensure they understand how the Department's policies are to be operationalized, and to provide officers with skills they need to safely and constitutionally resolve the broad spectrum of incidents they encounter on the street while minimizing the need to resort to force. The Department has failed to provide such training. The Department is likewise charged with investigating incidents of force to ensure they comply with its policies and the law, and where they do not, remedying officers' conduct through retraining and discipline, as appropriate. The Department has failed to exercise proper oversight over incidents of force and address deficiencies when they occurred, allowing officers to continue using unreasonable force and unsafe tactics. In addition, BPD fails to adequately prepare officers for their interactions with individuals with disabilities or in crisis, and to partner effectively with other social service providers in these incidents. Thus, the responsibility for the pattern or practice of unconstitutional force we observed lies with the Department as an agency.

a.   **BPD's Deficient Policies Have Contributed To and Permitted BPD's Pattern or Practice of Excessive Force**

Deficiencies in BPD's policies regarding the use, reporting, and investigation of force have contributed to officers' systemic use of excessive force. Overall, BPD's policies regarding when and how to use force: (1) are missing critical elements; (2) are scattered across multiple documents, making it difficult for officers to synthesize their guidance; (3) included elements that were not enforced; and (4) are sometimes inaccessible to some officers. These policies fail to provide officers with clear and consistent guidance that officers need to safely and constitutionally conduct their law enforcement activities. BPD issued revisions to its policies governing officers' uses of force on July 1, 2016. The policies appear to have improved in some respects and the Department is to be commended for its initiative and efforts. However, the recent updates may require additional amendments to correct the patterns or practices of unconstitutional force our investigation uncovered.

BPD's policies on use of force, and on use of specific weapons were, until very recently, missing critical elements. BPD implemented its first policy governing officers' use of batons in

2016. The Department's first policy governing the use of oleoresin capsicum, or "OC" spray was implemented in 2015. Despite the previous lack of policy guidance on the use of these weapons, the Department had issued these weapons to its officers for decades. It is a fundamental responsibility of the Department to provide controlling guidance to officers regarding when they are permitted to use the weapons the Department has supplied them. Previously, officers' use of these weapons was governed only by "Training Guidelines," but these training guidelines did not establish clear standards for officer conduct.

While the Department implemented a policy on Electronically Conducted Weapons, or tasers, in 2007, this policy failed to provide officers with necessary guidance on when it would be appropriate to use a taser. Training Guidelines regarding tasers, which were issued in 2010, similarly failed to provide any restrictions on officers' use of these weapons. Instead, both the policy and Guidelines simply provided officers with descriptions of the various modes that the weapon may be used in, without providing proper limitations on those uses. Neither the policy nor the training guidelines were updated when the Department of Justice's Office of Community Oriented Policing Services, in conjunction with the Police Executive Research Forum, released ECW Guidelines in March 2011, which recommended restrictions such as not using a taser more than three times on a particular individual.

Importantly, until its 2016 policy update, BPD did not require a number of types of force by BPD officers to be reported. This included takedowns, punches, control holds and pain compliance techniques, unless a subject complained of pain, or injury resulted. Our review of BPD's reports suggests that, in practice, force involving an officer's hands was generally only reported if the subject sustained injuries requiring medical attention. Our review of BPD's force cases, interviews with community members in Baltimore, as well as interviews with officers, demonstrated that a significant volume of force by BPD officers involves officers using their hands against individuals in close encounters—types of force that BPD did not require officers to report until very recently. Force that is not documented cannot be managed or monitored. In our interviews with community members, many members of the public described experiences in which officers used force such as takedowns and control techniques without sufficient justification. These incidents have led to the deep frustration that some members of the public feel towards BPD.

Until July 2016, BPD policies on force failed to encourage any de-escalation strategies. It is critical that officers be provided guidance not only on when and how force may be used, but also that they be encouraged to use tactics that minimize the need for force. Using force against members of the public is not only an intrusion to the subject of force, it also creates risks for officers entangled in these encounters by heightening tensions and creating situations in which officers may also, in turn, be injured. BPD's new policies have taken some steps to incorporate de-escalation principles, but significant work remains to ensure that de-escalation strategies are understood and utilized throughout the Department. Additionally, although BPD implemented a policy governing contacts with youth in June 2015, the policy fails to provide any guidance on the unique qualities of youth behavior and development or prescribe specific techniques for officers' approach and interactions with youth.

Second, in addition to missing critical elements, BPD's guidance on when and how to use force, as well as to report, investigate, and review uses of force is scattered throughout many policies, training guidelines, and their various updates. For example, the rules governing officers' uses of their service weapons are contained in at least four separate policies and a "Training

Guideline" on the use of deadly force, rather than a single, cohesive policy. Additionally, when the Department updates a policy, each update is written in a new and separate document. One policy can have many updates, and thus officers are expected to keep track of many different documents simply to understand a single policy. To understand all of the applicable policies governing force, officers must be aware of and synthesize dozens of documents. There is no cohesive, comprehensive guidance for officers that is digestible and workable. Having this critical guidance scattered throughout dozens of disparate documents makes it difficult to understand and operationalize what guidance the Department does provide its officers about use of force. In interviews, officers expressed concern that policies were simply implemented and distributed without sufficient guidance regarding the meaning of provisions. A number of officers we spoke with expressed confusion about the contents of recently updated policies, including the Department's new use of force policy.

Third, until recently, officers had insufficient access to Departmental policies. Officers received a policy manual in the Academy upon joining the Department, but later updates to policies were not distributed in a manner that ensured officers received and reviewed the updated policy. Officers receive policy updates through their email, which many officers do not frequently check or have access to because Department computers in the precincts are old, outdated, and frequently break down. Officers were not required to sign off on whether they had received policy updates and the Department had no tracking mechanisms in place to ensure that all officers had received, much less understood, policy updates. To its credit, the Department has realized that this is a significant problem, and has purchased a new software application to track the distribution of new and updated policies and proficiency testing of officers on the new or updated policies, but that application had not yet been rolled out by June 2016.

Finally, the Department does not uniformly and consistently enforce its policies. For example, a 1999 policy on reviewing and investigating firearm discharges that was in effect until 2012 included a requirement that each discharge be reviewed by an "ad hoc board" consisting of a number of chiefs and other personnel appointed by the Commissioner. To our knowledge, based on the documents we reviewed, such a review board was never constituted under this policy during the period of our review. Instead, under former Commissioner Batts, a new policy regarding a Use of Force Review Board was implemented in 2014, under which a number of reviews were conducted. As we describe in more detail in Section III(A) below, the Department's failure to consistently enforce its policies has contributed to the pattern or practice of excessive force that we found.

These deficiencies in policy guidance, organization, distribution, and enforcement contribute to the pattern or practice of unconstitutional force we observed.

b. BPD's Training On Force Is Severely Lacking, Leading To Officers' Systemic Constitutional Violations

BPD officers are trained in the Academy when they initially join the Department, and then through mandatory annual in-service training. Training at both levels—at the Academy and through in-service—is lacking. As described in more detail in Section III(A)(1) below, BPD's training generally fails to provide officers with sufficient instruction on how to operationalize policies. It lacks the integrated, scenario-based training that equips officers with the tactical skills necessary to conduct law enforcement activities in a safe and constitutional manner, including strategies that decrease the need for force.

BPD's Defensive Tactics training teaches officers an erroneous legal standard for excessive force. It separates excessive force into (1) "perceived" excessive force; (2) "intentional" excessive force; and (3) "unintentional" excessive force. This separation between "perceived," "intentional" and "unintentional" excessive force has no place under well-established Fourth Amendment standards governing excessive force. An officer's subjective intent is irrelevant for Fourth Amendment purposes. *Graham*, 490 U.S. 386, 397 (1989) ("the reasonableness inquiry in an excessive force case is an objective one: the question is whether the officers' actions are objectively reasonable in light of the facts and circumstances confronting them, without regard to their underlying intent or motivation") (internal quotations and citations omitted). Indeed, the Supreme Court explicitly rejected the notion that excessive force required intent or malice decades ago, declaring that "[a]n officer's evil intentions will not make a Fourth Amendment violation out of an objectively reasonable use of force; nor will an officer's good intentions make an objectively unreasonable use of force constitutional." *Id.* According to BPD's Defensive Tactics training, the "appropriate" consequence for "unintentional" excessive force, a category of force that does not exist in the legal landscape, is "remedial training"—no other consequence is identified. This training is a disservice to officers, because it is inconsistent with how courts will consider their use of force. The category of "perceived" excessive force is also problematic because it appears to discredit the complainant—whether the complainant is another officer or a community member.

BPD's training on "Characteristics of an Armed Person" also appears to be ineffective. While instructors teach students that eighty percent of individuals who show characteristics of an armed person—such as wearing loose or baggy clothing, or grabbing their waistbands while running—will *not* be armed, this issue of false positives does not appear to be taught in an effective manner. No scenarios involving false positives are employed in the training that would allow officers to internalize and retain this lesson. Additionally, it is critical to learn how to safely and constitutionally approach and investigate an individual who may be armed. In a training on the same subject, sponsored by the Department of Justice and the IACP and held at BPD's training center for law enforcement agencies throughout the region, the instructor spent a significant amount of time refreshing students' knowledge of Fourth Amendment law and principles. In that training, the instructor repeatedly reinforced throughout the course that a person who displays one of these characteristics is not necessarily armed; each characteristic should be one factor in an officer's analysis. It does not appear that BPD's own training on "Characteristics of an Armed Person" provides officers with such critical guidance.

Additionally, until recently, BPD had no comprehensive training on de-escalation strategies to guide officers on how to resolve incidents without resorting to force. It created a short course on de-escalation in 2015, a positive step forward. However, given the novelty of de-escalation tactics within BPD's curriculum, it is important that leadership within the Department make clear to officers that this skill-set is critical to keeping officers, as well as community members, safe. The Department must ensure that de-escalation is sufficiently emphasized and integrated into all of its courses involving force such that officers understand it is a critical tool for resolving incidents.

Similarly, officers have been provided with little to no training on tactics and techniques for interacting with youth, including on how to engage with juvenile witnesses or victims. Because their developmental state affects the manner in which adolescents comprehend, communicate, and behave, BPD officers must be trained on these unique realities and equipped with skills and techniques to account for them when interacting with youth.

The Department provided a brief training, running from May through June of 2016 for officers on its new use of force policy and 26 other policies the Department reviewed and updated. We were able to attend one of the first sessions of the training and hear from consultants about a later session. Our observations based on the first session we attended gave us serious initial concerns about the adequacy of the training, but it appears the training substantially improved with time. We applaud the Department's desire to issue new guidance and training to its officers, but we have some concerns about the adequacy of the training being provided, given the ambitious scope of what the Department intends to cover. It is clear to us, however, that the Department is committed to improving the guidance it provides to officers on use of force, and we look forward to working with the Department to make sure it is successful in its efforts.

c. BPD's Lack of Oversight Of Officers' Uses of Force Has Contributed to the Pattern of Excessive Force

As a whole, BPD fails to exercise oversight of its officers' uses of force. Of the 2,818 force incidents that BPD recorded in the nearly six-year period we reviewed, BPD investigated only ten incidents for excessive force based on concerns identified through its internal review. Of these ten incidents, it found only one use of force to be excessive. During the same period, twenty-five officers were sued four or more times in cases alleging violations relating to use of force, stops, searches, arrests, or discriminatory policing. The few incidents that the Department internally noted as problematic are also striking considering the many incidents we determined to be unconstitutional.

Like that of many departments, BPD policy sets out different investigative requirements for different levels of force that officers use. BPD officers' use of force is investigated through one of two routes. First, for most incidents of force other than shootings, officers notify their supervising sergeant after using force. The sergeant travels to the site where force was used, and conducts an investigation at the scene. The chain of command then reviews the sergeant's investigation and either returns it for further investigation or makes a decision on whether the officer's force was reasonable. The process for these investigations is outlined in a policy that has been in place since 2003; it remained in place until July 2016. Until November 2014, all uses of force other than shootings were to be investigated in this manner by an officer's chain of command. For ease of reference, we refer to these as "chain of command investigations."

In these chain of command investigations, if BPD investigators or reviewers believed that a use of force may have been unreasonable or out of policy, in order to investigate that concern, a supervisor in the chain of command would have to file an internal complaint of excessive force with Internal Affairs. Internal Affairs would then also separately investigate the complaint through its processes. We found that, in practice, internal complaints were exceedingly rare—the data we reviewed indicated only ten such complaints had been made during the period of our review. Indeed, one sergeant we spoke with about his force investigations of officers under his command indicated that he would not feel comfortable filing a complaint with Internal Affairs if he suspected an officer under his supervision had used unnecessary or unreasonable force. Instead, he would call his chain of command and inform them of the situation, leaving it to them to make the decision of whether to file a complaint about the officer for Internal Affairs to investigate.

The second route that an administrative investigation of force may take is reserved for officers' use of deadly force. The process for investigating these deadly force cases changed a number of times during the period of force incidents we reviewed. From the beginning of our period of review, in 2010 until early 2014, this second route was reserved for officer-involved shootings, which were investigated by officers in BPD's Homicide Unit. In January 2014, BPD instituted a specialized "Force Investigation Team" (FIT) to investigate shootings and other uses of force that have "the potential to cause serious physical injury or death." The FIT functioned only until July 31, 2015, when it was replaced as an interim measure by the Homicide unit in 2015, and then by a Special Investigation Response Team (SIRT) in September of 2015. The SIRT has the same jurisdiction as the former FIT and currently investigates shootings as well as other serious use of force cases. For ease of reference, we refer to these as "deadly force investigations."

Based on our review of BPD's force investigations and our interviews with BPD officers and sergeants, it appears that the chain of command fails to thoroughly and objectively evaluate officers' uses of force. BPD's investigative files of force incidents are missing critical elements necessary to allow the chain of command to understand and adjudicate the force incidents. This is perhaps unsurprising, because, until this year, BPD provided no training whatsoever for sergeants on how to investigate their officers' uses of force, or for lieutenants, captains or majors, regarding their responsibilities and obligations in reviewing force investigations. Similarly, BPD also fails to thoroughly and objectively investigate officers' uses of deadly force. BPD's deadly force investigations likewise lack critical information necessary to evaluate the force used and reflect bias on the part of investigators. These investigations are also subject to unreasonable delays, to the detriment of both officers and the community.

i. BPD's Investigations of Less-Lethal Force Cases are Missing Critical Elements that are Necessary to Evaluate the Propriety of the Force Used

In BPD's chain of command investigations, critical information that is necessary to investigate force incidents is routinely missing. Investigators routinely fail to interview any civilian witnesses, witnessing officers, the involved officer, and the person against whom force was used. In many cases, there are no witnesses—civilian or officer— interviewed even though witnesses were present on the scene. For example, in one 2014 narcotics arrest at a public housing complex during which a taser was deployed, there were reportedly 20 to 30 civilian witnesses gathered at the site of the arrest, and the officer felt it necessary to call in additional units for backup to deal with the crowd. However, the force report did not include a single civilian witness statement. Although the report states that "[t]here were no civilian witness[es] who wished to provide a statement," there is no indication of the efforts the officers made in attempting to obtain statements from witnesses.

From our interviews, it appears that some people may refuse to speak with officers because of the distrust they have of the police. While BPD's policy on use of force reporting requires that "notations of a neighborhood canvass for witnesses must be included," many other reports we reviewed did not include such a notation. Even in the instances where it appeared an investigator spoke with a civilian who had witnessed the incident, investigators did not record the civilian's statement or provide the civilian's account in their own words. Instead, the investigator summarized the civilian's statement for the investigative file. If the investigator misses relevant information, or misunderstands a civilian's statement in any way, or if the investigator biases the civilian's statement in any way—whether intentionally or not—this cannot be remedied by the chain of command's review.

We also found that, in cases where a civilian's account appeared to be inconsistent with information provided by an officer, investigators appeared to summarily dismiss the civilian's account or credit officers' accounts over civilians' without sufficient investigation. For example, in a 2014 incident, a sergeant responded as back-up to assist two plainclothes officers with an arrest for CDS possession. He observed them "engaged in an ongoing struggle in the street" when he arrived on the scene. Even though the sergeant was on the scene in a supervisory role when the use of force was taking place, he also investigated the officers' force. When attempting to locate witnesses, he reported "several citizens in the block" stated, "They didn't have to beat him like that," "Another case of police brutality," "They picked that man up and dumped him on his head," and "Somebody has it on video. It will be on youtube tomorrow," though he was unable to gain contact information for the person with video. Shortly after the incident, a woman formally complained to the Department about the incident, and the same sergeant responded to address her complaint. Despite these statements from witnesses, the sergeant dismissed the five complaints of the force used and determined "[b]ased on the facts of this incident, witness interviews, and reviews of CCTV footage" that the officers had used appropriate force.[106] In addition to our concerns about how the different witness and officer accounts were reconciled in this investigation, this is one of a number of cases we saw where sergeants who were involved in an incident where force was used investigated that incident. The sergeant's supervision of the use of force undermines the integrity of his investigation of the force as well as the individuals' complaints of the incident—he lacked the independence and objectivity to investigate either the force or the complaints.

Officers' statements, when they were provided, were only in written form, often lacked details of the force used and why it was necessary, and used vague and boilerplate language, preventing reviewers from understanding the nature of the threat that officers faced and the nature of the force that officers used. Often, the only documented basis for using force was that the subjects were "resisting," with no detail about which actions taken by the suspect while he or she "resisted" necessitated force by the officer. Descriptions of the force itself were likewise often vague. In some cases where a taser was used, officers reported they used the taser on an individual "a few" or "several" times or until he or she "complied" or "became subdued," rather than specifying the number of times that they deployed their taser. The specific number of times that a taser is deployed is critical to assessing the reasonableness of its use under the circumstances and must be reported. Similarly, in almost all instances in which officers employed a takedown technique, the officers did not specify the type of technique used, such as a straight arm bar, joint manipulation, or pressure points. Without knowing the specific actions that officers took, it is difficult to evaluate whether they acted reasonably under the circumstances. For example, during a 2010 incident, three plainclothes officers approached two men, who they believed were involved in distributing narcotics, to arrest them. Reportedly, as the officers approached, one of the two men punched one of the officers and ran. Two of the officers gave chase. When they caught up with the individual, the involved officers reported that the individual began to "violently resist" and "during the struggle," was reportedly "tackled to the ground several times," during the course of which the suspect "struck his head against a fence." According to the investigating sergeant's report, the

---

[106] The sergeant requested video from "Citiwatch," but the video was "on pan mode during the entire incident." He reported that the parts which "capture the incident are grainy, but gave no indication that unnecessary force was used." The video was not produced to us with the investigative file.

suspect suffered head injuries in this altercation requiring 37 staples. It is difficult to assess whether the officers' force here was reasonable without more information about how the suspect resisted the officers and what techniques the officers used on the suspect that caused a head injury requiring 37 staples. The suspect in this case was not interviewed, depriving BPD of critical information to assess the incident. In their review of this incident, the chain of command approved the force without asking for any additional information, despite the vagueness of the officers' accounts. This was the case in many of the incidents we reviewed.

Officers' written statements, when any were provided, were also often nearly identical—facially lacking in independence. The officers' accounts appeared to have been copied after they agreed upon a single account of the incident. Indeed, because of this, officers' accounts sometimes referred to themselves in the third person because the account had been electronically copied into the force report. We also found that the language investigators used in their reports indicated a lack of objectivity, such as a description that officers "were forced to use" a taser, baton, OC spray, or other weapon. This language does more than simply state the facts, and indicates bias in favor of the involved officers.

We also found that inconsistencies between officers' statements were not routinely reconciled or addressed. In one incident, in which a sergeant pointed out inconsistencies between officers' accounts, it appears the chain of command took issue with the sergeant's investigation and report that highlighted the inconsistencies. In a 2011 incident, an investigating sergeant, to his credit, explicitly reported that two officers' "versions of events differ[ed]" regarding whether a juvenile was sprayed with OC spray before or after he was handcuffed—a significant fact that could affect the reasonableness of the force used, and whether it had been in or out of policy. *See Tracy v. Freshwater*, 623 F.3d 90, 98–99 (2d Cir. 2010) (jury could find officer's application of pepper spray to be unreasonable where plaintiff claimed he was handcuffed and not resisting); *Henderson v. Munn*, 439 F.3d 497, 502–03 (8th Cir. 2006) (officer not entitled to qualified immunity at summary judgment where jury could find that he had applied pepper spray to non-resisting plaintiff's face while plaintiff was lying on his stomach and handcuffed with his hands behind his back); *Vinyard v. Wilson*, 311 F.3d 1340, 1347–49 (11th Cir. 2002) (officer not entitled to summary judgment where he had pulled over and applied pepper spray while arrestee was yelling and arrestee had been arrested for minor offenses, was handcuffed and secured in backseat of police car, posed no threat to the officer or herself, and there was a partition separating her from the officer). According to the sergeant's report, when he realized that the officers' reports varied on this point, he called them both into his office to "question them, about what had happened." The witnessing officer stated that "his administrative report was correct" and submitted it. The officer who used OC spray "with-drew his administrative report, stating he was getting worried about how this investigation was progressing and stated that he wanted to talk to the FOP prior to submitting his administrative report." The sergeant reported these facts—that the officers reported inconsistently about whether force was used on a handcuffed person, and that the involved officer withdrew his report—to his chain of command. He submitted his investigation for approval. A lieutenant colonel responded, "NOT APPROVED; RETURNED FOR CORRECTIONS," and stated, "YOU NEED TO SEE ME IMMEDIATELY REGARDING THIS SUMMARY!" There is no documentation of the conversation between the sergeant and the lieutenant colonel. In the final report produced to us, the second page of the witnessing officer's report is missing; the document specifically notes that it is two pages long, yet only the first page is provided. The first page of the witnessing officer's report simply states the facts about the beginning of the incident and provides no information about the force that was used and whether it was used after the juvenile was handcuffed. Ultimately, it appears the sergeant identified an inconsistency in this case, and the chain of command not only refused to address it, but may have attempted to cover up the report that identified potentially problematic officer conduct.

Witnesses' accounts, both officers' and civilians', are important not only for determining whether an officer's use of force was within policy, but also in assessing whether the officer's tactics were appropriate, and whether there are any issues on which the officer would benefit from additional training, mentoring, or guidance. The lack of specifics in these statements prevents supervisors from improving officers' performance and preventing future misconduct. One sergeant informed us during an interview that judging an officer's tactics is simply not part of a use of force investigation; he did not deem it to be his job to "second-guess" an officer's tactics. This is a failure in supervision—it is a sergeant's job to mentor officers in areas where they may benefit from additional guidance. The sergeant's statement here reflects a lack of understanding of the role of a supervisor, and indicates a Departmental failure to train sergeants on how to be effective supervisors.

Our investigation also found that critical evidence was often missing from the chain of command force investigations. We did not see a single chain of command investigation in which photographs of the subject's injuries were provided. These photographs are taken by Crime Lab technicians, but, as a matter of protocol, they are not kept with the investigative file. Among the over eight hundred chain of command investigative files we reviewed, we did not see any indication that a lieutenant or major had requested to see photographs of the subject's injuries in any case. Similarly, taser downloads verifying the number of times that officers deployed their tasers were not included in investigative files, thereby preventing the chain of command from confirming the accuracy of officers' reports. These deficiencies in chain of command investigations prevent supervisors from being able to exercise real oversight over officers' uses of force. Without details of incidents provided by civilian witnesses, involved and witnessing officers, and evidence such as taser downloads or photographs of injuries, officers' use of force cannot be critically examined.

Finally, we found evidence that serious incidents involving use of force by officers went entirely unreported. Indeed, because it was not required to be reported by policy, much of the force used by officers with their hands was not reported, even when it—and not the force reported—was the source of injuries to officers. In the 2011 incident involving a juvenile above at page 105, for example, the sergeant reported that the officers "fought" with the juvenile. The involved officer was transported to a hospital and treated for abrasions and bruises to his knee. His knee injuries were severe enough that he was unable to work for a number of days. However, the use of force report was created to report on the officers' use of OC spray. An injury report alleges the juvenile kicked the officer in the knee but the use of force report does not provide any specific information about the fight between the officers and the juvenile that caused the officer's injury, other than that the youth was making threatening statements, and "kicking" and being "combative" while officers were attempting to handcuff him. It does not include any details about the officers' use of their hands during the fight. These failures in exercising oversight of officers' use of force are attributable in part to BPD's prior deficient policy on reporting use of force. The policy on reporting use of force, through multiple provisions, allowed investigators and reviewers to ignore allegations of excessive force. It stated that "[w]hen allegations of excessive force arise[]," investigating sergeants were to inform the complainants of the "the reporting requirements for complaints of excessive force" and provide the complainants with the telephone number and address of the Internal Affairs Division. The policy did not require an investigating sergeant to address the complaint him- or her-self in any way or to ensure that Internal Affairs was notified of the complaint. These policy failures allowed significant force, and allegations of excessive force, to go entirely uninvestigated.

ii. BPD's Deadly Force Investigations Lack Critical Analysis and Information that is Necessary to Evaluate the Threat Faced and Force Used

Like its chain of command investigations, BPD's investigations of officers' use of deadly force, including officer-involved shootings, lack critical information needed to evaluate the propriety of the force, reflect a bias in favor of involved officers, and include unreasonable delays. This is concerning, as "[t]he intrusiveness of a seizure by means of deadly force is unmatched. The suspect's fundamental interest in his own life need not be elaborated upon. The use of deadly force also frustrates the interest of the individual, and of society, in judicial determination of guilt and punishment." *Garner*, 471 U.S. at 9. Officers' uses of deadly force must be critically examined to ensure that they conform with the Department's policies and law. Even when the use of deadly force is justified, much can be learned by critically examining incidents to improve tactics and lessen the need to use such force.

In our investigation, we requested investigative files for all deadly force incidents, including all officer-involved shootings, between January 1, 2010 and May 1, 2016. Troublingly, BPD informed us that they could not locate the investigative files for twenty officer-involved shootings that occurred in that timeframe, and could provide no explanation for their absence. These included lethal shootings of members of the public, including one lethal shooting, as well as firearms discharges against animals and unintentional discharges. Failing to maintain files of such high risk incidents is a serious omission, inhibiting effective oversight and eroding public confidence that BPD takes seriously its responsibility to oversee its own use of force.

Our review of BPD deadly force investigations revealed many of the same problems that were present in the chain of command investigations. Transcripts of interviews were routinely excluded, and it appears that they were not created in many cases. Inconsistencies between witness accounts, officer statements, and physical evidence were frequently not investigated. Moreover, documents and evidence that one would expect to see in an administrative investigation of an officer-involved shooting, such as crime scene logs, photographs of the subject or the scene, and crime lab reports, were frequently missing from the investigative files we reviewed. As in the chain of command investigations, we saw evidence that involved officers conferred with other involved and witnessing officers about the incident before speaking with investigators. Investigators also failed to question officers about their conduct before the shooting, to ascertain—even if the shooting was lawful—what tactical, training or other issues could be identified.

We also found that significant delays in BPD's deadly force investigations diminished the integrity of the investigations. As a matter of practice, BPD investigators do not interview officers who discharge their weapons until after the State's Attorney's Office issues a letter declining to prosecute the officer for any potential criminal act. Often, the State's Attorney's Office takes many months, and in a number of cases, over a year, to determine whether to prosecute, and, if not, to issue a declination letter. In one extreme case, for a shooting that occurred on August 29, 2010, the State's Attorney's Office did not issue a declination letter until October 16, 2012, over two years later. Many law enforcement agencies conduct parallel administrative investigations of officer-involved shootings, understanding that precautions can be taken to ensure that the officer's statements are segregated and do not taint any potential criminal investigation. BPD does not conduct such parallel investigations.

We also found significant differences between BPD's practices when interviewing witnesses and its practices when interviewing officers that suggest a bias in favor of the officer. For example, when interviews of the officers finally did occur, they were conclusory and superficial, often lasting no longer than ten or fifteen minutes, with some ending after five minutes. Officers were generally not asked any critical questions about the threat they faced or their decision-making process leading up to their deadly force. For example, in a lethal 2013 shooting, the Internal Affairs detective's interview of the shooting officer lasted only five minutes, which included form questions about the nature of the interview which were not particular to the facts of that case. The actual substantive interview of the officer lasted three minutes. BPD's interviews of civilian witnesses, on the other hand, often last hours, and the investigators ask specific, probing questions, demonstrating their ability to be thorough and exacting. We also found that BPD has a practice of conducting "pre-interviews" with officers before turning on the recording device; at times, investigators stated that they had done a "pre-interview" on the record. For example, in another 2013 officer-involved shooting, an investigator from Internal Affairs stated, "Sir, please just as we did before we went on the tape, just tell us what happen [sic]." The officer then provided a canned and prepared presentation about a shooting, summarizing the incident, from beginning to end. The entire interview, on tape, lasts only eight minutes. Pre-interviews impede the integrity of the investigation. Because of this, pre-interviews in investigations of officer-involved shootings have been discouraged since the at least the early 1990s. *See, e.g.*, JAMES G. KOLTS & STAFF, THE LOS ANGELES COUNTY SHERIFF'S DEPARTMENT 140 (1992), available at http://www.clearinghouse.net/chDocs/public/PN-CA-0001-0023.pdf.

These investigative deficiencies prevent BPD from being able to evaluate whether officers who used deadly force faced an immediate threat of serious harm, and whether their force was justified. Moreover, by failing to critically evaluate officers' tactics and decision-making prior to their use of deadly force, including opportunities to de-escalate, the Department fails to help officers improve their skills and potentially decrease the need to resort to deadly force. To effectively oversee its use of force, BPD must take steps to remedy these deficiencies.

d. BPD Has Inadequate Policies, Programs, and Training to Guide Officer Interactions with Individuals with Disabilities or in Crisis, and Fails to Coordinate Adequately with Other Social Services Providers

BPD's inadequate policies, training, and programs regarding officer interactions with individuals with a disability or in crisis also contribute to the systemic use of excessive force in violation of the Fourth Amendment and the failure to provide reasonable modifications necessary to avoid discrimination in violation of the Americans with Disabilities Act. The vast majority of individuals with mental health disabilities, including substance use disorders, or intellectual or developmental disabilities (I/DD) in Baltimore are working, learning, and living in the community and will live their lives without any involvement with BPD. Some individuals with disabilities, however, who are not able to access sufficient home- and community-based services to meet their needs may be unable to avoid crisis, maintain housing and employment or, for youth, to engage with school, leading some to come into contact with law enforcement. According to a 2009 Baltimore

City Community Health Survey, 23 percent of residents reported having unmet mental health needs.[107] The rate was notably higher for black residents (33.4 percent) and for all individuals with less than a bachelor's degree in education (28.6 percent).[108] This disparity was reflected again in a 2011 Maryland Behavioral Risk Factor Surveillance System study, which found that 19.5 percent of black residents and 15.1 percent of white residents reported that their mental health was "not good" for eight or more out of the past 30 days.[109] Law enforcement officers are often the first responders when people with mental health disabilities are experiencing a crisis, and the same is true in Baltimore.[110] It is therefore incumbent upon BPD to provide clear guidance to its officers on how to interact with individuals in crisis, but that guidance is lacking.

i.   BPD's Crisis Intervention Practices Are Inadequate

BPD's crisis intervention policies and procedures are inadequate to safely and lawfully serve individuals in crisis. Based upon our investigation, including our review of use of force files, reports, and training materials, as well as interviews with BPD employees, community members, and service providers, it is clear that BPD officers are not prepared to effectively and safely respond to individuals experiencing crisis. Consequently, BPD officers frequently resort to unreasonable force against individuals in crisis and fail to make reasonable modifications necessary to avoid discriminating against people with disabilities.

BPD itself recognized the challenges that police officers face when responding to individuals in crisis. But the program it launched in 2004, called Behavioral Emergency Services Team (BEST) has proven to be ineffective.[111] First, since 2009, BEST training has been offered only to new recruits in the training academy. Crisis calls are among BPD's most challenging calls for service, and officers early in their careers are typically not well prepared to handle these complex incidents while also adjusting to their many new duties as a police officer. An effective crisis intervention response program would provide at least a basic level of crisis intervention training to all officers, including new officers in the academy, but it would also ensure that at least some of its more experienced officers had received a high level of crisis intervention training. These experienced, highly-trained officers are the ones well positioned to handle the complex situations that interactions with individuals in crisis present. Because BPD only offers crisis intervention training to new recruits, many officers are not trained to identify whether an individual is in crisis or engaging in behavior related to a disability, to interact effectively with people with disabilities, to de-escalate a crisis, and to connect the individual with local resources to provide treatment or support. BPD should regularly provide in-service training to refresh the lessons recruits learned in the academy once they have experience in patrol. Our investigation revealed that insufficiently trained BPD officers have

---

[107] *See* BALTIMORE CITY HEALTH DEP'T, HEALTHY BALTIMORE 2015, at 11 (2015), http://health.baltimorecity.gov/sites/default/files/HealthyBaltimore2015_Final_Web.pdf.

[108] *Id.*

[109] *See* BALTIMORE CITY HEALTH DEP'T, HEALTHY BALTIMORE 2015: INTERIM STATUS REPORT 28(2013) available at http://health.baltimorecity.gov/sites/default/files/HB2015InterimUpdateOct2015Optimized_2.pdf.

[110] *See, e.g.*, Law Enforcement and Mental Health, NAT'L ALL. ON MENTAL ILLNESS, https://www.nami.org/Get-Involved/Law-Enforcement-and-Mental-Health (last visited May 25, 2016) ("With our failing mental health system so inadequate, law enforcement agencies have increasingly become *de facto* first responders to people experiencing mental health crisis.").

[111] The BEST program has trained over 800 officers since its inception. During the first five years of the project, it trained an average of 70 officers each year. Since 2009, the training numbers average 136 officers per year.

escalated interactions that did not initially involve criminal behavior, resulting in the arrest of, or use of force against, individuals in crisis, or with mental health disabilities or I/DD, or unnecessary hospitalization of the person with mental health disabilities or I/DD.[112] When BPD officers have discretion about whether to make an arrest, agency policies and procedures should direct them to consider whether it would be appropriate to decline to arrest or issue a citation, and instead connect individuals to community-based services without further criminal justice involvement.

Second, dispatchers do not receive training on BPD's BEST program and BPD has no mechanisms in place to ensure that BEST-trained officers are dispatched to crisis-related calls for service. Nor does the Department collect data on whether and how often BEST-trained officers respond to calls involving individuals in crisis. Moreover, other officers and community members do not know to request a BEST-trained officer when a crisis does occur. During an interview on crisis intervention, for example, one district commander bluntly stated "We don't do that here." Similarly, many Baltimore City mental health service providers indicated they were unaware of the program or had only a limited familiarity with the concept of BEST training, and an even smaller number stated that they request BEST-trained officers to respond to individuals in crisis.

Third, BPD policy does not require that a BEST-trained officer be dispatched to calls involving individuals in crisis. In fact, the only BPD policy we found that specifically addresses individuals in crisis is an order describing the process for executing a petition for an emergency evaluation. And until BPD amended the policy in July 2015, it failed to provide any guidance to officers on how to identify and interact with an individual in crisis or mention utilizing BEST-trained officers. Indeed, this policy is both underdeveloped and unnecessarily restrictive. The policy suggests that de-escalation techniques and BEST-trained officers are only needed in situations where someone is going to be taken to the hospital for an emergency petition evaluation. It is unsurprising, therefore, that many BPD officers see detention for an emergency petition, arrest, or inaction as their only options when responding to a crisis situation.

Officers in the field also stated that it is not a common practice to seek out BEST-trained officers for assistance with crisis calls. Similarly, during our review of force reports, there was no indication that BPD officers rely on BEST-trained officers to help them respond to crisis calls, even when they request back up for a call involving an individual in crisis. We reviewed one force file where BPD officers, responding to a call for an assault where people experiencing homelessness were known to stay, encountered an individual clearly in crisis, naked, hiding in the woods, bleeding and yelling. Instead of requesting the assistance of a BEST-trained officer, BPD officers asked dispatch to request that an officer armed with a taser respond to the scene. When one arrived, the officers yelled at the man to walk out of the woods, and that he would be tased if he did not comply. The officers' report indicated that the man had his arms "tucked up under his arm pits" and "positioned himself into a fighting stance[.]" Allegedly believing that the man might charge, the

---

[112] Under Title II of the ADA's "integration mandate," public entities must administer services, programs, and activities in the most integrated setting appropriate to the needs of qualified individuals with disabilities. 28 C.F.R. § 35.130(d). The Supreme Court in *Olmstead v. L.C.*, 527 U.S. 581 (1999), further held that Title II prohibits the unjustified institutionalization of individuals with disabilities. The Court held that public entities are required to provide community-based services to persons with disabilities when (a) such services are appropriate; (b) the affected individuals do not oppose community-based treatment; and (c) community-based services can be reasonably accommodated, taking into account the resources available to the entity and the needs of others who are receiving disability services from the entity. *Id.* at 607.

officer tased him, striking him in the groin and causing him to fall to the ground. When they approached him, he started kicking his legs and grabbing at the trees. The officers responded by cycling the taser five additional times. None of the four officers present on the scene were BEST-trained.

Not every encounter with an individual in crisis will or should result in arrest or an emergency petition evaluation. Employing sound crisis de-escalation techniques could prevent unnecessary and unreasonable force with individuals in crisis and also prevent needless incarceration and hospitalization.

ii.   BPD Does Not Partner Effectively with Community Service Providers

Our investigation found that there are existing services in the community that BPD fails to utilize sufficiently, many of which may prevent an individual from experiencing a crisis or may prevent recurring instances of crisis. The City of Baltimore provides a range of services for people with disabilities to which the police should be connecting individuals, including community mental health clinics where individuals can receive mental health and substance use assessments, individual and group therapy, and medication management; Assertive Community Treatment teams, which are mobile teams of psychiatrists, social workers, nurses and mental health professionals who provide mental health treatment and support services; and the array of crisis services, such as community-based psychiatric crisis intervention and addictions treatment services. These include a telephone crisis hotline, mobile crisis teams (mental health professionals including psychiatrists, social workers, and nurses who can be dispatched to any Baltimore City location to provide immediate assessment, intervention, and treatment), medical detoxification for individuals addicted to substances, and in-house and community case management.

Although there appears to be a sufficient array of services to meet the needs of many individuals with disabilities, there does not appear to be sufficient capacity in many of those services to meet the need. Gaps in Baltimore City's community mental health service system increase the community's reliance on the police as mental health first responders. If a person with mental health disabilities is not adequately connected to services or is not getting her mental health needs met by the mental health system, she may end up in crisis, and BPD will likely be called to intervene. BPD, alone, cannot solve the problem of insufficient mental health services or capacity—although BPD's collaboration with the mental health service system could result in greater reliance on the mental health system to serve people in crisis, rather than law enforcement. What BPD can control, however, is how effectively it uses the resources that exist in the community.

BPD's BEST program does not partner effectively with the behavioral health community, consumers of these services, and their families. Until relatively recently, BPD's approach to crisis intervention has been limited to its academy training program. Beginning in 2014, the BEST coordinator formed the Collaborative Planning and Implementation Committee (CPIC) with the purpose of bringing together a body of stakeholders from the behavioral health community to act as an advisory board for further developing BPD's BEST program. CPIC is a substantial undertaking, and we are encouraged that BPD is taking this important step toward greater collaboration between BPD and Baltimore's behavioral health community, and, ultimately, toward providing effective crisis intervention services to the people of Baltimore. Progress has been slow, however, and during our site visits, it was apparent that BPD officers had not been trained on diversion to community-based treatment as an alternative to jail or short-term acute hospitalization, demonstrating that additional work remains for CPIC. BPD should continue to find ways to build and strengthen relationships with local providers that serve individuals with disabilities or in crisis.

Finally, BPD should better track when it connects people to service providers. It is difficult to fully assess BPD's efforts to connect individuals with disabilities to services because BPD does not aggregate data on mental health calls and does not track connection to services.

iii. To Remedy the ADA Violations, BPD Should Strengthen its Crisis Intervention Policies, Training, Community Partnership, and Data Collection Practices

In order to prevent further ADA violations, BPD should strengthen its crisis intervention policies, training, community partnership, and data collection practices. BPD must develop and implement policies and procedures for all officers on responding to individuals with mental health disabilities to ensure that officers make reasonable modifications necessary to avoid discrimination. BPD must develop and implement effective training for all officers and dispatchers that focuses on identifying individuals with mental health disabilities and effectively responding to individuals with mental health disabilities, including making reasonable modifications and diversion to treatment services. To better ensure the success and efficacy of these efforts, BPD should work collaboratively with the mental health community, including mental health agencies, providers, advocates, and consumers and their families, to develop the policies, procedures, and trainings. BPD must ensure appropriate officer accountability for protecting the civil rights of people with disabilities. BPD should collect, aggregate, and analyze information on officer interactions with individuals with mental health disabilities. BPD should use the data and information to make further improvements to policy, procedures, training, and accountability measures as necessary to avoid discrimination.

6. BPD's Transport Practices Create a Significant Risk of Harm

Our investigation revealed significant deficiencies in BPD's transport practices that place detainees who are being transported at significant risk of harm. A lack of video monitoring and data collection surrounding BPD's transport practices prevented us from reaching a conclusive determination regarding a practice of "rough rides" or constitutional violations in transportation. Nonetheless, we found evidence that BPD officers routinely fail to safely secure arrestees in transport vans with seatbelts. In multiple instances in the past, this failure has resulted in serious injuries and, in some circumstances, death. This risk of harm should be remedied.

a. BPD Has a History of Not Securing Arrestees

BPD relies on specially outfitted vans to transport detainees from the location of arrest or crisis to the district station, Central Booking, or the emergency room.[113] BPD's use of these vans has, at times, been the subject of considerable controversy and has led to some reforms, but these have not been consistently carried through in practice. For example, in 1997, BPD arrested Jeffrey

---

[113] Most BPD cruisers do not have partitions, or "cages," and are therefore unsuitable for transporting people who have been arrested.

Alston for speeding. According to testimony at a later trial, he was placed into a chokehold by BPD officers during the arrest and thrown unsecured into a transport van. As a result of the treatment and transport, Alston was left quadriplegic. A civil jury found in favor of Mr. Alston, and the City ultimately settled with him for $6 million. Following this incident, BPD issued a General Order requiring officers to ensure every individual placed in a van is secured with seat or restraint belts. The Police Commissioner reaffirmed this requirement in 1999, issuing a memorandum stating that it is the responsibility of the officer to "[e]nsure that prisoners transported in prisoner transportation vehicles are secured with a seat belt."

Despite its longstanding policy that officers must secure detainees, BPD has received repeated indications that officers routinely fail to comply with seatbelt policies, sometimes with tragic results:

- In 2005, Dondi Johnson, Sr. was arrested for urinating on a public street and transported in a van by a BPD officer. During a subsequent trial, officers admitted that neither the driver of the van nor the arresting officers secured Mr. Johnson in the back of the van. While transporting him, the driving officer testified that she heard several bangs from the back of the van, and that she reached the district station in half the time it would have taken if she had driven at the speed limit. When the van was opened, Mr. Johnson was found face-down on the floor and in pain. Hospital records revealed that Mr. Johnson described being hurt while falling after the van took a sharp turn, and an expert witness testified that the nature of the injury was such that the van must have been driven in an aggressive manner. Mr. Johnson died shortly afterward due to complications from paralysis. A jury found in favor of Mr. Johnson's family, awarding $7.4 million in damages.

- In 2013, Christine Abbott sued BPD officers, alleging that she and her boyfriend were subjected to a "rough ride" in addition to other constitutional violations. The suit stated that officers threw her into the back of the police van, failed to secure her, and drove erratically. Ms. Abbott claimed she was violently thrown around the interior of the van during the ride and sustained injuries. In a deposition, the transporting officer acknowledged that Ms. Abbott was not secured during the ride. The City settled the case with Ms. Abbott for $95,000.

b. BPD Continues to Place Detainees At Risk During Transport

Our investigation found that BPD continues to place detainees at significant risk during transport. Following each of the Johnson and Abbott lawsuits, BPD undertook inspections of its transport vans to determine if officers were properly securing arrestees. An audit conducted by BPD from April 12, 2012, through May 14, 2012, inspected 18 vehicles, two from each BPD district. The audit found that *none* of the 34 arrestees in those vehicles were secured with seatbelts.

BPD conducted similar audits of nine vehicles in April 2014 and September 2014, and another shortly after the death of Freddie Gray in April 2015. With each audit, BPD inspected one transport vehicle from each of the districts, one time. The April 2014 audit found that one out of 11 arrestees was not secured by a seatbelt. The September 2014 audit found that all of the 15 arrestees in the inspected vehicles were secured. The April 2015 audit found that 13 out of 14 detainees were secured. While this represents a significant improvement from 2012, the audits were limited in scope and sample size, and as described below, are contradicted by the statements of officers about BPD's actual practices. According to the documents produced to us in our investigation, BPD has not conducted any further inspections of the transportation process, nor has it gathered any data to ensure that detainees are consistently secured in vans.

Given the limitations of the BPD audits, we attempted, through several methods, to obtain information from BPD about injuries that occur during transport. BPD neither collects data about injuries that detainees incur during transport nor tracks data on the source of injuries reported by detainees after they are accepted at Central Booking or the emergency room. Thus, we attempted to obtain injury data directly from Central Booking and to match it to injury data available in BPD's incident and force reports. These data were insufficient for us to reliably match and analyze them.

We also attempted to obtain videos BPD maintained of detainees during transport. BPD transport vans originally contained cameras to show drivers the detainees in the rear of the van. Many of these cameras ceased to function shortly after the vans were put in use, however, and have not been repaired. Because of these failures, we were unable to obtain video of detainees and conduct an evaluation of their treatment during transport. Without functioning video, data collection on injuries, or more frequent inspections, we could not confirm that detainees are still routinely being transported while unsecured.

Given such difficulties in obtaining data about BPD transport practices, we conducted an anonymous poll of recent arrestees during bail review hearings throughout the month of March 2016, with assistance from lawyers at the Maryland Office of the Public Defender. Sixty of the 298 polled arrestees reported that they had been unsecured for at least a portion of the ride to Central Booking—more than 20 percent of the arrestees polled. Several of the respondents indicated that they hit their head, neck, or back during the ride, and/or reported minor injury. While this survey was limited in scope, it was larger than any of the audits conducted by BPD. And, despite its limitations, the results suggest that BPD continues to fail to secure arrestees during transport, placing them at significant risk of harm.

We also obtained significant anecdotal evidence from officers that detainees were often unsecured while being transported by BPD officers, particularly before Freddie Gray's transport last year. One officer who spoke to us described the transportation process before Freddie Gray's death as "load and go," often with little regard for seatbelts. Other officers repeatedly told us that they knew of or had heard about "rough rides" that had taken place in the past, although they declined to give us specifics.

c. BPD Transport Equipment Continues to Place Detainees At Risk

Our evaluation of BPD transport vans heightens our concern regarding transportation practices. Many vans used by BPD remain unsuitable for safe transportation because of a lack of functioning seatbelts and video observation equipment, although BPD has made a number of changes over the last few months to address this problem. Until recently, all vans featured a rear compartment split down the middle by a dividing wall, creating two parallel sections to enclose detainees, with three seats facing inward in each section. While each seat features a seatbelt, this was not always the case: for some time, many vans had no seatbelts. Moreover, though vans are now equipped with seatbelts, we observed on our ride-alongs that some are broken. The space inside each of the transport vans is limited, making it possible for detainees being transported, if not properly secured, to strike their head on the divider or walls relatively easily; and there is virtually no padding to protect the person from injury. The physical layout of the van also creates significant concerns for officer safety. In order to belt in multiple individuals, the officer has to climb into the van, exposing his weapons and equipment to those seated in the first two seats. Once inside the compartment, the officer runs the danger of being harmed by an individual in the van or even locking himself inside. Officers reported to us that such lock-ins occur with some frequency.

BPD is currently retrofitting older vans with a partition, or "cage," that has a different format. The new cage features an open compartment accessed from the rear doors of the van, with seating for four people; two on each side of the van, facing inward. There is a separate, smaller compartment, accessed from the side of the van, with seating for two people sitting side by side, facing the door. Each seat is equipped with a seatbelt and a strap for the detainee to grip for stability while seated with hands cuffed behind his or her back. The newer vans also have video cameras in the rear compartments that can be viewed by the driver and have the capability to record.

However, significant challenges remain, even with the new system. Officers reported that the video recording function has yet to be enabled. There is no clear line of sight from the driver to the rear compartments and sounds are muffled by the barrier. Accordingly, if any person in the rear compartment is hurt or otherwise requires assistance, the driver may remain unaware of the person's condition. This is contrary to a recommendation by the International Association of Chiefs of Police that officers should maintain visual contact with people they transport at all times, through either video or direct observation.[114] Similar to the older vans, the interiors are small and lack padding, so anybody riding in the back, if unsecured, could be injured if the manner of driving caused them to hit the walls, seats or floor. Even when functioning, the seatbelts are positioned in such a way that a person with hands cuffed behind his back can unbuckle himself by turning his body. This raises additional concerns for people in crisis, as well as for officer safety with uncooperative detainees.

BPD has also made other efforts to improve their transportation practices and procedures. After the 2012 audit, officers were briefed on the requirement to seatbelt arrestees. Following Freddie Gray's death and the 2015 audit, BPD sent officers who operate the transport vehicles to academy training, and conducted a brief training during "roll-call" at the beginning of shifts. The training and certification program is short, however, consisting of only four hours of instruction. And while it purports to cover a wide range of topics, from proper handcuffing and search techniques to identification of mental health and medical issues, the training does not cover driving techniques. BPD has also indicated that new patrol cars coming into the departmental fleet will be equipped with protective partitions allowing for the transport of detainees, but it is not clear when BPD will have a sufficient number of equipped cars to eliminate the need for transport vans.

Thus, despite such improvements, BPD still has a great deal of work to do. Most fundamentally, BPD must improve its oversight and monitoring of its transportation practices to ensure that its own policies are followed, and that arrestees are consistently transported in a manner that is safe and secure.

---

[114] IACP Law Enforcement Policy Center, "Transportation of Prisoners Concept and Issues Paper," originally published August 1990, revised October 1996, March 2005, and September 2015.

D. BPD Unlawfully Restricts Protected Speech

The people of Baltimore have a constitutional right to observe and verbally criticize the police. "Since the day the ink dried on the Bill of Rights, the right of an American citizen to criticize public officials and policies is the central meaning of the First Amendment." *McCurdy v. Montgomery County*, 240 F.3d 512, 520 (6th Cir. 2001) (internal quotation marks and citations omitted). We found that BPD officers routinely infringe upon the First Amendment rights of the people of Baltimore City, typically in one of three ways. First, we found that BPD unlawfully stops and arrests individuals for speech they perceive to be disrespectful or insolent. Second, we found that officers retaliate against individuals for protected speech through the use of excessive force. Third, we have concerns that BPD improperly interferes with individuals who record police activity.

1. BPD Unlawfully Detains and Arrests Members of the Public for Protected Speech

BPD detains and arrests individuals for speech perceived to be rude, critical, or disrespectful. These arrests—described by the officers in their own words in incident and arrest reports—violate the First Amendment. For example, an officer in downtown Baltimore in 2011 "felt . . . that it was reasonable" to order a young African-American man to leave the area because he "had no respect for law enforcement" and was "making idle threats towards a uniformed officer." As the young man walked away accompanied by a friend, the two made additional comments mocking the officers and the BPD; 15 minutes later, the officer again spotted the two men in the same area and placed both under arrest for failure to obey. "The freedom of individuals verbally to oppose or challenge police action without thereby risking arrest is one of the principle characteristics by which we distinguish a free nation from a police state." *City of Houston v. Hill*, 482 U.S. 451, 462–63 (1987) (striking down municipal ordinance that made it illegal to oppose or interrupt a policeman as constitutionally overbroad under the First Amendment).[115] By ordering the young men to leave, and then arresting them for their comments, the officer violated their First Amendment right to peacefully and verbally criticize or oppose law enforcement officers without actively interfering with the officers' lawful performance of their duties.

In another incident from 2011, BPD officers arrested a man for disorderly conduct after he refused to leave a public area following an order issued without just cause, and yelled "fuck you" repeatedly at the officer. This arrest was also unlawful, as individuals may not be punished for using vulgar or offensive language unless they use "fighting words," that is, words that "by their very utterance inflict injury or tend to incite an immediate breach of the peace." *Chaplinsky v. New Hampshire*, 315 U.S. 568, 572 (1942). Use of profanity alone is not sufficient to rise to the level of inflicting injury or inciting a breach of peace. *See Hess v. Indiana*, 414 U.S. 105, 107–08 (1973) (finding that profane words were not fighting words because they were not a personal insult); *Lewis v. City of New Orleans*, 415 U.S. 130, 132–34 (1974) (invalidating New Orleans ordinance that made it unlawful to curse at a police officer on duty); *Buffkins v. City of Omaha*, 922 F.2d 465, 467–68, 472 (8th Cir. 1990) (arrest was unlawful as use of the word "asshole" towards officers did not constitute fighting words). From our review of their reports, some BPD officers appear to believe that use of vulgar or profane language provides probable cause to arrest or grounds for ordering a person to leave a location.

---

[115] As discussed in Section *supra* at 36-39, this order and arrest also likely violate the Fourteenth Amendment's Due Process clause.

Indeed, in another case, an officer patrolling the inner harbor on the Fourth of July complained that a man, "Nicholas," bumped his shoulder while walking past. As Nicholas continued walking, the officer said, "Hey, you ran right into me," to which Nicholas replied "fuck you" and continued walking. Although no crime had been committed, the officer pursued Nicholas and demanded his identification. Nicholas continued to walk away from the officer, who attempted to grab his arm. Nicholas swore at the officer again and continued to pull away, at which point the officer informed him he was under arrest. According to the officer's report, after attempting to place the man under arrest, the incident ended in a physical altercation between officers, Nicholas, and his brother, with the brother eventually being tased. Though Nicholas made repeated attempts to walk away peacefully, the officer pursued him and escalated the encounter. According to the officer's report, he believed that Nicholas's attitude and actions indicated "he was purposely looking for a confrontation with law enforcement[.]" However, Nicholas made no obvious threats or aggressive movements toward the officer. His use of profanity did not rise to the level of "fighting words" and was protected by the First Amendment. The officer's pursuit, detention, and eventual arrest was an unlawful exercise of government power to exact personal vengeance for a perceived slight.

BPD officers also violate the First Amendment by arresting individuals who question the lawfulness of their actions. In one reported use of force, an officer described the arrest of a man who approached him during a traffic stop to ask why the officer had stopped his friend. The proffered justification for the arrest was that the man refused to leave the area when ordered to do so by the officer. Nothing in the officer's report indicates that the man physically interfered with the officer's duty or was otherwise committing a crime. He was arrested merely because he continued to stand "near" the officer. Arrests for failing to leave a crime scene are also unlawful. The man had a right to "voice his objection to what he obviously felt was a highly questionable detention by a police officer." *Norwell v. City of Cincinnati, Ohio*, 414 U.S. 14, 16 (1973); *see also Wilson v. Kittoe*, 337 F.3d 392, 402 (4th Cir. 2003) (officers lacked probable cause to arrest an attorney who did not obey officers' orders to leave the scene of the arrest of another person, and that the subsequent arrest of the attorney unlawfully infringed upon his First Amendment rights). The man sustained an injury to his head while struggling during the course of being taken into custody following the unlawful arrest. Despite a clear lack of probable cause, supervisory review found that the officer had acted properly and within policy.

In a similar incident from 2014, BPD officers arrested a man for disorderly conduct because he was shouting at the officers. The man believed they had assaulted his nephew and stolen from him while detaining him on suspicion of "gambling." When he approached the officers, demanding to know which of them had punched his nephew, a crowd gathered, and he was placed under arrest. The man was within his rights to question the officers' actions, and the arrest unlawfully suppressed his speech. Officers arrested him for objecting to their actions and for making vocal inquiries into their conduct.[116] In making these arrests, BPD officers violated these individuals' right to question and criticize police actions. *See Norwell*, 414 U.S. at 16 (speech protesting officers' actions is protected even if "loud and boisterous" or "annoying" to officers).

---

[116] Although one officer later told a supervisor that the man had adopted a "fighting stance" before the decision to arrest, this was not corroborated by other officers or civilian witnesses on the scene, who reported that the man merely refused to leave and made repeated demands to know who had assaulted his nephew.

"[A] clear and present danger of crowd violence" may be a consideration in determining whether a First Amendment violation occurred. *Smith v. McCluskey*, 126 Fed. Appx. 89, 94 (4th Cir. 2005) (per curiam) (unpublished) (internal quotations omitted). But the presence of other people alone is insufficient to render otherwise protected speech grounds for arrest, unless such speech "is directed to inciting or producing imminent lawless action and is likely to incite or produce such action." *Brandenburg v. Ohio*, 395 U.S. 444, 447 (1969). *See also State of Texas v. Johnson*, 491 U.S. 397, 409–10 (1989) (rejecting the argument that "the potential for breach of peace" satisfies the *Brandenburg* standard); *Patterson v. United States*, 999 F.Supp.2d 300, 316 (D.D.C. 2013) ("[C]ursing at an officer in the presence of a crowd, without some indication of a likely violent reaction from that crowd, does not give rise to probable cause to believe that the speaker is engaged in disorderly conduct."); *Dormu v. District of Columbia*, 795 F.Supp. 2d 7, 21 (D.D.C. 2011) ("[D]isorderly conduct does not occur merely because a crowd gathers to watch a citizen-police encounter."). And unlike the plaintiff in *Smith v. McCluskey*, the individuals in the above described incidents had not been placed under valid arrest at the time their speech was suppressed. Neither the man's demand to know which officer had struck his nephew, nor the woman's shouts or profanity were evidently directed to produce imminent lawless action on the part of the crowd. Accordingly, their suppression by arrest was unlawful.

These and other arrests for protected speech demonstrate that BPD officers may consider speech critical or disrespectful of their activities to be assaultive or disruptive, and therefore sufficient to justify suppression through the unlawful use of police powers to detain and arrest.

2. BPD Retaliates by Using Force Against Individuals Who Engage in Protected Speech

BPD uses unreasonable force to retaliate against individuals who engage in protected speech critical of law enforcement, in violation of both the First and Fourth Amendments.[117] *City of Houston*, 482 U.S. at 461; *Hartman v. Moore*, 547 U.S. 250, 256 (2006) ("the law is settled that as a general matter the First Amendment prohibits government officials from subjecting an individual to retaliatory actions . . . for speaking out."). We reviewed a number of troubling incidents where BPD officers appeared to use force against individuals simply because they did not like what those individuals said. In one case from 2011, officers tackled and used a taser to drive-stun a young black man who was, in their view, "loitering" near a market during business hours in downtown Baltimore. When told to move, the young man refused and swore at the officers, who then tackled him. Nothing indicated the man was armed, violent, or presented a danger to the officers or others. Supervisors who investigated and approved the incident failed to recognize that the force appeared to be retaliatory, even though the man, when interviewed, told them he believed he was tackled because he cursed at the officers.

Furthermore, we have reviewed many incidents in which BPD officers believe they are justified in using force or arresting a person, based solely on profane or insulting words. We reviewed an incident, for example, in which an officer tased a young man who, according to the officer's report, had removed his shirt and was yelling at club patrons and staff. The officer justified

---

[117] Retaliatory force also violates the Fourteenth Amendment when used against individuals who have been arrested are being held as pretrial detainees, for example during prisoner transport. *See Orem v. Rephann*, 523 F.3d 442, 446 (4th Cir. 2008), abrogated on other grounds by *Wilkins v. Gaddy*, 559 U.S. 34, 39 (2010).

using the taser on the basis that the man approached the officer in an aggressive manner while swearing. Although the report is not altogether clear on what the officer meant by "aggressive," the report does make clear that the man's "mouth"—his words—constituted the weapon or means of attack:

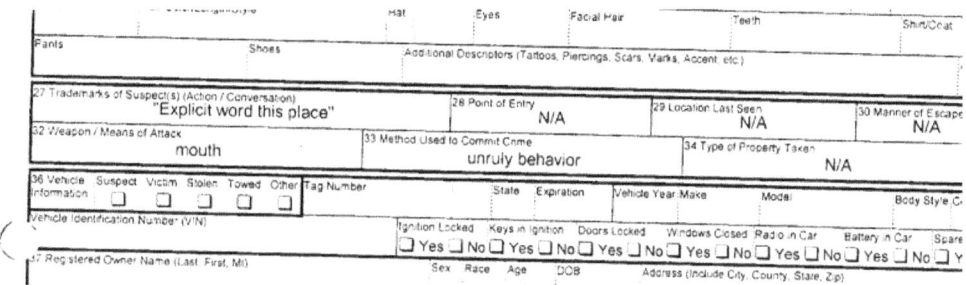

Indeed, this report appears to indicate the officer felt he was justified in tasing an individual—a high level of force—for this reason. Moreover, the report noted that the individual's "trademark" was "[e]xplicit word this place." If this was in fact the officer's justification for tasing this individual, it is grossly insufficient, and it would violate both the First and Fourth Amendments. Although we make no finding about this specific incident because of the vagueness of word "aggressive" in the report, it is notable that the officer's direct supervisor signed off on the report, and a review of the use of force found it to be justified without need of clarification.

We reviewed a number of substantially similar incidents where BPD officers only resorted to force after an individual swore at them. These uses of force in retaliation for protected speech violate the First and Fourth Amendments, and they undermine public confidence in the BPD.

3. Concerns that BPD Interferes with the Right to Record Public Police Activity

We also have serious concerns that BPD officers interfere with individuals who attempt to lawfully record police activity, although we do not make a finding of constitutional violations in this area because we did not find a sufficient number of incidents to warrant such a finding at this time. We nevertheless received and reviewed a number of allegations that BPD officers seize, view, and destroy video and audio recordings that constitute private property without just cause to do so. In 2012, we provided guidance to BPD on the First, Fourth, and Fourteenth Amendment considerations related to the recording of public police activity in a Statement of Interest filed in *Sharp v. Baltimore City Police Dep't.*, No. 1:11-cv-02888-BEL (D. Md. Jan. 12, 2012), 2012 WL 9512053.

That case was brought by the ACLU of Maryland on behalf of a man whose cellular phone was seized by BPD officers during an incident at the Pimlico Race Course in 2011. The City settled the case in 2014 for $250,000. The plaintiff alleged that BPD officers seized, searched, and deleted the contents of his phone after he used it to record officers using force during an arrest of his acquaintance. When BPD returned the phone to him, all of the videos on the device were deleted, including a number of personal videos of his young son. After the man filed suit, BPD moved for partial summary judgment, and the Department of Justice opposed that motion in our Statement of Interest. Shortly thereafter, on May 14, 2012, in advance of the parties' settlement conference, we sent a letter to both parties. In our letter, we described in more detail how these constitutional interests play out in practice, and we gave technical assistance on their implications for policy and training. The parties settled, and, as part of the settlement, BPD agreed to implement a new policy and training program concerning the right to audiotape, videotape, and photograph BPD members during the public exercise of their duties. The new policy was published in 2014. Nonetheless, in the time period since *Sharp*, we have received numerous allegations that BPD officers continue to interfere with the individual right to record police activity, in violation of the First Amendment and their own policy.

One example of the allegations we received stems from an incident in 2015. According to the complainant, a young man was charged with three offenses after filming BPD officers arresting his friend for trespassing outside a nightclub in Baltimore City. The friend was engaged in an argument with security officers at a bar complex about refunding his admission fee. When BPD Officers informed him that he was trespassing and began handcuffing him, his companion, allegedly standing approximately 20 feet away, began to film the incident using his phone. Two other officers on the scene turned and confronted him, grabbing his phone and placing him in handcuffs. While the alleged trespasser was released with only a ticket, the man filming was arrested and charged with three offenses: failure to obey, trespassing, and assault (for what appears to be a later-discovered alleged assault against the nightclub's bouncer). During the arrest process, the man watched as an officer openly went through his phone. When BPD released the man after he spent two nights in jail, he discovered that the video of the incident had been deleted. Ultimately, a state court entered a judgment of acquittal for the assault and failure to obey charges, and the man was acquitted of the trespassing charge at trial. According to the man, the sole justification for his arrest was his attempt to record the officers' interaction with his friend. We also note that, to the extent that the officers thought that the man recording their activities was somehow interfering in their enforcement efforts, the officers do not appear to have made any effort to instruct the man who was recording them to move to a less-intrusive place where he could continue recording.

In addition to these apparent First Amendment violations, BPD officers also appear to have violated the Fourth and Fourteenth Amendments by searching the phone following the arrest, apparently without a warrant, and by deleting the video. When individuals record police officers in the public exercise of their duties, they have a Fourteenth Amendment property right to maintain the possession of their belongings, including recordings and recording devices. *See, e.g., Helton v. Hunt*, 330 F.3d 242, 247–49 (4th Cir. 2003) (striking down statute allowing police to seize and destroy video gaming machines without due process). BPD's policy accordingly prohibits employees from erasing, deleting, or instructing others to erase or delete any recordings from a recording device. By going through the man's phone and deleting the video, BPD destroyed valuable evidence and disregarded the owner's property rights and the Department's own policy.

First Amendment violations acutely affect a community's trust in the legitimacy of law enforcement operations. BPD's sensitivity to criticism and recording of their activity is ultimately both a symptom and a cause of mutual mistrust with the community. There is emerging evidence that video recording can be a valuable tool to reduce use of force incidents and complaints, and protect the rights of both community members and officers.[118] To create an atmosphere of mutual respect and accountability, officers will need to demonstrate the ability to work within the confines of the First Amendment.

---

[118] *See, e.g.,* IACP. *The Impact of Video Evidence on Modern Policing: Research and Best Practices from the IACP Study on In-Car Cameras,* available at: http://www.theiacp.org/Portals/0/pdfs/WhatsNew/IACP%20In-Car%20Camera%20Report%202004.pdf (last accessed June 10, 2016).

*   *   *

In sum, BPD takes law enforcement action in retaliation for individuals' engaging in protected speech or activity in violation of the First Amendment.

E. BPD's Handling of Sexual Assault Investigations Raises Serious Concerns of Gender-Biased Policing

Our investigation also raised serious concerns about how BPD responds to and investigates reports of sexual assault.

1. Evidence of Gender Bias in BPD's Response to Sexual Assault

a. Treatment of Victims of Sexual Assault

By its very nature, sexual assault is a crime about which it can be difficult to ascertain the facts: for example, sexual assault often occurs in a private setting, with no witnesses other than the people involved as the victim[119] and suspect, and victims of sexual assault are often reluctant to report the assault, particularly to law enforcement. For that reason, victim advocates—who act as confidantes and guides for victims as they navigate the criminal justice system, and whose role affords them a unique perspective from which to identify patterns in their clients' experiences—play a critical role in providing information about sexual assaults to BPD.

The information provided to us by victim advocates, and, in some cases, by victims of sexual assault themselves, together with our review of BPD's sexual assault case files and related documents, raise serious concerns about gender bias in BPD's treatment of victims of sexual assault. For instance, officers and detectives in BPD's Sex Offense Unit often question victims in a manner that puts the blame for the sexual assault on the victim's shoulders—for example, with questions suggesting the victims should feel personally responsible for the potential consequences of a criminal report on a suspect or for having engaged in behavior that invited the assault. In their interviews of women reporting sexual assault, for example, BPD detectives ask questions such as "Why are you messing that guy's life up?" BPD officers and detectives also asked questions suggesting that they discredit the reports of victims who delayed in reporting the assault to the police. This type of questioning is inappropriate in a detective interview of a potential victim of sexual assault and suggests gender bias by the detectives.

We were also troubled by statements of BPD detectives suggesting an undue skepticism of reports of sexual assault. One victim advocate told us about a detective in the BPD Sex Offense Unit making comments at a party, in the company of BPD officers and victim advocates, that, "in homicide, there are real victims; all our cases are bullshit." When another person suggested the detective soften the statement, the detective added, "Ok, 90 percent." We also reviewed e-mail correspondence between a BPD officer and a prosecutor in which they openly expressed their contempt for and disbelief of a woman who had reported a sexual assault: the prosecutor wrote that "this case is crazy. . . I am not excited about charging it. This victim seems like a conniving little whore. (pardon my language)."; the BPD officer replied, "Lmao! I feel the same."

---

[119] Throughout this findings letter, we have used the terms "victim" and "victim of sexual assault" to refer to people having experienced sexual assault because it is the term generally used in criminal legal definitions of sexual assault and in the criminal justice system. We appreciate, however, that many prefer the terms "survivor" or "victim/survivor," and encourage respect for those preferences.

In addition, we found indications that BPD disregards reports of sexual assault by people involved in the sex trade—a particularly troubling trend given the vulnerability of those individuals to rape.[120] According to one case report, the suspect had approached the victim with a gun, the victim had called the police right away, and the suspect's interview was almost entirely consistent with the victim's account of the assault—all evidence that could have supported an investigation and prosecution. Nonetheless, the BPD detective made no attempt to corroborate the victim's account of the assault with witness interviews or other evidence and told the suspect that he would not be charged with anything other than possession of a gun.

b. BPD's Treatment of Transgender Individuals

We received allegations of BPD officers' mistreatment of transgender individuals and have concerns that BPD's interactions with transgender individuals reflect underlying unlawful gender bias. We heard allegations that BPD officers make disparaging and inappropriate comments to transgender individuals, and that BPD officers refuse to acknowledge transgender women as women. One transgender woman, for example, described an incident after a traffic stop in December 2015 in which she was asked by the officer whether she identified as male or female, and told the officer that she identified as female. Despite her response, the arresting officer then said to another officer at the scene, "Well, are you going to transport him?" We also heard from the transgender community that their interactions with BPD are degrading and dehumanizing and that, as a result, transgender individuals are afraid to report crime to law enforcement. The same transgender woman described above, for example, alleged that when she arrived at intake, the female supervisor who was called to search her said, "I am not here for this shit. I am not searching that." When she then tried to ask the supervisor to show her some respect, the supervisor said, "Like I said, I don't know you. I don't know if you're a boy or a girl. And I really don't care, I am not searching you." This is not the only example we heard about BPD officers conducting inappropriate searches of transgender individuals. We heard several reports that indicate that BPD officers lack guidance on the appropriate process for conducting searches of transgender individuals, including ensuring that searches are conducted by a person of the appropriate gender.

BPD's treatment of women victims of sexual assault and of transgender individuals should not reflect gender-based stereotypes and assumptions that may compromise the effectiveness and impartiality of BPD's response to reports of sexual assault and discourage women and transgender individuals from engaging with the criminal justice system.

2. BPD Fails to Adequately Investigate Reports of Sexual Assault

BPD seriously and systematically under-investigates reports of sexual assault, and the sexual assault investigations it does conduct are marked by practices that significantly compromise the effectiveness and impartiality of its response to sexual assault. These are not new issues for BPD. BPD's handling of sexual assault was subject to widespread public scrutiny in 2010, spurred by media reports of BPD's misclassification of rape cases, failure to identify and investigate reports of sexual assault, and substantial backlog of rape kits. Victim advocates, for example, criticized the

---

[120] See, e.g., Michele R. Decker et al., *Violence Against Women in Sex Work and HIV Risk Implications Differ Qualitatively by Perpetrator*, 13 BMC PUB. HEALTH 876 (2013), available at http://bmcpublichealth.biomedcentral.com/articles/10.1186/1471-2458-13-876.

manner in which BPD treated victims of sexual assault—including interrogating rape victims, questioning women in the emergency room, threatening to hook up women reporting sexual assault to lie detectors, and not informing victims about the status of their cases. Moreover, victim advocates reported that BPD's Sex Offense Unit was only minimally investigating reports of sexual assault; for example, they were not making efforts to identify witnesses or submitting rape kits for testing.

Despite some attempts at reform by BPD and Baltimore City leaders, most of these problems either remain or have returned. BPD's response to reports of sexual assault is, overall, grossly inadequate: for example, BPD allows more than half of its rape cases to linger in an "open" status, often for years at a time, with little to no follow-up investigation, while fewer than one in four of its rape investigations are closed due to the arrest of a suspect, a rate roughly half of the national average; BPD detectives request testing of rape kits in fewer than one in five of BPD's adult sexual assault cases, leaving these rape kits to sit untested in BPD's evidence collection unit; and BPD detectives rarely, if ever, seek to identify or interview suspects and witnesses, even in cases where they are clearly identified by the woman reporting the assault. In addition, BPD investigative policies and practices significantly undermine the quality, effectiveness, and fairness of BPD's response to reports of sexual assault, making it more difficult to uncover the truth when sexual assault allegations are made.

a. Failure to Develop and Resolve Preliminary Investigations

In the majority of BPD's sexual assault cases, BPD fails to pursue investigations beyond the immediate, preliminary response to a report of sexual assault. According to BPD's own data, for example, between 53 and 58 percent of its sex offense cases were in an "open" status each year between 2013 and 2015. In our own review of a sample of BPD's sexual assault cases between 2010 and 2015, we found that more than half of these cases were described by BPD as being in an "open" status and that only a preliminary investigation had been done in a substantial proportion of those "open" cases. One sexual assault case, for example, was identified by BPD as "open," despite the fact that there had been no activity on the case since February 2013. In this case, there had been no request for a lab test kit, no follow-up with the suspect's lawyer to interview the suspect or test DNA, and no indication of communication with the victim over the past three years. Indeed, it appeared from the file that communication with the victim, and BPD's investigation of the case, had slowed and ultimately stopped after the suspect hired a defense attorney.

b. Failure to Identify and Collect Evidence to Corroborate Victims' Complaints

Similarly, BPD makes little, if any, effort to corroborate victims' accounts of their assaults, either by identifying and interviewing witnesses, gathering other types of evidence, or identifying and interrogating suspects. BPD routinely fails to contact witnesses to sexual assaults in the first instance and, where their initial attempts to contact witnesses fail, BPD almost never make a second attempt to contact those witnesses. Even when a victim describes having reported the assault to others in the immediate aftermath of the crime, BPD makes no effort to identify and interview these "outcry" witnesses—in other words, the people who first heard the allegation of sexual assault. In one case, for example, the victim had immediately told her father and other witnesses about the assault; however, BPD made no attempt to contact any of these outcry witnesses to corroborate the victim's story. Similarly, BPD persistently fails to make any efforts to contact eye witnesses to sexual assaults. In one case, for example, the victim and the suspect had been in two different bars together before the assault. The victim believed that the suspect had drugged her, and she had injuries all over her body. After the assault, the victim had run out of a bar and immediately reported the crime. Given these facts, it is reasonable to expect that there would have been numerous people who would have seen the victim and the suspect together at or around the time of the assault and who could have corroborated details of the victim's account. But BPD made no attempt to contact the bartenders of the bars or to identify any other eye witnesses.

In addition to failing to seek out corroborating witness testimony, BPD persistently fails to seek other types of evidence that could corroborate a victim's account of the assault. In the case just described, for example, in addition to neglecting to identify and interview witnesses, BPD made no attempt to review surveillance camera recordings from the two bars visited by the victim and the suspect, no effort to have the victim tested for drugs, and no attempt to gather physical evidence from the scene.

BPD persistently neglects to request lab testing of rape kits and other forensic evidence. Rape kits are only tested if a detective makes a request and all too often, detectives do not request that rape kits be tested. Between 2010 and September 2014, for example, rape kits were tested in only 15 percent of BPD's cases involving sexual assaults of adult victims. Similarly, between January and September 2015, BPD detectives requested testing of rape kits in only 16 percent of BPD's cases involving sexual assaults of adult victims. In the few cases where BPD is requesting rape kit tests, we found that there are long delays in making those requests. In one case, for example, BPD requested a lab test nine months after receiving a report of the sexual assault; it took another five months for BPD to get the results of the lab test.

Similarly, BPD detectives consistently neglect to gather DNA evidence and to request lab tests for DNA evidence from swabs or clothing. In one case, for example, a taxi driver drove an intoxicated woman to his home instead of to the address given to him by a bartender; the woman reported that the taxi driver had then raped her at his home. BPD subsequently interviewed the taxi driver, and he admitted to having taken the woman to his home. A rape kit was submitted and tested positive for semen. However, BPD made no attempt to get a DNA sample from the taxi driver.

BPD also makes minimal to no effort to locate, identify, interrogate, or investigate suspects. We found this to be true even in cases where the suspects had been identified or were easily identifiable on the basis of the victim's testimony. For example, in one case, involving an attempted sexual assault of a woman by the driver of an unauthorized taxi, the detective was able to identify the suspect based on the woman's detailed description of the suspect's car. The detective made no attempt to contact the suspect, however, and the investigation progressed no further. Because sexual assault is a crime that frequently occurs in private settings, it is critical that law enforcement make efforts to gather, preserve, and analyze evidence, especially corroborative evidence, as quickly as possible. BPD's persistent failure to seek out and develop such corroborative evidence, including suspect interrogations, constitutes a significant and damaging omission from their investigations of sexual assault.

BPD fails to identify and follow up on indications of serial suspects in its sexual assault cases. Serial suspects are believed to be responsible for a substantial proportion of sexual assaults—one oft-cited study concluded, for example, that two in three rapists who had never been prosecuted for their crimes were repeat rapists[121]—and thus there may be enormous public safety consequences when law enforcement fails to identify and hold accountable serial rapists. We were troubled to find evidence of such failures in BPD's investigations of sexual assault. For example, we reviewed numerous cases of forcible rapes of women by strangers that presented circumstances suggesting there might be serial rapists involved; however, BPD detectives did not take the steps necessary to make that determination, such as searching for cases presenting similar factual scenarios or identifying other victims in Baltimore or neighboring jurisdictions.

c. Missing or Inadequate Documentation of Investigation

BPD's sexual assault case files, as a general matter, are missing critical information and lack sufficient documentation of the investigation to allow detectives, their supervisors, and prosecutors to effectively evaluate the quality of investigation and to assess and respond to the reported crimes. For instance, we found that BPD's sexual assault case files frequently lack video recordings of victims, witnesses, and suspects, even where the notes in the case file indicate that those interviews had taken place and been recorded. BPD's sexual assault case files generally lack notes from officers and detectives. Where case files do include such notes, the notes provide insufficient information about officers' and detectives' impressions and observations, or about their reasons for making investigative decisions, to present a comprehensive, factual picture of the reported assault. Indeed, across the board, we found that we learned far more about victims' impressions and recollections of their assaults from the forensic medical exam reports than from BPD's own reports.

d. Failure to Collect and Review Data About, and to Appropriately Report and Classify, Reports of Sexual Assault

The information provided to us by BPD in response to our requests for data regarding the department's cases of sexual assault suggests to us that BPD continues to have problems with improperly identifying, reporting, and classifying reports of sexual assault, as well as with collecting, reviewing, and analyzing data about sexual assaults reported to BPD. BPD has previously been subject to public scrutiny for its misclassification of cases of sexual assault and for its failures to appropriately identify or report cases of sexual assault. In June 2010, the *Baltimore Sun* reported that BPD patrol and detectives had classified more than 30 percent of their rape cases as "unfounded"—a classification that is appropriate only for a report of rape that is found, after an investigation, to be either false or baseless; BPD's "unfounded" rate for rape cases at that time was five times the national average.[122] A subsequent review of unfounded cases conducted by the Baltimore City Sexual Assault Response Team (SART) audit unit found that, of the cases reviewed by the SART audit unit, more than half of the sexual assault cases classified as "unfounded" by BPD detectives

---

[121] David Lisak & Paul M. Miller, *Repeat Rape and Multiple Offending Among Undetected Rapists*, 17 VIOLENCE AND VICTIMS 73–84, 78, 80 (2002).

[122] *See, e.g.,* Justin Fenton, *City Rape Statistics, Investigations Draw Concern*, BALTIMORE SUN (June 27, 2010), http://articles.baltimoresun.com/2010-06-27/news/bs-md-ci-rapes-20100519_1_rosalyn-branson-police-detective-police-figures.

had been misclassified.[123] According to data from BPD, the proportion of rape cases classified as "unfounded" by BPD has dropped dramatically since 2010; BPD's data reflected a rate of 9.6 percent of rape cases classified as "unfounded" between January 2010 and March 2016. We are concerned, however, that these statistics mask a continuing problem with BPD's understanding and application of the appropriate definitions and uses of the classification categories, as well as with its practices for identifying and reporting sexual assaults. In 2015, for example, BPD described approximately 56 percent of its rape cases as "open." Meanwhile, only 17 percent of BPD's rape cases in 2015 were closed by arrest – a rate less than half the national average for the proportion of rape cases closed by arrest. Also in 2015, according to both data and anecdotal evidence from the Baltimore City SART, only a handful of BPD's cases were closed as "unfounded;" SART data indicated a rate of 6.6 percent of rape cases classified as "unfounded" by BPD between January and September 2015, and BPD presented only a handful of cases classified as unfounded to the SART audit committee for their review. Taken in the aggregate, this data suggests that BPD is keeping the majority of its rape cases in an "open" status, thus drastically reducing the rate of its rape cases closed as "unfounded"—and creating the illusion of having made meaningful reforms to its procedures for identifying and classifying sexual assaults.

In addition, we were troubled by the fact that BPD was unable to provide us with responses to our requests for basic data about the victim and suspect population, the incidence and nature of cases of sexual assault reported to and handled by the department, and the incidence of cases of sexual assault involving BPD officers. The inability to collect and produce such data suggests to us that BPD, at present, lacks the capacity to effectively assess the effectiveness its own response to sexual assault, to identify trends in the incidence of sexual assault, both in the Baltimore community and within its own department, and to make decisions about how to adjust or improve its response to sexual assault. Particularly in light of the public attention to the serious flaws in BPD's identification, reporting, and classification of cases of sexual assault, BPD's failure to remedy its procedures for collecting and reviewing data about sexual assault represents a significant weakness in the department's handling of sexual assault.

e. Lack of Supervisory Review

Although a supervisory review form is included as a matter of course in BPD's sexual assault case files, these supervisory review forms are almost always left blank. In the rare circumstances where the supervisory review forms are filled out, they include little information and appear to reflect a limited review of what steps have been taken in the investigation, and not an examination of the quality of the investigation or the reasoning for the outcome of the investigation. Similarly, although a "State's Attorney Contact Log" form is included as a matter of course in BPD's sexual assault case files, this form is rarely completed and, when it is filled out, contains very little information. The extremely limited nature of the information provided by the supervisory review form and State's Attorney Contact Log form raises concerns for us about the inadequate supervision and review, both within and external to the police department, of BPD's sexual assault investigations.

---

[123] Md. Coal. Against Sexual Assault, *Baltimore City Sexual Assault Response Team Annual Report* 10 (Oct. 5, 2011), http://www.mcasa.org/_mcasaWeb/wp-content/uploads/2011/11/BaltimoreCityAnnualReport_print.pdf.

III. SYSTEMIC DEFICIENCIES IN BPD'S PRACTICES CONTRIBUTE TO CONSTITUTIONAL VIOLATIONS, ERODE COMMUNITY TRUST, AND INHIBIT EFFECTIVE POLICING

The constitutional violations described in our findings result in part from critical deficiencies in BPD's systems to train, equip, supervise, and hold officers accountable, and to build relationships with the broader Baltimore community. *First*, BPD fails to adequately supervise its officers. This lack of supervision manifests itself in multiple ways, including a failure to guide officer activity through effective policies and training; a failure to collect and analyze reliable data to supervise officer enforcement activities; and the lack of a meaningful early intervention system (EIS) to identify officers who may benefit from additional training or other guidance to ensure that they do not commit constitutional violations. *Second*, BPD lacks meaningful accountability systems to deter misconduct. BPD does not consistently classify, investigate, adjudicate, and document complaints of misconduct according to its own policies and accepted law enforcement standards. Indeed, we found that BPD personnel sometimes discourage complaints from being filed and frequently conduct little or no investigation—even of serious misconduct allegations. As a result, a culture resistant to accountability persists throughout much of BPD, and many officers are reluctant to report misconduct for fear that doing so is fruitless and may provoke retaliation. *Third*, BPD fails to have proper agreements in place to coordinate its activities with other agencies that are operating within its jurisdiction. *Fourth*, BPD fails to adequately support its officers through effective strategies for recruitment, retention, and staffing patterns, and does not provide them with appropriate technology and equipment. *Fifth*, BPD does not engage effectively with the community it polices. BPD's failure to use accepted community policing strategies and transparency mechanisms erodes the community trust that is central to productive law enforcement.

These systemic deficiencies impair officer safety and effectiveness and lead directly to violations of the Constitution and federal law.

A. BPD FAILS TO ADEQUATELY SUPERVISE ITS OFFICERS' ENFORCEMENT ACTIVITIES

1. BPD Does Not Provide Adequate Policy Guidance and Training to its Officers

BPD's inadequate policies and training contribute to the Department's pattern or practice of constitutional violations. Clear, comprehensive, and legally accurate policies and training are essential to the proper functioning of a police department. They provide crucial guidance for officers regarding what practical steps to take to remain in compliance with departmental rules and legal requirements, allow supervisors to properly monitor and instruct officers, and provide consistent guidelines for officer discipline. Here, we find that certain BPD policies and trainings do not fulfill these functions. BPD officers thus lack sufficient guidance to ensure that their enforcement activities are effective, safe, and consistent with the constitutional rights of the people they serve. While BPD has made admirable efforts to update its policies in 2015 and 2016, some outdated and contradictory policies remain in effect, diminishing the impact of the new policies and procedures.

a. Deficient Policies

As we described above in our findings, critical deficiencies in BPD's policies contribute to officers violating the constitutional rights of Baltimore residents. For example, officers' frequent use of tasers to apply constitutionally excessive force is connected to the Department's failure to have any policy governing the use of electronic control weapons until 2015. BPD similarly lacked any policy on baton use—also a frequent source of constitutional violations—until 2016. The Department likewise lacked a fair and impartial policing policy until 2015, despite longstanding notice of concerns about its policing of the City's African-American population. And policy deficiencies also contribute to officers' frequent illegal stops, searches, and arrests by misstating the law on the justification required to stop or frisk individuals suspected of criminal activity. Indeed, several BPD policies do not adequately capture the current state of the law, and others provide insufficient guidance to officers to allow them to align their conduct with constitutional requirements.

Beyond these specific policy deficiencies, however, we found systemic problems with BPD's method of drafting, distributing, and implementing policies that has made it difficult for officers to understand proper procedures and adapt to changing rules. BPD fails to follow widely accepted principles in developing, distributing, and implementing new policies. The International Association of Chiefs of Police, for example, has developed a set of best practices for effective development of operational policy and procedures. Among other recommendations, these principles indicate that staff should be involved in the development of the manual and kept informed of any changes. Chief W. Dwayne Orrick, *Best Practices Guide: Developing a Police Department Policy-Procedure Manual*, International Association of Chiefs of Police, http://www.theiacp.org/portals/0/pdfs/BP-PolicyProcedures.pdf (last visited June 17, 2016). Empirical research has also suggested that officers are more likely to support and comply with policies when they have been provided opportunities to give input, and supervisors clearly explain decisions that they have made. Nicole E. Haas et. al., *Explaining officer compliance: The importance of procedural justice and trust inside a police organization*, 15 Criminology & Crim. Just. 4, 16 (Sept. 2015).

BPD does not follow these accepted methods of policy development. Instead, the Department has historically developed and published policies and amendments in a manner that officers find to be confusing and opaque. As many officers told us, the numbering system alone is a source of confusion. Generally, BPD policies have been organized with titles that included letters and numbers. During one period, however, the letter-and-number system was replaced with a system that included numbers alone. The new system only applied to newly implemented policies, however, and the majority of policies were still classified by letter-and-number. Policies from different eras are written in different formats, and often modified by annexes, memoranda, amendments, and rescissions, instead of replacing the old policy completely, making it difficult for officers to be confident that they had the current, complete policy. While the policy manual has a table of contents, there is no index, and new additions and revisions can quickly make older manuals difficult to navigate. In fact, during our investigation, BPD was unable to locate one of its own amendments to disclose to us. In short, BPD policies do not provide officers with clear guidance that can be rapidly digested and put into practice in the field. Although in early 2016 BPD made efforts to provide clearer and more effective guidance to its officers by distributing a binder of updated, core policies that each officer can use in the field, significant work remains to ensure that all of BPD's policies are clear, internally consistent, and readily available to officers.

BPD likewise fails to provide officers the opportunity to provide input on the policy as it is developed. We spoke with many officers, including supervisors and others in positions of authority, who were frustrated by the lack of input they were able to have on policy development, including the policies developed in 2016. With nearly 3,000 sworn officers and another 1,000 personnel, BPD will likely receive conflicting input in addition to the helpful ideas generated if it seeks input from officers. Without seeking this input, however, BPD fails to learn critical lessons from the field, and, as importantly, it risks alienating its officers and undermining adherence to the policies it develops. Indeed, during our interviews and ride-alongs, we found that large numbers of officers expressed a lack of confidence in the policy guidance BPD provides.

To ensure that its policies provide officers with sufficient guidance to police within the bounds of the Constitution, BPD must update its policies to make them reflect current legal requirements and develop a system to distribute and maintain policies and procedures in a way that promotes officer confidence and allows officers to use the policies effectively.

b. Deficient Training

Compounding the problems with policy development, BPD relies on deficient training on a broad array of substantive policing functions. This contributes to the pattern or practice of violations of the Constitution and federal law that we observed. Officers have not been properly trained on numerous important topics, from the use of force and de-escalation to stops, searches, and arrests, to how to supervise and investigate misconduct. Absent effective training on how to properly conduct these actions, it is not surprising that BPD officers frequently violate federal law when interacting with the community. Our observations of training programs, review of internal documents, and conversations with BPD personnel revealed that training deficiencies within the Department arise from foundational issues in BPD's overall approach to training. The Department has failed to establish a robust training program and lacks the basic organizational capacities, infrastructure, and support required to effectively train police officers to respond to situations that arise in law enforcement encounters.

i. Training Has Not Been a Top Priority Within BPD

Our investigation revealed that one of the fundamental causes of the breakdown in training is the Department's indifferent attitude towards its training program. Numerous members of BPD, from line officers to command staff to training personnel, conveyed to us that training is not a priority within the Department. Indeed, BPD's former director of the Training Academy released a needs assessment in 2015 that highlighted an "internal culture of placing training second," "expectations for 'rushed' training," and "outside pressure to condense training programs" as threats to the current program. *See Baltimore Police Department Training Academy Needs Assessment* (July 2015), at 5. Unfortunately, after the training director sent the needs assessment to BPD leadership, he did not receive a response for months. He also organized three different meetings with patrol commanders to begin making changes based on the needs assessment, but no commanders attended the meetings.

We found that this lack of emphasis on training has a pervasive influence on the Department. A significant number of officers we spoke with had no training beyond Maryland's basic requirements. Officers who had furthered their training did so because of their own personal interest or ambition, often using private funds and overcoming obstacles posed by supervisors or work schedules. Rather than encouraging additional training, supervisors view training as a peripheral activity that is consistently superseded by the need to keep officers on the street. Strikingly, training personnel are also subject to being pulled from their training duties to other tasks: basic training is frequently postponed or shifted due to overtime details for training personnel, leading to the extension of time basic recruits spend at the Academy. *See id.*

Training is crucial for effective and lawful policing in Baltimore. Indeed, keeping officers on the street without proper or up-to-date training is a disservice not only to community members, but to officers because of the impact on officer safety.

ii. BPD Lacks Basic Infrastructure to Train its Officers

The failure to invest in training infrastructure underscores BPD's failure to prioritize this critical component of effective policing. BPD lacks adequate staff to train its officers efficiently; its training facilities are outdated, ill-repaired, and often unable to accommodate modern training methods; and BPD lacks mechanisms to track officer attendance and performance to ensure that officers receive and understand the training they need to engage in safe, effective, constitutional policing.

The training academy is notably under-resourced. The program lost about two-thirds of its staff over the past three years: training staff fell from approximately 60 in 2013 to 20 currently. During the course of our investigation, thirty classes had no primary instructor. Multiple training units, including the ones responsible for supervisor training for new sergeants and lieutenants, were entirely vacant with no personnel staffing them. We also found that student-to-instructor ratios during training classes were often extremely high, undermining effective communication of the material. The Fraternal Order of Police has also highlighted this concern, noting that class sizes for new recruit training have averaged 35–50 officers. *See FOP Blueprint for Improved Policing* (July 11,

2012), at 7. Minimal staffing also poses difficulties for BPD instructors to attend outside courses to develop their training skills.

BPD training facilities are in a similarly troubling state. During the course of our investigation, we were informed that BPD has only 17 computers available to train its nearly 4,000 personnel. The buildings themselves are in disrepair: water cannot be consumed from the faucets, and the buildings often lack workable air conditioning and heating. According to the Academy's recent needs assessment:

> The decrepit state of the academy itself gives the impression of a lackadaisical and uncommitted attitude towards the necessities of training the modern police officer. Recruits, sworn personnel, visiting law-enforcement experts, and civilians get the impression that they are party to a fly-by-night, poverty-stricken department when they find themselves in a crumbling, drafty building.

See Baltimore Police Department Training Academy Needs Assessment (July 2015), at 12. The needs assessment additionally describes a long list of basic equipment and structures missing from training facilities, from protective headgear to mats for defensive exercises. Our observations confirmed many of these shortcomings.

Equally problematic is BPD's inability to evaluate and track officer training, thus failing to properly enforce training requirements. According to internal documents produced to us during the investigation, practical training exercises do not have a comprehensive evaluation tool that measures the skill and comprehension levels of students; instructors are unable to properly assess recruits' proficiency with defensive tactics or their ability to determine when situations require force; and the current curriculum lacks pre- and post-testing procedures for evaluating how training changed recruits' comprehension of relevant information. Nor is there a mechanism to track the follow-up remedial training required after a disciplinary incident. Numerous personnel conveyed that they do not have a workable tracking system for determining when officers require training or have failed to attend a class. Rather, the current system relies on a single officer updating an Excel spreadsheet with the activities of thousands of officers and formulating a training schedule. Likely due to this deficient tracking system, members of the training staff noted that they often find that officers are "missing" significant amounts of required training.

iii.   Despite Efforts to Improve Training, Much Work Remains to Fix the Program

Individuals throughout the Department have highlighted that the Department needs to significantly improve its training program. For example, in 2012, the Fraternal Order of Police's *Blueprint for Improved Policing in Baltimore* includes an entire section focused on training issues and recommendations. *See FOP Blueprint for Improved Policing* (July 11, 2012), at 6–8. More recently, BPD's July 2015 Training Academy Needs Assessment provides a program analysis, describing major issues in personnel, curriculum, equipment and structures, and budgeting. It also notes that the Academy has been working to address some of these issues. This includes topic-area trainings on, for example, the use of force, de-escalation, and understanding youth. The Academy has also begun to create training videos and providing roll-call trainings on current law, two important steps forward.

While this is encouraging, these new initiatives will not be successful without a considerable change in the overall approach to the Department's training. Much work remains, and this work will require dedication from all members of the Department to provide BPD's training programs with the necessary resources and to create an atmosphere that actively encourages training and preparation.

Three particular types of training will need significant work if the Department wants to effectively implement reforms. First, the Department lacks sufficient scenario-based training for its officers. This "real world" training is critical for building officers' skills. The FOP has also noted this deficit: according to the FOP, simulation training on real-life scenarios should be an area of focus for BPD, and officers have frequently noted that simulation training is crucial because it teaches officers how to react in situations that regularly arise. *See FOP Blueprint for Improved Policing* (July 11, 2012) at 7. Such training, especially within a defensive tactics or crisis intervention curriculum, helps students determine the most appropriate actions during law enforcement activities, such as the level of force to be used in an encounter. Fortunately, leaders in the Department have also recognized this need, but much work remains to address it.

Second, BPD's Field Training Officer, or FTO, program needs significant improvement. An effective FTO program is a critical tool for the Department to reinforce the training and values communicated to a new officer during the academy. Likewise, a poor FTO program can undermine the investment the Department has made in a recruit before that training has become ingrained. Generally speaking, BPD does not currently attract and retain the right officers for the FTO positions, and those who do become FTOs receive only one week of training. There is a dearth of qualified FTOs throughout the Department; some districts lack FTOs entirely. The importance and benefit of a strong FTO program have long been recognized. *See, e.g.*, Michael S. McCampbell, *Field Training for Police Officers: The State of the Art* (1987) (discussing research showing that FTO programs can help reduce civil liability complaints and increase a police agency's effectiveness in the community). To achieve the reforms required, BPD needs to invest in this program to ensure that the new officers it adds to the Department have a solid foundation to engage in effective and constitutional policing.

Finally, supervisor and leadership training is a critical need within the Department. Across all levels of BPD, we found that training for these positions was deficient. Our interviews revealed that many Department commanders do not have the opportunity to receive command development training, and the FOP noted a similar lack of training. *See FOP Blueprint for Improved Policing* (July 11, 2012) at 6. The Blueprint describes management training overall as "very insular," because department managers generally "stay in Baltimore." *Id.* In an agency of BPD's size, command-level and supervisory training is critical to ensuring that the values of the agency are reinforced by its leaders on a consistent, day-to-day basis. To create the type of cultural transformation required to address the constitutional violations we found, strong, capable leadership is required. Effective leadership, combined with procedural justice internal to the agency, results in officers who are more likely to behave according to agency standards when interacting with members of the community. *See, e.g. The Final Report of the President's Task Force on 21st Century Policing* (May 2015) at 54.

2. BPD Does Not Adequately Supervise Officers or Collect and Analyze Data on their Activities

Serious deficiencies in BPD's supervision of its enforcement activities, including through data collection and analysis, contribute to the Department's failure to identify and correct unconstitutional policing.

a. BPD Does Not Effectively Use Data to Oversee Officer Activity

BPD fails to collect and record important data on a broad range of police activities, and that, when it does collect data, BPD does not use the data to manage and supervise officer activity. As discussed in Section II.A4, *supra*, BPD's own internal audits and other indications demonstrate that officers fail to record any information on a large portion of the stops and searches conducted on Baltimore streets, contrary to BPD's own policies and procedures. When officers do record the existence of a stop, they do not consistently record important information connected to it. We found that officers likewise often fail to report using force against individuals. And as with stops and searches, even where force is reported, officers do not consistently document important supporting information, such as statements from witnesses and other officers on the scene. These omissions violate BPD's own policy requirements. The policies and procedures are also under-inclusive, however, and do not require information to be gathered that is essential to supervise officer activity effectively.

Even where data is collected, BPD fails to store it in systems that are capable of effective tracking and analysis. Chief among the data analysis challenges is BPD's failure to use integrated systems to maintain information. Information technology officers with the Department informed us that BPD uses 232 separate databases to store information, most of which cannot link to each other. Moreover, most files do not contain unique identifiers that allow supervisors to identify and review information about a single incident that may be stored in separate databases. For example, BPD uses different programs or databases to record stops, arrests, and incident reports. The different information captured on these activities is siloed: BPD's systems do not allow a supervisor reviewing the record of an arrest or use of force that stemmed from a pedestrian stop to access the stop record that is maintained separately. BPD's failure to respond to its pattern of conducting unlawful arrests illustrates the consequences of segregating related data in unconnected systems. As explained above, Maryland maintains data on all arrests by BPD officers for which booking officers find "no probable cause" or otherwise result in prosecutors declining to bring charges. Many of these problematic arrests stem from stops, searches, or other incidents described in various BPD reports. Yet the Department lacks any mechanism to connect problematic arrests to information about the enforcement actions that precipitated them because that information is maintained in separate programs or databases. BPD supervisors thus lack critical information to correct these constitutional violations.

Moreover, BPD conducts minimal pattern analysis of officer activities. The Department does not generate any reports or otherwise track patterns in officers' stops, searches, arrests, uses of force, or community interactions. For example, supervisors do not have access to information about how frequently officers search suspects during stops, the proportion of stops and searches that find weapons or contraband, how often stops or arrests lead to officers using force, or how often arrests lead to charges being dismissed. Because the Department does not track these activities, it lacks information to assess the effectiveness of its policing strategies and resource utilization.

BPD's inadequate data collection and analysis reflects broader deficiencies relating to officer supervision that allow constitutional violations to go uncorrected. As explained throughout our findings on stops, searches, arrests, and uses of force, supervisors conduct minimal substantive review of officers' justifications for these activities. A number of supervisors informed us that they view their role as "documenting" activity rather than assessing whether the activity conformed to policy, or that they believe internal affairs—not direct supervision—is the appropriate vehicle for assessing whether an enforcement action meets policy or constitutional requirements. Indeed, our review did not identify a single stop, search, or arrest that a front line supervisor found to violate constitutional standards—even though numerous incident reports for these activities describe facially unlawful police action. Supervisory review of officers' use of force is similarly limited. As explained further in Section II.C.5, *supra*, the Department sustained only one excessive force complaint that came from internal channels between 2010 and 2015, despite the over 2,800 uses of force that BPD recorded during that time period. These failures are compounded by the data collection and analysis deficiencies highlighted above. Supervisors lack important information about the activities and effectiveness of officers under their command.

BPD's failure to implement systems to collect and analyze data undermines not only BPD's ability to supervise its own activities, but also the ability of City leadership and the community to review the activities of their own police force. The lack of data and data analysis renders BPD opaque to any external entity, making it difficult to ascertain whether BPD is policing in a manner that accords with the priorities of City leadership or the communities BPD serves. BPD must institute more effective data management, so that it can be accountable to its community and leadership.

b. BPD Does Not Use an Adequate Early Intervention System

Related to BPD's failure to supervise its officers and collect data on their activities, the Department lacks an adequate early intervention system, or EIS, to identify officers based on patterns in their enforcement activities, complaints, and other criteria. An effective early intervention system allows sergeants, lieutenants, and commanders to proactively supervise the officers under their command and to continually assess officers' risk of engaging in problematic behavior. EIS is a forward-looking tool that helps supervisors interrupt negative patterns before they manifest as misconduct or unconstitutional activity. Likewise, early intervention systems help supervisors recognize positive patterns that should be encouraged. BPD's EIS does not achieve these goals.

Despite BPD's longstanding notice of concerns about its policing activities and problems with its internal accountability systems, the Department has failed to implement an adequate EIS or other system for tracking or auditing information about officer conduct. Rather, BPD has an early intervention system in name only; indeed, BPD commanders admitted to us that the Department's early intervention system is effectively nonfunctional. The system has several key deficiencies. First, BPD sets thresholds of activity that trigger "alerts" to supervisors about potentially problematic conduct that are too high. Because of these high thresholds, BPD supervisors often are not made aware of troubling behavioral patterns until after officers commit egregious misconduct. Second, even where alerts are triggered, we found that BPD supervisors do not consistently take appropriate action to counsel the officer, consider additional training, or otherwise intervene in a way that will correct the behavior before an adverse event occurs. Third, critical information is omitted or expunged from the EIS that could help address officer training or support needs or help prevent future misconduct. For example, BPD expunges discipline imposed from "command investigations"—more than half of all internal investigations handled by the Department—within one year where an officer voluntarily accepts the command punishment. This expungement is problematic for officer discipline, which is not the function of EIS, but it also inhibits a functional EIS because this critical information is omitted. Together, these deficiencies impede BPD's ability to identify and interrupt patterns of behavior that may compromise safety or lead to future misconduct. Moreover, under the State Law Enforcement Officer Bill of Rights, all complaints that do not result in a sustained finding are eligible to be expunged within three years and thus no longer captured in the Department's EIS system.

It is clear that the Department has been unable to interrupt serious patterns of misconduct. Our investigation found that numerous officers had recurring patterns of misconduct that were not adequately addressed. Similarly, we note that, in the past five years, 25 BPD officers were separately sued four or more times for Fourth Amendment violations. BPD has likewise failed to identify officers in need of support through its EIS. For example, one of the officer-involved shooting files we reviewed revealed that the involved officer—who unloaded his entire magazine at a car driving toward him—had been previously involved in two other officer-involved shootings in the past five years, in addition to a long history of complaints for harassment and excessive force. When interviewed about the most recent shooting, the officer told detectives that he believed he still had post-traumatic stress related to the other shootings. Even under BPD's high EIS thresholds, the officer's conduct had triggered alerts. But based on the records we reviewed, the Department failed to respond to those alerts in a way that could have uncovered the officer's condition or otherwise allowed for an intervention. The officer was criminally charged in the shooting. BPD's lack of an effective EIS exposes officers, the Department, and the public to risk that should be avoided.

B. BPD Fails to Adequately Support its Officers

BPD fails to support its officers through effective strategies for recruitment, retention, and staffing patterns, and does not provide them with appropriate technology and equipment. The Department must address a number of internal challenges—namely, current and projected manpower shortages, and outdated technology, facilities, equipment and insufficient resources— in order to ensure that officers are adequately supported. BPD districts are short-staffed, an issue that is further complicated by challenges the Department is facing in retaining experienced officers, and in recruiting qualified cadets. Additionally, the Department's technology, equipment, and facilities are outdated, creating inefficiencies for officers and the Department, and negatively impacting the Department's relationship with the community. The Department also lacks critical resources to support officers, such as psychological counseling for officers following a traumatic incident.

First, BPD does not have a Department-wide plan to address staffing shortages in patrol; instead, each district deals with its own shortages independently. Districts address their staffing shortages by "drafting," or requiring, officers to work additional hours after their regular ten-hour shift. Officers are "drafted" to work up to an additional ten hours after their regular shift, making for, potentially, a twenty-hour day. Only one district indicated that they attempt to draft officers who are not working the following day after being drafted. Each district has crafted its own process of drafting, and there are variations in each district's procedures. The Department has, however, indicated it is in the process of creating a policy to more consistently address staffing shortages. The Department does not record, track, or assess which officers are drafted, how frequently they are drafted, or for how many hours they are drafted per day or over any period of time. Officers we spoke with consistently informed us of the serious negative impact that drafting has on their morale. Additionally, the potential negative impact that drafting has on officers' decision-making skills after working for up to twenty hours is equally troubling. It would be difficult even for officers who are well-trained and guided by proper policies – which BPD officers are not – after working fourteen to twenty hours, to exercise restraint and good judgment in their interactions with the public. It is difficult to expect ill-trained officers who are provided little to no guidance to do so in such circumstances.

It appears BPD's staffing shortage will not be resolved in the short term. We heard from officers, supervisors, and command staff that many officers join BPD to gain experience in a high-activity environment, and after three to five years, leave the Department for less-demanding and higher-paid positions with neighboring agencies. *See FOP Blueprint for Improved Policing* (July 11, 2012) at 4, 13. This is a significant drain on the Department's resources, as these experienced officers, if they remained, would be the future leaders of the Department, and critical to the success of the Department's law enforcement efforts. The Department also appears to be confronting challenges in recruiting qualified officers – it has only met a fraction of its goals for the 2016 Academy class. At least one of the Department's background check processes—its psychological testing—has been investigated for allegedly rushing those evaluations, sometimes conducting psychological evaluations for aspiring officers in as little as fifteen minutes.[124] The Department must ensure that in its efforts to recruit a sufficient quantity of officers, it does not sacrifice the quality of officers that the Baltimore community and current employees of the Department deserve.

---

[124] Kevin Rector, *Provider of mental health evaluations for Baltimore police under investigation*, The Baltimore Sun, Aug. 5, 2015 (9:23 PM), http://www.baltimoresun.com/health/bs-md-police-psych-evals-20150805-story.html.

Second, officers are also challenged by BPD's outdated technology, equipment, and facilities. The Department is hampered by significant technological infrastructure gaps and historically has underestimated the infrastructure required to implement technology. While we applaud the Department's advances, such as its commitment to equipping all officers with body-worn cameras, BPD must also ensure that it updates its technological infrastructure to support such initiatives, as necessary. Likewise, officers suffer from being supplied with outdated, broken, or in some cases, no equipment. As one officer noted to the Fraternal Order of Police in a focus group, "How am I supposed to pull someone over for having a taillight out when my car has two?" *See also FOP Blueprint for Improved Policing* (July 11, 2012) at 10. Officers have no computers in their cars, forcing them to return to the district station to type reports, and even those computers are often not working. Although the Department uses the "PocketCop" application on departmentally issued cell phones, we found that many officers did not have access to it for various reasons, and that it could not be used for many reports. This absence of technology for field-based reporting creates an additional drain on the Department's already limited resources. Taking officers off the street to type reports at the district takes away from time that could be spent on law enforcement or community building activities. It also creates inefficiencies for officers who often must write reports on paper in the field while their memories of incidents are fresh, and then type the same information into computer databases after arriving at the district station at the end of their shift.

These equipment issues not only create inefficiencies for officers and drain the Department's resources, they also negatively impact officer morale. The dilapidated state of some of the Department's district stations also lowers officer morale, and affects community relationships. The Department also lacks critical support services for officers, such as adequate psychological counseling or peer support program following a shooting or other traumatic event. Despite its budgetary issues, the City of Baltimore will need to make an investment in its public safety facilities and resources to ensure that officers have the tools necessary to properly serve the residents and businesses of the City.

C. BPD Fails to Hold Officers Accountable for Misconduct

BPD relies on deficient accountability systems that fail to curb unconstitutional policing. For years, the Department's process of investigating and adjudicating complaints has been plagued by systemic failures, including: discouraging individuals from filing complaints; poor investigative techniques; unnecessary delays; minimal review and supervision; and a persistent failure to discipline officers for misconduct, even in cases of repeated or egregious violations. BPD likewise fails to provide information about officer misconduct in a transparent manner or receive input on the accountability process from the community it serves. As a result, a cultural resistance to accountability has developed and been reinforced within the Department. This culture further undermines accountability by discouraging officers from reporting misconduct and discouraging supervisors from sustaining allegations of it. BPD's persistent failure to hold officers accountable for misconduct contributes to an erosion of the community trust that is central to effective law enforcement.

Central to BPD's accountability systems is the Internal Investigation Division, or IID. IID investigates and resolves complaints of officer misconduct, both complaints received internally from other officers or BPD employees, and those received from members of the community. Within the IID, "Ethics" detectives investigate complaints that officers engaged in potentially criminal activity, or other allegations that, though not criminal, implicate an officer's integrity or truthfulness. "General internal affairs" detectives investigate all other allegations of serious officer misconduct, including most instances of excessive force. Outside of the IID, each of the nine patrol districts, along with each Specialized Unit within BPD's Operations Bureau, housed a "Command Investigations Unit," or CIU, until January of 2016, when the Department centralized all Command Investigation Units at the IID. Before centralization, each CIU operated independently of the other CIUs and of the IID. The CIUs investigate minor violations of BPD policy, and BPD has authorized district and unit commanders to impose minor discipline in the event an accused officer agrees to the discipline.

When IID sustains the allegations in an investigation,[125] or an officer refuses to accept discipline at the command level, the case is sent to the Office of Administrative Hearings to coordinate the drafting of administrative charges and, if necessary, to arrange disciplinary proceedings. Under the State's Law Enforcement Officer's Bill of Rights (LEOBR), officers are then entitled to an adversarial hearing, or trial board, before the Department can discipline them. At BPD, trial boards convened to adjudicate certain minor violations of BPD's command discipline policy typically consist of one person, drawn from a pool of BPD commanders. Trial boards convened to adjudicate major discipline are composed of two commanders and one BPD member of the same rank as the accused officer. If the trial board finds the officer is not guilty of violating BPD policy, that finding terminates the case and the Department cannot discipline the officer. But if the trial board finds the officer is guilty, it hears a presentation of mitigating evidence, and then recommends discipline. Ultimately, the commissioner determines the appropriate discipline, but

---

[125] When BPD completes an internal investigation, there are four possible outcomes. The Department can sustain an allegation, which means investigators found, by a preponderance of evidence, that a policy violation occurred. Allegations can be found "not sustained," which means that investigators were unable to tell either way. Allegations can be unfounded, meaning the investigator determined that the violation did *not* occur. Or allegations may be exonerated, meaning that the action alleged did occur, but that it did not violate Department policy.

may only do so if the trial board first finds the officer guilty. The commissioner may depart from the Board's recommendation and impose less or more discipline. But if the commissioner imposes greater discipline, the officer is entitled to another opportunity to be heard. The officer may then appeal any discipline imposed by the Department to the state courts in Maryland.

We found deficiencies throughout these accountability systems that undermine adherence to BPD's policies and procedures and contribute to the violations of federal law that we found.

1. BPD Lacks Adequate Systems to Investigate Complaints and Impose Discipline

BPD's systems for holding officers accountable are plagued by several deficiencies. We found that BPD discourages members of the public from filing complaints; improperly classifies complaints to mask misconduct; delays investigations of complaints unnecessarily; uses poor investigative techniques to gather evidence about misconduct; fails to consistently document the results of its investigations; and does not receive input from the community or share information about its investigative processes. As a result, the Department is rarely able to impose discipline for misconduct, and many officers believe that disciplinary determinations are not made fairly or consistently.

a. BPD Discourages Members of the Public from Filing Complaints

BPD discourages members of the public from filing complaints against officers through the procedural requirements BPD has imposed on filing complaints, and BPD officers and supervisors have actively discouraged community members from filing complaints. These practices pose significant barriers to members of the Baltimore community who try to alert the Department to misconduct by its officers.

As an initial matter, BPD places unnecessary conditions on the filing of complaints. While the Department ostensibly accepts complaints made in person, by telephone, or over email, it requires complaints alleging many common types of misconduct—including excessive force, abusive language, harassment, false arrest and imprisonment—to be signed, notarized, and filed in person at one of just a few locations throughout the City.[126] Additionally, complaints alleging excessive force must be sworn under penalty of perjury. Although IID commanders we interviewed informed us that, despite these requirements, the Department investigates all complaints even if they are not notarized or submitted in person, our review of BPD's files indicated that, in practice, BPD does not investigate unless these requirements are met. For example, in 2013 an individual called BPD's internal affairs to complain about an officer who grabbed him by the neck and called him a "punk ass faggot." Although the individual gave a statement describing the incident over the phone, BPD supervisors closed the case because the complainant did not show up in person at BPD's Internal Investigation Division to "fill out a CRB form and to have his statement notarized." Indeed, the BPD investigator claimed that the man "failed to cooperate" by not submitting a notarized form. These requirements all but ensure that numerous anonymous complaints, or those received over the phone, by email, or in person at any of BPD's nine police districts, will go unexamined.

In addition, we found examples of BPD officers expressly discouraging civilians from filing

---

[126] If the complaint is made by a juvenile, the juvenile must be accompanied by an adult.

complaints, sometimes mocking or humiliating them in the process. Some civilians wishing to alert BPD to officer misconduct had to endure verbal abuse and contact BPD multiple times before investigators would move forward with any investigation. As described *supra* at 69-70, for example, BPD officers ridiculed an African-American man attempting to file a complaint that officers used excessive force and racial slurs during an arrest: when the man arrived at the district headquarters to make the complaint, officers told him, "you can take your black ass down to Kirk Avenue before the bus leaves because you know how you black people like the bus." Kirk Avenue is the location of BPD's Internal Investigation Division. In another incident, a woman alleged that a BPD supervisor flatly refused to accept a complaint that officers used excessive force when arresting her son. According to the woman, the supervisor refused to accept the complaint, telling the woman "she could not go against her officers."

To ensure that it learns about potential constitutional violations and other misconduct by its officers, and to rebuild its relationship with many of the communities it serves, BPD must reform its complaint intake procedures and make them accessible to the public.

b. Supervisors Misclassify Complaints and "Administratively Close" Them Without Investigation

After intake of a complaint, BPD investigators frequently misclassify those complaints or administratively close them with little attempt to contact the complainant.

First, BPD investigators often inappropriately categorize complaints as minor allegations that may be resolved at the command level without IID involvement. Appropriately categorizing a complaint is critical because it affects which internal affairs component will investigate, the level of investigation undertaken, and the possible discipline imposed. BPD's policy on command discipline lists categories of cases which "may" be handled by the district, but this fails to provide guidance for officers and detectives about when cases should be referred to IID, or who is responsible for making that decision. Instead, we were told that BPD officers and IID investigators categorize complaints based on "common sense." Moreover, we found that BPD does not use its internal affairs database to consistently review how complaints are categorized, and that is its only mechanism for doing so. This process vests considerable discretion in supervisors, and we found that supervisors frequently use this discretion to classify allegations of misconduct that result in minimal investigation. Indeed, we found that the Department resolved the majority of the approximately 38,000 allegations[127] made against BPD officers from 2010 through 2015 at the command level without referral to IID, resulting in significantly less investigation. Moreover, of these 38,000 allegations, 9,694 allegations were categorized as "supervisor complaints," which, according to BPD commanders, require no investigation at all. Accordingly, allegations handled as supervisor complaints virtually never result in discipline. We found that BPD "administratively closed" 67 percent of supervisor complaints and sustained just 0.27 percent of them, or 1 out of every 370 allegations.

Many complaints that were sent to command investigations or classified as "supervisor complaints" alleged serious misconduct, including allegations that officers committed criminal assault, theft, and domestic violence. In 2014, for example, although a complaint on intake alleged a

---

[127] A single complaint may contain multiple allegations.

"sexual assault," the case was assigned to a command investigations unit and categorized as "misconduct/improper search" and "discourtesy." In 2011, a sergeant likewise misclassified a complaint alleging that that BPD officers had been harassing an African-American woman's nephew over the past month by repeatedly stopping him near their home in West Baltimore. Though the woman wished to make a complaint of harassment, the sergeant categorized the complaint as a "supervisor complaint" and closed the case without conducting any interviews of the involved officers or the woman's nephew. This is troubling, particularly given our findings that BPD officers engage in unlawful stops and discriminatory policing.

Second, even where complaints are nominally "accepted," BPD supervisors often "administratively close" them with minimal investigation. Indeed, BPD supervisors administratively closed 33 percent of all allegations received from 2010 through 2015—ensuring that the allegations would result in no further investigation or officer discipline. Administrative closures frequently occur after supervisors make only minimal efforts to contact the complainant. Some of the files we reviewed contained no indication that investigators attempted to contact complainants at all. Many other files showed that investigations languished for months before investigators made any effort to reach out, or that investigators closed cases after complainants failed to respond to a single letter, answer a phone call, or appear for a scheduled interview. By administratively closing complaints, BPD investigators evade BPD policy that requires all complaints to be labeled as sustained, not sustained, exonerated or unfounded. Some BPD officers we interviewed believed it was appropriate to administratively close a complaint when the complainant withdrew his or her complaint, or could otherwise not be reached. Others believed "complaints" that failed to allege a "real" violation of BPD policy should be administratively closed. These administrative closures, combined with BPD's failure to ensure that complaints are appropriately classified, undermine BPD's system of accountability and contributes to the perception shared by officers and community members alike that discipline is inconsistent and arbitrary.

c. BPD Fails to Investigate Complaints in a Timely Manner or with Effective Techniques

When investigations of complaints do proceed, they are hampered from the start by poor investigative techniques and unreasonable delays. These failures limit the Department's ability to discipline its officers by preventing investigators from gathering evidence of misconduct and subjecting evidence to attack during administrative proceedings.

i. Delays Impede Investigations

BPD's misconduct investigations are frequently plagued by delays that compromise the evidence-gathering process and undermine community confidence. As an initial matter, even when BPD nominally "accepts" an external complaint and assigns the case to an investigator, the Department's practice in most cases is to not investigate that complaint until the individual appears in person at BPD's Internal Investigation Division during business hours and participates in a formal, taped interview. By that point, key evidence that could corroborate claims may be lost or destroyed. We found instances in which investigators waited months before canvassing neighborhoods in which alleged misconduct occurs. After such delays, physical evidence is often destroyed, witnesses cannot be located, and witness memories have faded. Other important evidence, such as surveillance video, may also be unavailable.

These delays not only impede effective investigations, they communicate to the community that BPD does not take complaints seriously—even those alleging egregious officer behavior. For example, a man alleged in 2013 that two plainclothes officers punched him in the face, placed him in a chokehold, and spit in his face during an arrest. The man, whose arrest prosecutors declined to pursue, participated in a formal interview at IID during which he provided the investigator with the name of a witness to the incident, and the witness's wife, who could help investigators locate him. The investigator made no effort to follow up with the civilian witness until eight months after the incident occurred. At that time, the investigator went to the car wash where the witness's wife had been working at the time of the incident and was told by the owner that she was no longer employed there. The investigator then recommended to close the complaint as "not sustained" because "[w]ithout testimony from independent witnesses," along with the officers' denial, "there exists insufficient evidence to prove or disprove the allegations." BPD's investigation of a second 2013 complaint alleging serious misconduct suffered even longer delays. The complainant alleged he was hospitalized after two officers slammed him to the ground and unlawfully arrested him for "hindering" and failing to obey due to his refusal to leave the area while officers questioned his brother-in-law. The complaint was not investigated for thirteen months while two command investigation units sent the complaint back and forth. After the case was rediscovered after an audit of IA Pro, it lingered for another four months before a supervisor finally assigned the case to an IID detective. BPD ultimately found the complaint not sustained for "lack of cooperation" when witnesses failed to show up for interviews *seventeen months* after the complaint was filed. According to the investigative file, the Department never interviewed the accused officers.

In another egregious example, an investigator made minimal delayed attempts to look into a woman's complaint that two BPD officers fondled her when conducting a search and called her a "junkie, whore bitch." The investigator assigned to the case made no attempt to contact the woman until four months after she made these serious allegations. And at that point, the investigator merely sent the woman a certified letter seeking information. Two months later, after the letter had come back unclaimed, the investigator went to the residential address the woman had originally provided, only to discover she had been evicted months before. Moreover, the delays precluded investigators from identifying relevant video evidence. The incident occurred in a public location—the Lexington Market—that was likely captured on video surveillance. Yet the detective made no attempt to gather the footage until ten months after the incident. By that time, any video had been deleted. Investigators also waited ten months to reach out to a witness, even though the complainant had provided the witness's contact information at the time she filed the complaint. Ultimately, the investigator learned that the complainant had passed away several months before he first contacted the witness. BPD then found the complaint "not sustained."

In these and many similar cases we reviewed, unnecessary delays precluded BPD investigators from gathering important evidence about allegations of serious misconduct. Going forward, collecting and assessing such evidence in a timely manner will be a critical piece of the accountability system that BPD must build to identify officers' constitutional violations and impose appropriate discipline.

ii. BPD Uses Ineffective Methods to Investigate Misconduct Allegations

In addition to frequent delays that limit the information available about misconduct allegations, poor investigative techniques further compromise BPD's investigations. We identified several key failures that recur throughout the Department's investigative files, including the failure to adequately consider inconsistencies in investigations, as well as inappropriate interviewing methods and notice of allegations.

First, investigators fail to adequately consider evidence and statements from witnesses or other officers that contradict explanations provided by officers accused of misconduct. Indeed, BPD appears to apply a standard that favors officers when evaluating statements made by complainants and involved officers. While BPD's Internal Affairs Manual encourages investigators to be wary of a complainant's inconsistent statements, the Department permits officers to submit addendums that clarify their original statements. And when inconsistencies arise—either from such addenda or other evidence—investigators generally discredit or discount entirely evidence contradicting the accused officer's account. We found investigations in which this took place even where the accused officer's account is contradicted by physical evidence, including photographic or video evidence.

Second, BPD investigators compromise officer interviews by failing to probe beyond reports the accused officer already provided, and performing unrecorded "pre-interviews" with accused officers. As we described in Section II.C.5, *supra* at 107, regarding force investigations, these pre-interviews compromise the integrity of an investigation. Similarly, we also found numerous instances in which officers reviewed their statement or administrative report related to the incident before the interview, and the interview then consisted merely of the accused officer orally reciting his administrative report.[128] IID investigators did not probe beyond this oral recitation. These interview techniques inhibit the function of IID investigators to obtain reliable information from officers accused of misconduct.

Third, BPD risks compromising investigations by providing accused officers with a detailed notice describing the alleged misconduct, often right after a complaint has been filed and before any investigation occurs. While LEOBR provides that officers must receive basic notice of allegations and five days to obtain counsel prior to questioning, BPD frequently notifies officers almost immediately after the Department receives a complaint.[129] This notice often takes place before a detective undertakes any investigation or even attempts to contact the complainant to set up an

---

[128] BPD officers' collective bargaining agreement provides the opportunity to review statements and reports prior to being interviewed .

[129] Until early 2016, LEOBR entitled officers to a ten day notice period to obtain counsel prior to being questioned. We note that these waiting periods prescribed by LEOBR may, in many instances, impede effective investigations, and that a similar waiting period is not afforded to members of the public who may have been involved in an incident or were witnesses to the incident. In some instances, we saw evidence that BPD required witnesses to be interviewed immediately, even while the witness's friend or family member was being taken to the hospital as a result of the incident. The best practice is to interview the officer as soon as possible. Additionally, the International Association of Chiefs of Police "opposes any special and/or additional protection for law enforcement officers. Officers' rights should be no greater than those of other private and public sector employees." LEGISLATIVE AGENDA FOR THE 114TH CONGRESS, INTERNATIONAL ASSOCIATION OF CHIEFS OF POLICE 20, http://www.theiacp.org/Portals/0/documents/pdfs/IACP114thLegislativeAgenda.pdf.

interview. Moreover, the notice specifically articulates the allegations against the officer—sometimes including the date and time of the incident in question. Providing such detailed notice at the outset of an investigation, which is not required by LEOBR, may compromise certain investigative steps and opens the possibility that a complainant may be retaliated against or intimidated prior to speaking with investigators. Indeed, the Department's own internal affairs audit identified these same potential problems in 2014. The Department nonetheless continues to use its early notification practice.

iii. BPD Fails to Adequately Supervise Investigations

The deficiencies in BPD's investigative techniques persist in part because of ineffective supervision and training. Indeed, we found that most investigators receive no formal investigative training. Lack of training coupled with minimal supervision results in some investigators continuing to rely on poor investigative techniques. For example, one CIU detective who was responsible for all command investigations for an entire district told us that his practice was to allow accused officers to be interviewed by questionnaire—which officers could complete off-site with the assistance of their attorneys—rather than submit to in-person interviews. Although BPD formally discontinued the use of written questionnaires years ago, the practice persists because of inadequate training and oversight. Indeed, this practice has continued even after it was criticized by the Department's own internal affairs audit.

Moreover, BPD supervisors fail to identify deficiencies or questionable findings in investigations. We found that commanders consistently approve investigative findings, even where investigative files are deficient or incomplete. In our review, we found that files frequently omitted basic information, such as the outcome of the investigation or any discipline imposed. We also found key pieces of evidence referred to in the investigator's narrative—including witness statements, photographs, and video footage—were left out of the case file itself. Nevertheless, across all the case files we reviewed, we saw virtually no evidence that supervisors sent cases back for further investigation or clarification. Nor do supervisors meaningfully review investigators' determinations about whether to sustain complaints. Indeed, CIU investigators told us they were not required to have supervisors review and sign off on investigations that resulted in findings of "not sustained," although supervisors must approve an investigation that results in a finding of "sustained."

Additionally, BPD's internal affairs files and database indicate that BPD does not adequately supervise investigators to ensure that they meet investigative deadlines, especially in the command investigations units. Under LEOBR, in order to discipline an officer for misconduct, the Department must complete the internal investigation and bring administrative charges within one year. We reviewed complaints where investigators recommended closing cases because the investigations had extended past the one-year deadline. Indeed, BPD's internal affairs database itself includes possible "findings" that indicate cases were closed due to "expiration."

Finally, BPD has not taken sufficient steps to ensure that investigators do not have a conflict of interest. We found instances in which conflicts of interest could have compromised an internal investigation. For example, one internal affairs detective we interviewed told us that he had been detailed to serve under the supervision of an officer he was investigating at that time, and that the commander knew of the investigation. This is troubling, and it communicates to officers, investigators, and the community that internal investigations are not a priority of the Department.

BPD's failure to ensure that investigations are thoroughly and fairly investigated limits its ability to hold officers accountable for misconduct. Without adequate evidence, the chances of sustaining allegations of officer misconduct are diminished. And even where allegations of misconduct are sustained, the Department's ability to marshal adequate evidence at trial board proceedings is compromised. Consequently, officers frequently do not face internal discipline even where evidence of misconduct exists.

d. BPD Fails to Sustain Complaints and Apply Discipline Consistently

Deficiencies in BPD's complaint intake and investigation contribute to BPD's extremely low rate of sustaining allegations of officer misconduct, which in turn leads to a lack of discipline and accountability in the Department. Discipline for allegations of serious misconduct is rare. Of the 1,382 allegations of excessive force that BPD tracked from 2010 through 2015, only 31 allegations, or 2.2 percent were sustained. These allegations arose out of fourteen separate incidents. In light of the significant evidence of excessive force we found in our investigation, the low rate of sustaining excessive force complaints is troubling. Similarly, BPD completed investigations into 1,359 allegations of discourtesy from 2010 through 2015, and sustained just 2.6 percent of those allegations, arising out of just fifteen incidents. This low number of sustained outcomes is also concerning, considering the number of community members we spoke to who described BPD officers behaving in a rude or abusive manner during encounters with community members.

When complaints of misconduct are sustained, however, the trial board process that follows in order for discipline to be imposed also has several problems that impede accountability. First, the process is beset by delay. The Department reported to us, for example, that some trial boards conducted in 2015 were to resolve cases BPD began investigating in 2011. Delays of this magnitude send a message to officers that misconduct is tolerated, frustrating officers and supervisors who are trying to follow and implement Department policies and procedures. They also signal to the public, and in particular to the complainant, that officers who commit misconduct are unlikely to be held accountable.

Second, officers facing the trial board have substantial powers granted to them by LEOBR and BPD's collective bargaining agreements to shape the membership of the trial board that will hear their case, undermining accountability. Trial boards convened by BPD to adjudicate allegations of misconduct are typically composed of three officers selected from a pool determined by the commissioner. Under LEOBR, each board must include one officer who is "the same rank as the law enforcement officer against whom the complaint is filed."[130] The accused officer has the right to reject assigned Board members a total of three times through the use of peremptory strikes. The officer can exercise these strikes up to and including the day of the hearing itself, potentially dismissing all members of the board. We heard from numerous sources, including many within BPD and City leadership, that this use of peremptory strikes permits officers to assemble a trial board sympathetic to their interests, particularly because the pool of eligible command staff in the Department is limited, and because the command staff members are also part of the same union.

---

[130] Md. Code Ann., Pub. Safety § 3–107.

The Maryland legislature amended LEOBR in early 2016 to authorize jurisdictions within the state to allow up to two voting or nonvoting civilians to serve on trial boards if authorized by local law or if negotiated through collective bargaining with the police union. To date, BPD does not allow civilians to serve on the trial board.

Although BPD produced a very limited amount of information about trial board proceedings, we saw indications that the construction of the trial boards undermines confidence in the equity of the process. We requested information on all trial boards conducted between 2010 and 2015, and BPD produced only twelve transcripts of trial board proceedings, and no summaries and no written findings for the 139 trial boards the Department reported took place between 2010 and 2015, despite our request that the Department produce "all documentation" concerning trial board cases. In addition, BPD's attorneys told us the Department will only create a transcript of a trial board that results in a guilty finding if the officer challenges the discipline imposed in court. This lack of information is consistent with BPD's own assessment: according to an internal audit, BPD has historically failed to fully track information related to disciplining officers. Such minimal documentation of the trial board process prevents the Department from fully evaluating the proceedings or identifying patterns or deficiencies that may contribute to the Department's failure to discipline an officer.

This lack of consistency and fairness in imposing discipline has a profound effect on officer morale, and it also affects how officers interact with the public. Throughout our interviews and ride-alongs with officers, we heard officers express that discipline is only imposed if an incident makes it into the press or if you were on the wrong side of a supervisor, not because of the magnitude of the misconduct. Similarly, some officers felt that command staff creates an appearance of addressing problems after a high-profile incident by rushing to issue new policies, without any officer input, and often in conflict with existing policies. By BPD rushing to issue these new policies, officers felt that they were not provided with adequate training to follow the new rules, exposing them to risk even as the Department appeared to address the problem and respond to City politics. This lack of internal procedural justice—officers' sense that they are being treated fairly by their Department—diminishes officer morale and diminishes officers' adherence to Departmental rules. This, in turn, can make officers less likely to treat members of the public fairly and in accordance with BPD policies and procedures, potentially contributing to violations of federal law we found in our investigation. *See, e.g.,* Nicole E. Haas et. al., *Explaining officer compliance: The importance of procedural justice and trust inside a police organization*, Criminology & Criminal Justice, p. 14 (January 2015) (finding that "the perception of procedural justice and trust is associated with higher levels of endorsement of rules and regulations on the use of force").

e. BPD Lacks Effective Civilian or Community Oversight

BPD's accountability system is shielded almost entirely from public view, and the civilian oversight mechanisms that are currently in place are inadequate and ineffective. These flaws damage the Department's legitimacy in the community.

Community members are unable to obtain information about BPD's complaint and discipline systems at almost every step in the process. Complainants face many hurdles in filing complaints, but once they are filed, it is difficult for complainants to obtain information about how the complaints are progressing or whether and when they will be acted upon. Indeed, even when discipline is imposed, notice of this action is only given to a small group within the Department, not to the complainant or to the public except in unusual circumstances where the Department determines that a broader announcement of the discipline is in the public interest. Trial board proceedings have been closed to the public historically. Although they were opened to the public in early 2016, it is too early to determine what effect this has on the community's ability to affect the accountability process. The Maryland Public Information Act, or MPIA, further limits BPD's transparency to the public. The MPIA prohibits disclosure of documents that constitute "personnel records." *See* Md. Code Ann. § 10–616. The statute does not define the scope of this prohibition, but Maryland appellate courts have held that it applies to all materials related to hiring, promotions, and discipline, as well as "any matter involving an employee's status." *See, e.g., Montgomery County v. Shropshire*, 23 A.3d 205, 215 (Md. Ct. App. 2011). We heard from numerous sources that this provision has repeatedly blocked attempts to access information about the resolution of complaints and other issues of public concern related to BPD's policing activities.

In addition, Baltimore's Civilian Review Board, or CRB, has proven to be ineffective at changing this dynamic, in large part because it has never been provided with adequate authority or resources to perform its intended function. Established in 2000, the Board was meant to be a crucial check on police misconduct by providing an alternative investigative and review process. The Board is made up of civilian representatives from each of the City's nine police districts selected by the Mayor and approved by the City Counsel, along with members without voting power from local advocacy organizations and the local chapter of the Fraternal Order of Police. The Board may accept complaints that allege excessive force, abusive language, harassment, false arrest, and false imprisonment directly from the community. BPD is also required by policy to forward all complaints containing these categories of allegations to the Board. The Board may review BPD's investigations, or it may conduct an independent investigation and make recommendations directly to the commissioner that the complaint be sustained, not sustained, unfounded, or exonerated. It can also request that BPD undertake additional investigation.

The Board has faced several impediments to serving as a meaningful community backstop for accountability. First, the Board relies upon BPD to forward complaints that fall within its authority, except when a complaint is filed directly with the Board, and BPD often fails to forward complaints in a timely manner. Indeed, CRB staff members told us of cases BPD forwarded to the Board only after BPD had already closed its investigation, despite BPD's obligation to share the complaint with the Board within 48 hours of receipt. The Board has no authority to audit BPD to determine if it has received all the complaints that should have been forwarded to it. Second, the Board has insufficient resources and authority to conduct its own investigations. During 2010 to 2015, the Board only had a single investigator to investigate all the complaints that fell within its authority. The Board also cannot compel officers to participate in investigations; indeed, LEOBR provides that sworn law enforcement officers can only be "interrogated" by other sworn law enforcement officers. Finally, when the Board makes recommendations to the commissioner about investigative findings, or recommends that the IID conduct additional investigation, the Board has no way of knowing if BPD acts on its recommendations, much less requiring that BPD do so. The lack of resources and authority that the City currently invests in the Board render it ineffective, heightening community perceptions that BPD is resistant to accountability.

We note that we are encouraged that the Civilian Review Board was recently able to hire several new staff members, and is now coordinating a new mediation initiative for police and community members. Although these are steps in the right direction, the Board will still be unable to fulfill its mission if it is not granted more authority and supported with adequate resources to perform its duties.

2. BPD's Internal Culture is Resistant to Effective Discipline

The longstanding deficiencies in BPD's systems for investigating complaints has contributed to a cultural resistance to accountability that persists in the Department. The cultural opposition to meaningful accountability within the Department is reflected by the lack of discipline for serious misconduct and widespread violations of minor policy provisions; the failure to take action against officers with a known reputation for repeatedly violating Department policy and constitutional requirements; and the reluctance of officers to report observed misconduct for fear that doing so will subject them to retaliation.

a. BPD Has Allowed Violations of Policy To Go Unaddressed Even When They Are Widespread Or Involve Serious Misconduct

In part because of the above failures in investigating complaints against officers, BPD allows policy violations to go unaddressed, even when they occur in large number or involve serious misconduct. For example, the most common allegations of policy violation that fall under command investigations level is that officers fail to appear in court. The Department's internal affairs database indicates that 6,571 allegations were made that officers failed to appear in court between January 1, 2010, and March 28, 2016. For 1,698 of these allegations, the Department did not record any disposition at all, although a "completed date" has been entered for all but a handful of these incidents, indicating that the investigation has concluded. Additionally, the Department "administratively closed" 1,142 of the cases. Thus, nearly half of these policy violations—43 percent—resulted in no action being taken against the officer for failing to appear in court. Without the arresting or witnessing officer's testimony, many of these cases lack adequate evidence to proceed, and are dismissed.

Moreover, we found evidence that some BPD officers engage in criminal behavior that BPD does not sufficiently address. We heard complaints from the community that some officers target members of a vulnerable population—people involved in the sex trade—to coerce sexual favors from them in exchange for avoiding arrest, or for cash or narcotics. This conduct is not only criminal, it is an abuse of power. Unfortunately, we not only found evidence of this conduct in BPD's internal affairs files, it appeared that the Department failed to adequately investigate allegations of such conduct, allowing it to recur.

For example, BPD investigators became aware of one officer's alleged misconduct in March of 2012 when they conducted a "prostitution initiative" "for the purposes of gathering intelligence and obtaining confidential informants relating to police corruption." One of the women interviewed informed BPD investigators that she met with a certain officer and engaged in sexual activities in the officer's patrol car once every other week "in exchange for U.S. Currency or immunity from arrest." The Department administratively closed the case nine months later, without, it appears, referring the matter for criminal prosecution or interviewing the accused officer, or any other potential witnesses.

Ten months after closing the first investigation, the Chief of BPD's Office of Professional Responsibility received an anonymous "Crime Stoppers" tip that the same officer was "having sex in his patrol vehicle" with a different person involved in the sex trade. The Department initiated a new investigation, and assigned the case to a different detective. One day after opening the investigation, an assistant state's attorney directed the detective to subpoena the woman's phone records for a six month-period. The detective waited more than a month to do so, and then did not review those records for another six months, until May of 2014. The records confirmed that the officer and the woman exchanged 237 text messages and five phone calls in the six-month period for which records were subpoenaed. Approximately four months later, the State's Attorney's Office declined to prosecute the officer, though BPD's administrative investigation remained open.

Four months after the State's Attorney's Office declined to prosecute, in February of 2015, BPD received a third, new tip that the same officer was engaging in sexual activities with the same woman involved in the sex trade who was mentioned in the "Crime Stoppers" tip. The new tip came from a neighboring Police Department, which interviewed the woman and subpoenaed her phone records in the course of an investigation. Though BPD's administrative investigation into the "Crime Stoppers" tip remained open, BPD opened a third, separate investigation into the new tip, assigning a new, third detective to investigate the same officer's conduct. The case was assigned "low" priority. The third BPD detective attempted to interview the woman but postponed the interview because she was in ill health. Two days later, the woman passed away. The investigators finally reviewed the officer's phone records, which indicated that the officer had exchanged text messages—some sexually explicit—with several other women whose numbers were linked to online profiles for sex trade services. Finally, months later, Department investigators interviewed the officer two times in connection with the two open investigations. The allegations resulting from the "Crime Stoppers" tip and the third investigation were eventually sustained in the fall of 2015, based largely on the evidence provided by the neighboring Police Department. The officer was allowed to resign from BPD. It is unclear from BPD's files whether any state authorities were notified of the officer's sexual misconduct.

This was not the only case in which allegations were made that officers coerced sex in exchange for immunity from arrest. We found other complaints of this nature were also not properly investigated. Failing to properly investigate allegations that officers were engaged in sexual misconduct is troubling in light of the concerns of gender bias discussed *supra* at 122-27. Failing to properly investigate and address repeated policy violations and serious misconduct also does a disservice to community members and the vast majority of law-abiding BPD officers who are unfairly tainted by the misconduct of a few. By failing to timely address repeated policy violations and misconduct the Department does harm to its internal credibility and external legitimacy.

b. BPD Has Failed To Take Action Against Offenders Known to Engage in Repeated Misconduct

Our investigation also found substantial evidence that BPD fails to take disciplinary action against officers BPD knows have engaged in serious or repeated misconduct. One example of this problem is the so-called "Do Not Call" list. BPD has had notice, including from the State's Attorney's Office, that particular officers may be engaging in behavior that is, at a minimum, unethical and impacts their credibility and integrity. Through at least 2011, the State's Attorney's Office maintained a formal "Do Not Call" list of officers prosecutors would not call to testify because they believed their testimony would be undermined by issues of credibility or integrity. The size of this list varied over time, and included as many as a dozen officers. BPD was aware of the list—the State's Attorney's office regularly discussed the officers on the list with the Chief of BPD's Office of Professional Responsibility—but failed to take action on the information. Instead, the officers listed remained on the streets, making arrests that could not be credibly prosecuted. At one point, we were told, an entire squad's members were on the list, leading to a number of cases being dismissed. Although the formal "Do Not Call" list has been discontinued, the State's Attorney's Office continues to discuss problem officers with BPD.

BPD's ability to take disciplinary action against officers on the "Do Not Call" list is expressly circumscribed by LEOBR and BPD's contract with the police union. Specifically, BPD cannot take punitive action against the officer "based solely on the fact that [the] officer is included on the list," including demotion, dismissal, suspension without pay, or reduction in pay.[131] Because of this prohibition, BPD has not taken any action against officers that the State's Attorney's Office has notified BPD cannot be called to testify, and these officers remain on duty. Particularly given the evidence of numerous unlawful stops, searches, and arrests that we found, the fact that officers whose arrests are not able to be prosecuted remain on the street is troubling. While LEOBR may prevent the Department from taking disciplinary action against officers solely for appearing on the list, it does not prevent the Department from taking other action, including initiating its own investigation of officers' conduct to independently determine whether discipline, training, reassignment, or other action is appropriate.

We also found evidence that BPD fails to take action against officers with a long history of misconduct that is well known to the Department. Our investigation found, for example, that one officer currently employed by BPD has received approximately 125 complaints from complainants within the Department and from the community since 2010, and many of these complaints allege serious misconduct. Indeed, complaints from different individuals alleged remarkably similar facts—specifically, that the officer subjects civilians to unwarranted strip and cavity searches in public. But the Department has sustained only one complaint against the officer for minor misconduct—for not filing a proper vehicle inventory report, resulting in the loss of a camera valued at $1,200. The officer was "verbally counseled on the proper procedure" for filling out inventory reports. Although we were unable to conclusively determine whether other complaints should have been sustained based on the information BPD provided, such a large number of complaints, including unrelated complaints alleging similar behavior, is troubling. We have serious concerns that BPD is not adequately addressing repeated misconduct by its officers.

c. BPD Officers are Reluctant to Report Misconduct

BPD's systemic accountability failures have also contributed to a culture in which some officers are reluctant to raise concerns to supervisors about problematic policing practices or identify misconduct by their fellow officers. Several officers told Justice Department investigators that they

---

[131] Md. Code Ann., Pub. Safety § 3–106.1.

believe their fellow officers have retaliated against them for reporting misconduct or objecting to improper enforcement activities. Other officers expressed fears that they would face such retaliation, and that BPD supervisors would not address any retaliation that occurs. Our review of BPD's internal affairs files underscores these concerns.

Several examples highlight BPD's resistance to internal accountability. In 2014, a BPD lieutenant placed several signs next to the desk of an African-American sergeant with a reputation for speaking out about alleged misconduct in the Department. Among the signs were warnings to "stay in your lane," "worry about yourself," "mind your own business!!" and "don't spread rumors!!!" After the sergeant filed a complaint about the signs, the lieutenant admitted to creating them and placing them next to the sergeant's desk. Yet BPD took no meaningful corrective action. Though the complaint was sustained, the lieutenant received no suspension, fine, or loss of benefits. Instead, he was given only "verbal counseling" instructing him that such behavior is "unprofessional and inappropriate." This minimal response to admitted allegations that a supervisor warned his subordinate to "mind your own business" rather than report misconduct underlines BPD's failure to create a culture of accountability.

In a widely-publicized incident,[132] a former BPD detective in the Violent Crime Impact Division (VCID) faced retaliation after reporting two officers, including his sergeant, for alleged excessive force in the fall of 2011. According to the detective, the VCID unit arrested a man for drug possession after a chase that ended with the man breaking into the home of an officer's girlfriend to hide. According to the officers' reports of the incident, after the man's arrest the sergeant brought him back inside the home to "apologize" to the woman living there. When the man emerged from the home, his shirt was ripped open, he was bleeding, and he had suffered a broken ankle and other injuries. The sergeant claimed that the arrested man injured himself by attempting to head-butt the sergeant and falling to the ground. Concerned that the sergeant and off-duty officer had beaten the man inside the home, the detective asked a different BPD sergeant whether to report the incident to internal affairs. According to the detective, the sergeant discouraged him from reporting the incident, stating "If you're a rat, your career here is done." The detective reported the incident to prosecutors in the State's Attorney's Office, who indicted both officers on criminal charges stemming from the incident. After the detective testified against the officers at trial, a jury convicted the sergeant of misconduct and the off-duty officer of assault and obstruction of justice.

The detective faced significant retaliation for exposing this misconduct. The detective recounted that, after reporting the incident to prosecutors, fellow officers frequently called him a "rat." A sergeant left pictures of cheese on the detective's desk. The detective also told us that a lieutenant denied his transfer request to a violent repeat offender squad because the detective "snitched." The lieutenant allegedly said that the detective was "not the right fit" for the unit because they "have to do things in the gray area." And on two occasions, no one in the detective's

<hr>

[132] *See* Justin Fenton, *Whistle-blower officer files lawsuit against Batts, BPD*, The Baltimore Sun (Dec. 23, 2014, 6:55 PM), http://www.baltimoresun.com/news/maryland/baltimore-city/bs-md-ci-crystal-whistleblower-ratgate-lawsuit-20141223-story.html; Albert Samaha, *Breaking Baltimore's Blue Wall of Silence*, Buzzfeed (May 14, 2015, 9:09 PM), https://www.buzzfeed.com/albertsamaha/breaking-baltimores-blue-wall-of-silence?; Luke Broadwater, *Baltimore to pay $42K to whistle-blower former officer who found rat on car*, The Baltimore Sun (June 1, 2016, 7:14 PM), http://www.baltimoresun.com/news/maryland/baltimore-city/bs-md-ci-crystal-settlement-20160601-story.html.

unit responded to his calls for backup. The retaliation intensified as the officers' trials approached. In November 2012, the detective found a dead rat on his car with its head severed under his wiper blades. Shortly thereafter, a BPD sergeant allegedly told the detective "you better pray to God you're not the star witness" against the officers. The detective reported the dead rat incident to internal affairs, but stated that investigators did not contact him until May 2014, after the incident received substantial media coverage. The detective ultimately resigned from the Department in September 2014 and now works at a different law enforcement agency. The Department settled a lawsuit brought by the former detective in the spring of 2016.

The alleged retaliation against the detective received significant publicity and has had a chilling effect on other officers in the Department who witness misconduct. In one case, an officer in a specialized drug unit observed one of his fellow officers plant drugs on a suspect after a foot chase. The officer decided not to report the misconduct because he did not want BPD officers to "do me" the way they treated the detective.

Officers also told us that they have faced retaliation for raising concerns about the constitutionality of certain BPD enforcement practices. In 2015, a sergeant banned a patrol officer from working overtime for 30 days after the officer objected to the sergeant's frequent requests to "clear corners," which the officer believed required her to violate constitutional standards by making stops without reasonable suspicion. When the officer raised her concerns with the major in charge of the district, he allegedly defended the punishment by stating that the officer "hadn't made stats for six days." At the time supervisors banned her from working overtime, the officer was a single parent who was known to work overtime frequently to support her family. In a similar incident, detailed in Section II.B.2, *supra*, a sergeant reported that she was transferred and given a poor performance review after objecting to a lieutenant's instruction to target "black hoodies" for enforcement.

In short, resistance to internal accountability persists within BPD. The Department has failed to take adequate steps to ensure that officers feel comfortable reporting misconduct and make clear that it will not tolerate retaliation against officers who do so.

D. BPD Does Not Coordinate with Other Agencies Appropriately

BPD also fails to appropriately coordinate its efforts with other law enforcement agencies that it has granted authority to exercise concurrent jurisdiction, creating gaps in the reporting of stops, searches, and in the reporting and investigation of the use of force. These gaps impede BPD's ability to ensure that it is appropriately supervising its own enforcement activities and those of agencies exercising concurrent jurisdiction.

The Department has entered into a number of agreements with law enforcement agencies in and around Baltimore City, including the Baltimore School Police Force, and police forces serving the University of Baltimore and Morgan State University. For example, BPD has entered into an agreement with the Baltimore City Public School System, which operates the Baltimore School Police. This agreement considerably expands the school police force's jurisdiction, which otherwise would be limited to school property. Md. Code Ann., Educ. §§4–318 (c) and (d)(1)(2015) (limiting BSP's jurisdiction, in most circumstances, to "property operated or controlled by the school system"). Under the school police force's agreement with the Department, however, the Baltimore School Police are given "concurrent jurisdiction": school police may act with lawful authority— including with the power of arrest—throughout the City of Baltimore. According to the agreement, school police may "exercise full police power anywhere within the jurisdiction of the City of Baltimore" and assist in investigations and follow-up in criminal cases. School police must notify BPD when its officers act outside of school property and within the territorial jurisdiction of BPD. If school police officers make an arrest while exercising concurrent jurisdiction, they must write an official police report, and they must also use BPD field reports or identical forms for incidents occurring in areas of concurrent jurisdictions.

Early in our investigation, we learned that the City has essentially used the Baltimore School Police as an auxiliary force to BPD. During our ride-alongs with BPD officers, we frequently observed school police officers patrolling neighborhoods and responding to calls along with BPD officers. This was particularly true in districts that were understaffed. The files BPD produced to us confirmed that school police are often present with BPD officers during enforcement activities. School police were present, for example, at the scene of several incidents in which BPD officers used force, and school police officers were also mentioned in our review of BPD's internal affairs files.

We have several concerns with the City's use of the school police as an auxiliary force to BPD. First, based on our review of the agreement between BPD and the Baltimore City Public School System, the agreement does not clearly delineate which agency is in charge of an incident when officers from both agencies respond, as we observed numerous times during our ride-alongs. It is unclear whether this responsibility falls to the senior officer on the scene, regardless of that officer's agency, or to BPD officers because BPD is the agency granting concurrent jurisdiction to the school police (regardless of rank), or if the decision is based on other factors. When officers were questioned about it during our ride-alongs, they were also unclear about who would be in control in those circumstances. This creates considerable risks for both the officers and members of the public, because lines of authority are not clear if a crisis of some kind arises.

Second, the agreement is likewise silent on which agency's policies control decisions made during and after an incident, such as an incident involving the use of force. When use of force policies for each agency set different standards for when force may be used, BPD risks having a school police officer, acting under the concurrent jurisdiction granted by BPD, use force in circumstances that BPD would deem out of policy. Similarly, after the use of force occurs, the agreement does not make clear which agency—or both—would investigate the use of force if it involved officers from both agencies, or how that investigation would be conducted. This failure could lead to gaps in accountability for both agencies.

Third, the agreement does not set forth a process for how complaints about alleged officer misconduct will be handled, even if those complaints arise out of incidents where officers from both agencies are present. When we questioned commanders in BPD's Internal Investigation Division about this, they informed us that the Department's practice was to refer complaints received about school police officers to the school police force itself. We found incidents, however, where it appears BPD officers refused to take complaints about school police—and did not refer them to other agencies—without making any effort to ascertain whether the school police were acting with authority granted to them by BPD, or pursuant to the direction of BPD commanders. This failure similarly undermines accountability and community confidence in both BPD and the school police.

Finally, although the agreement requires school police officers to file arrest and field reports, we are concerned that the data from these reports, as well as from other reports on activities such as stops and searches that do not appear to be required by the agreement, are not being properly collected and analyzed. This impacts the ability of BPD and the school police to effectively supervise officer activities. Particularly where BPD is using the school police as an auxiliary force to aid in patrol and other activities when BPD is itself short-staffed, the failure to coordinate efforts to collect and analyze this data can lead to a skewed view of BPD's enforcement activities. As mentioned previously, reliable and accurate data about BPD's enforcement efforts is critical to effective supervision and prevention of unlawful stops, searches, arrests, and use of force.

BPD should take immediate steps to strengthen its agreements with agencies to which it has granted concurrent jurisdiction to remedy these deficiencies.

E. BPD FAILS TO ENGAGE IN EFFECTIVE COMMUNITY POLICING

From participation in grassroots organization meetings to police department interviews, our investigation revealed a significant divide between the police and members of the Baltimore community. Both community members and police officers expressed that the Department has overly focused on narcotics enforcement, gun recovery, and "clearing corners," even when such strategies are ineffective at addressing the community's desire to combat drug crimes and other enforcement priorities. Many officers openly admitted that community relations are BPD's weakest attribute. Some supervisors noted that it is "sad to see" how many of the city's residents, especially those in low-income, predominantly African-American neighborhoods, hate the police. This divide is a significant impediment to constitutional and effective policing in the City of Baltimore.

Central to this divide is the perception that there are "two Baltimores" receiving dissimilar policing services. One is affluent and predominately white, while the other is impoverished and largely black. The notion that residents in more affluent neighborhoods receive better policing services than residents in poor neighborhoods was evident in many of our conversations with community members. The disparities described to us go beyond aggressive behavior and misconduct; some residents spoke about a police non-response to poor, minority areas as well as a lack of thorough investigation into crimes committed in these communities. Many point to the police response following the unrest in April 2015 as an example. We heard from an African-American resident who told us that "during the unrest in Baltimore the rich white people's neighborhoods were protected but stores in the black neighborhoods were left unguarded." In another account, residents in a minority neighborhood at the center of the unrest described their frustration upon hearing that Bolton Hill, an affluent, majority-white area, was granted an increase in officer deployment while their request for foot patrol following a dramatic spike in drug trafficking was denied due to a lack of resources. One resident commented, "The city was pretty much saying Sandtown doesn't matter; the black neighborhood can burn. They were protecting the white people, the richer people." *See, e.g., Over-Policed, Yet Underserved: The People's Findings Regarding Police Misconduct in West Baltimore*, West Baltimore Commission on Police Misconduct and the No Boundaries Coalition (March 8, 2016) at 11.

Our investigation found that, through all levels of the Baltimore Police Department, from members of command staff down to officers on the street, the Department has not implemented fundamental principles of community policing. Community policing involves building partnerships between law enforcement and the people and organizations within its jurisdiction; engaging in problem-solving together with the community; and managing the police agency to support this community partnership and community problem-solving. *See, e.g., Community Policing Defined* 1–16 (U.S. Dep't of Justice, Office of Community Oriented Policing Services, 2014). Community policing is inherently proactive; it involves identifying leaders within a community that can aid the police in preventing and investigating crime, particularly among those groups that are most alienated from the police, and creating relationships with those leaders that allow the police and the community to work together to make the community safe. This strategy enables law enforcement agencies and the individuals and organizations they serve to develop solutions to problems and increase trust in the police. *See, e.g., Effective Policing and Crime Prevention: A Problem Oriented Guide for Mayors, City Managers, and County Executives* 1–62 (U.S. Dep't of Justice, Office of Community Oriented Policing Services, 2009); *The Collaboration Toolkit for Law Enforcement: Effective Strategies to Partner with the Community* 1–92

(U.S. Dep't of Justice, Office of Community Oriented Policing Services, 2011). To be effective, it must include all ranks, sectors, and units of a police department. *See, e.g., Community Policing Explained: A Guide for Local Government* 1–54 (U.S. Dep't of Justice, Office of Community Oriented Policing Services, 2003). This approach is currently not being implemented by the Baltimore Police Department, although leadership in the Department has made efforts to change this over the last few years. To remedy the constitutional violations we found in our investigation, a comprehensive community policing strategy must be a central component of police reform in Baltimore.

1. The Relationship Between the Police and the Community in Baltimore Is Broken

The relationship between the Baltimore Police Department and many of the communities it serves is broken. During our investigation, we participated in or observed dozens of community meetings, reviewed thousands of documents, including letters and complaints from Baltimore residents, and interviewed hundreds of additional Baltimore residents. Many residents throughout the City of Baltimore, and particularly in impoverished, primarily minority, neighborhoods, described being belittled, disbelieved, and disrespected by officers, spurring some groups to submit detailed accounts, documentation, and even formal reports to us about their experiences with the Department. *See, e.g., Over-Policed, Yet Underserved: The People's Findings Regarding Police Misconduct in West Baltimore*, West Baltimore Commission on Police Misconduct and the No Boundaries Coalition (March 8, 2016). These accounts included reports of verbal abuse during routine interactions and often involved cursing or threats. In one account, during a traffic stop, a resident politely asked an officer why he had been pulled over. The officer simply told him to get out of the car and, when asked again, began cursing at the resident, even threatening to tow his "fucking car." In another account, a woman asked police officers the reason for conducting a search of her home. She was told to "shut the fuck up bitch and sit the fuck down" because they were "the fucking law." Strikingly, the vast majority of the individuals we spoke with do not want the police to be less involved in their communities; they want police engagement, and they want this engagement to be respectful and collaborative, so they can feel safe in their own communities.

Our interactions with BPD officers and review of the Department's documents confirmed many of the accounts we heard from members of the public. Our review of the Department's own incident reports, for example, revealed numerous instances in which officers spoke in an unnecessarily rude or aggressive manner when interacting with suspects, witnesses, and the general public. And, as described previously *supra*, these aggressive interactions frequently escalated situations and, at times, led to the unnecessary use of force. Interviews with BPD officers throughout the chain of command also revealed that officers openly harbor antagonistic feelings towards community members. We found a prevalent "us-versus-them" mentality that is incompatible with community policing principles. When asked about community-oriented problem solving, for example, one supervisor responded, "I don't pander to the public." Another supervisor conveyed to us that he approaches policing in Baltimore like it is a war zone. A patrol officer, when describing his approach to policing, voiced similar views, commenting, "You've got to be the baddest motherfucker out there," which often requires that one "own the block." Officers seemed to view themselves as controlling the city rather than as *a part* of the city. Many others, including high ranking officers in the Department, view themselves as enforcing the will of the "silent majority."

Many BPD discretionary enforcement actions increase distrust and significantly decrease the likelihood that individuals will cooperate with the police to solve or prevent other crimes, as described in numerous incidents and statistics throughout this letter. In one report, an officer described telling two individuals, a mother and her son, who were standing in the block to leave. They refused, noting that were standing outside of their own home, but eventually moved to the steps of their front stoop. Ultimately, the son, a juvenile with no prior criminal record, was arrested for loitering outside his own home. Supervisors raised no issues with respect to the incident. Similarly, groups of people are often dispersed unless they have a clear reason for gathering in that location. In one internal report, a supervisor describes the actions of an officer, stating, "Officer approached the group to ascertain the reason for the crowd and if there was no legal reason they were going to disperse the crowd." The interaction concluded with an officer using OC spray on the entire group of people. These enforcement activities for behavior that is, at most, a minor offense if even unlawful, alienate community members and decrease their willingness to work with police.

Indeed, our review of documents and our conversations with Baltimore residents confirm that distrust is causing individuals to be reluctant to cooperate with police. It was not uncommon to see marked on incident reports that witnesses were hostile and unwilling to share basic information with police officers. And in many instances, BPD imposed unnecessary negative consequences for optional interactions. For example, a case manager requested that the police reach out to a juvenile who was friends with victims of a homicide case because she was concerned for his safety and wanted to check if he desired to be relocated. Detectives in the Homicide Unit arrived at his house, and the juvenile invited them inside his home to speak about the murder of his friend. During the course of the conversation, the detectives decided that they wanted a formal statement from the juvenile. However, after telephoning his grandmother, who advised him not to speak to investigators, he refused. The detectives insisted that he come downtown, which caused the juvenile to allegedly scream and ball his fists. Ultimately, officers placed him in handcuffs and transported him downtown. We also read numerous incident reports where the person who originally called the police or was in need of assistance refused to cooperate after becoming upset with the manner in which the police responded.

2. BPD Has Failed to Implement Community Policing Principles

Our investigation revealed that one of the fundamental causes of the breakdown in the relationship between the Department and the community it serves is that, throughout much of the Department, community policing principles are not being implemented. During our interviews with command staff, district commanders, and other supervisors, we observed that, in the vast majority of these interviews, the person was unable to accurately describe what community policing is or how BPD implements community policing efforts. Some district commanders had not even considered enlisting the community to help combat crime problems. Most could not identify community organizations willing to do violence prevention work or other partners for community policing on an ongoing basis. And none of the BPD majors we talked with had relationships with community groups who were able to put pressure on violent members of the community to stop the violence. These coalitions can be an effective tool in not only stopping the violence but also building important community relationships. Notably, when a district commander or member of command staff did have a stronger grasp of community policing principles, their description of the specific actions BPD is taking often differed widely from that shared with us by other Department leaders. The Department lacks a common vision for how it is engaging and working with its community.

The Department leadership's lack of vision for community policing has repercussions for the officers they supervise. Most of the officers we encountered during our investigation care deeply about doing a good job, but their approaches are narrowly aimed at enforcement, with an almost exclusive focus on offenders, and lack community-oriented problem-solving. Many officers described little interaction with the communities they patrol, noting that those on patrol simply handle calls for service. Supervisors confirmed this notion. One noted, "Officers basically just handle calls for service." Another described patrol officers by stating that they "go from call to call, so they have no time for community interaction . . . they're controlled mostly by the radio." Many police personnel openly admitted that officers do not regularly attend community meetings—that street cops focus on enforcement with little outreach to or investment in community needs.

Community policing efforts are ad hoc and officer- or major-specific. Those officers we saw interacting with the community in a positive manner did so due to their own interest, noting that such actions were not mandated by command staff. At the command level, one district commander described prioritizing sector officers and sergeants having as many "designed intentional moments" as possible with the community and tracking officers' foot patrol time to encourage such interactions. The same district has been involved in numerous outreach efforts, including listening campaigns, "Cocoa with a Cop," a shoe giveaway, and community walks. However, this district commander's efforts again appear to be an exception to BPD's overall policing strategy. The commander confirmed this, telling us, "I know it needs to happen—so I don't wait for someone to tell me to do it." Furthermore, although this district commander and some others focus on community policing, many patrol officers are receiving conflicting messages. For example, one officer told us, "Commanders say they want community policing, but then they come back around and ask 'How many arrests you made?'" As this question suggests, from command staff to officers, the Department struggles to embrace true community policing and fails to understand how community policing strategies can make it better and more effective at reducing crime and social disorder.

3. BPD Recognizes that It Must Improve Its Relationship with the Communities It Serves, But Much Work Remains

Over the past few years, leaders within the City and within Baltimore Police Department have recognized that the Department needs to do significant work to improve its relationship with the communities it serves throughout Baltimore, particularly those in impoverished and minority neighborhoods. During our investigation and before it, the Department began to make changes to the way it polices to better embrace community policing principles and more effective serve its community. Unfortunately, community policing is still not a philosophy that permeates all aspects of BPD's activities; rather, it currently is a single program that is not integrated with BPD's other law enforcement functions. Indeed, most officers think of community policing as distinct from their regular policing duties.

Currently, the Department's community policing efforts are undertaken exclusively by the Community Collaboration Division (CCD), except for the ad hoc efforts of certain officers and commanders described above. CCD is led by a Lieutenant Colonel, and its philosophy is based on four pillars: community-oriented policing, faith-based involvement, youth engagement, and re-entry programs. Structurally, CCD aims to have one sergeant and four officers per district—with each officer responsible for a "pillar" and the sergeants responsible for supervision. These officers are not under district command; instead, they work out of their own unit downtown.

While it is too early to conclusively evaluate these efforts, we are concerned that these new initiatives will not be successful without substantial changes in the Department's approach. First, the Department's community policing plan is currently too limited in scope, and does not embrace all aspects of the work of the Department. As currently understood by many members of the Department, community policing is the responsibility of the CCD, not the Department as a whole. To be effective, however, community collaboration and engagement has to be practiced by every member of the organization, especially by the uniformed patrol officers who are assigned to neighborhoods. At present, patrol officers largely view the policing strategy as someone else's job. This limited version of community policing will not be effective, particularly given the relatively small number of individuals dedicated to undertake these efforts.

Second, and relatedly, the Department's community policing efforts are not well-integrated with the work of the districts. We express no view on whether community policing efforts need to be led out of the districts or centralized, as they currently are in Baltimore in the CCD. Regardless of where these efforts are led, however, they must be closely coordinated and integrated with patrol and specialized units, and that integration is not yet occurring. This problem is exacerbated by the distinct nature of each district in Baltimore. According to some people throughout the Department, districts work as if they are a separate "kingdom," with distinctly different practices and approaches. This is consistent with our observations. Evidence of the difficulties this poses is already apparent. In some districts, the district commanders were appreciative of the help and support they received from the CCD; other commanders, however, were concerned that they were not aware when the unit was actually working in their area. A few also voiced frustration that they lack control of community engagement in their district, given their experience in the area. One commander noted that it can be difficult to engage and build relationships with some community groups, most notably the faith-based contacts, since this responsibility falls under the CCD. "It's harder for district commanders to have access to these folks," noted one. The major described how the district developed its own initiatives to facilitate community policing and engagement because of the difficulties in coordinating with the CCD.

Third, the Department is not building effective partnerships with existing community groups dedicated to serving their communities, and instead is trying to establish new programs that are led by the Department. During the course of our investigation, we observed a surprising lack of BPD representation at community meetings of grass-roots organizations throughout the City. At the majority of community meetings we attended, we found that members of the BPD—even the CCD—were not present. Often, the community and religious leaders hosting the meeting told us that they had personally reached out to the police department to invite officers to the meeting, but received no response. According to some participants, police officials used to attend their meetings but have not done so since the unrest following the death of Freddie Gray. By not participating in these meetings, the Department is missing valuable opportunities. Attending these meetings would allow officers to build partnerships, gain information, and solve problems that would facilitate effective policing. Notably, during our interviews with them, CCD leadership did not speak to the importance of partnering with grass-root organizations that are not traditional supporters of the police. Instead, the approach to police-community relations is primarily focused on establishing programs to support CCD's four pillars, which are police-led rather than partnering with others who have already established themselves in the community. It is perhaps unsurprising that community activists have described the Department's efforts to improve police-community relations as troubling—that the police are seeking "a 'community rubber stamp' to normalize 'problematic policing practices'" rather than working with the community to find an approach to policing that can gain buy-in.[133]

Fourth, the Department is not consistently enforcing its own requirements for officer community engagement. For example, the Department recently implemented a 30-minute foot patrol requirement, but this obligation is not uniformly enforced by command staff. Although we engaged in numerous ride-alongs with patrol officers, only a handful of the officers completed their foot patrol. Additional interviews confirmed that this requirement is not readily enforced across BPD. It is, therefore, unsurprising that some officers fail to integrate community policing efforts into their time on patrol. There are few incentives and little encouragement to do so.

Finally, BPD's policies and training do not consistently embrace community policing principles. BPD's community policing strategy involves few training modules on community policing and communication. We attended one of these in-service trainings, which focused on community policing and foot patrol. The segment on officers' role as "warriors versus guardians" focused primarily on the benefits of being a warrior. Indeed, it seemed that principles of community policing and the role of a police officer as a "guardian" is not yet well understood by the instructors, who emphasized the drawbacks of this approach, making it unlikely that officers will understand how to embrace such principles in their interactions. Better training is needed if the Department wants to teach officers effective community policing practices, and this training needs to be provided and tailored to personnel throughout all levels of the Department.

*   *   *

Community policing and engagement provide a promising route for ensuring officers act in accord with the Constitution and for repairing BPD's relationship with the community. A proactive community policing strategy has the potential to overcome divisive dynamics that disconnect residents and police forces, dynamics ranging from a dearth of positive interactions to racial stereotyping and racial violence. *See, e.g.*, Jack Glaser, *Suspect Race: Causes and Consequence of Racial Profiling* 207–11 (2015) (discussing research showing that community policing and similar approaches can help reduce racial bias and stereotypes and improve community relations); L. Song Richardson & Phillip Atiba Goff, *Interrogating Racial Violence*, 12 Ohio St. J. of Crim. L. 115, 143–47 (2014) (describing how fully implemented and inclusive community policing can help avoid racial stereotyping and violence); *Strengthening the Relationship Between Law Enforcement and Communities of Color: Developing an Agenda for Action* 1–20 (U.S. Dep't of Justice, Office of Community Oriented Policing Services, 2014). Thus, as the Department strives to correct the problems our investigation

---

[133] Maggie Ybarra, *A conversation with Police Commissioner Kevin Davis*, City Paper, April 27, 2016, http://www.citypaper.com/news/features/bcp-042716-feature-commissioner-davis-interview-20160427-story.html.

identified and to engender trust within Baltimore's diverse communities, a community policing strategy should be a central component of its approach moving forward.

CONCLUSION

For the foregoing reasons, the Department of Justice concludes that there is reasonable cause to believe that BPD engages in a pattern or practice of conduct that violates the Constitution or federal law. The pattern or practice includes: (1) making unconstitutional stops, searches, and arrests; (2) using enforcement strategies that produce severe and unjustified disparities in the rates of stops, searches and arrests of African Americans; (3) using excessive force; and (4) retaliating against people engaging in constitutionally-protected expression. We also identified concerns regarding BPD's transport of individuals and investigation of sexual assaults. BPD's failings result from deficient policies, training, oversight, and accountability, and policing strategies that do not engage effectively with the community the Department serves. We are heartened to find both widespread recognition of these challenges and strong interest in reform. We look forward to working with the Department, City leadership, and Baltimore's diverse communities to create lasting reforms that rebuild trust in BPD and ensure that it provides effective, constitutional police services to the people of Baltimore.